organisational consulting

organisational consulting

A RELATIONAL PERSPECTIVE

THEORIES AND STORIES FROM THE FIELD

Bill Critchley
Kathleen King
John Higgins

LIBRI
PUBLISHING

First published in 2007 by Middlesex University Press

This edition published in 2013 by Libri Publishing

Copyright © Libri Publishing

Authors retain copyright of individual chapters.

The right of Bill Critchley, Kathleen King and John Higgins to be identified as the editors of this work has been asserted in accordance with the Copyright, Designs and Patents Act, 1988.

ISBN 978 1 907471 63 6

All rights reserved. No part of this publication may be reproduced, stored in any retrieval system or transmitted in any form or by any means, electronic, mechanical, photocopying, recording or otherwise, without the prior written permission of the copyright holder for which application should be addressed in the first instance to the publishers. No liability shall be attached to the author, the copyright holder or the publishers for loss or damage of any nature suffered as a result of reliance on the reproduction of any of the contents of this publication or any errors or omissions in its contents.

A CIP catalogue record for this book is available from The British Library

Cover design by Helen Taylor

Design by Helen Taylor

Libri Publishing
Brunel House
Volunteer Way
Faringdon
Oxfordshire
SN7 7YR

Tel: +44 (0)845 873 3837

www.libripublishing.co.uk

contents

Acknowledgments

SECTION 1	**INTRODUCTION**	**1**
SECTION 2	**ADVOCATING SOME THEORY –**	**9**
	THE FACULTY PRACTITIONER PERSPECTIVE	

    Section Introduction   11

    Framing Bateson
    Conversation with Adrian McLean and Kevin Power   12

    Short Stories about Working with a Gestalt Perspective
    Conversation with Bill Critchley   23

    Towards Relational Consulting
    By Kathleen King   31

    Working from a Complexity Perspective
    Conversations with Caryn Vanstone (and Bill Critchley)   49

    Inquiry and Reflective Practice
    Conversations with Robin Ladkin   59

    Consulting from a Dialogic Orientation
    By Hugh Pidgeon   68

SECTION 3	**INQUIRING INTO PRACTICE –**	**79**
	THE GRADUATE PRACTITIONER PERSPECTIVE	

    Section Introduction – The Inquiry Process   81

    Kevin – As Good as it Gets   83
    Bill's Postscript to Kevin's Story –   97
    Looking through Six Theoretical Frames

    Jon – Man not Superman   100
    Bill's Postscript to Jon's Story –   111
    Looking through Six Theoretical Frames

    Dominic and **Liz** – Not Just Doing the Do   114
    Bill's Postscript to Dominic and Liz's Story –   126
    Looking through Six Theoretical Frames

    Francesca – Do Consultants Make a Difference?   129
    Bill's Postscript to Francesca's Story –   139
    Looking through Six Theoretical Frames

	Bill – The Old Gestaltist and the Global Media Company	142
	Bill's Postscript to Bill's Story – Looking through Six Theoretical Frames	153
	Iain – Consulting with Conviction	155
	Bill's Postscript to Iain's Story – Looking through Six Theoretical Frames	164
SECTION 4	**CONCLUDING CHAPTER – A PUNCTUATION IN AN ONGOING INQUIRY**	**169**
	John's Story about a Conference	171
SECTION 5	**APPENDICES**	**183**
	Appendix 1	185
	Appendix 2	190
	Appendix 3	195
	Appendix 4	201
	Contributor Photographs	205

ACKNOWLEDGMENTS

Our thanks go to all the consultants, clients and members of the AMOC faculty who have engaged so wholeheartedly in sharing and reflecting on their experience.

SECTION 1

Introduction

BATESON GESTALT

Introduction

This book is the result of a research project which follows the working lives of eleven graduates and faculty members of the Ashridge Masters in Organisation Consulting (AMOC). Details of the rationale and logistics of the research are outlined in Appendix 2. The research intended to explore the theoretical frameworks that underpin the AMOC curriculum and how they inform the practice of faculty and alumni.

This book seeks to give an account of what really happens in consulting relationships, rather that to produce the more common polished rationalisations. It does not intend to offer consulting recipes, tools or techniques; rather it hopes to inspire reflection and further inquiry.

Preview of the content

The first half of the book comprises six case studies either written by, or co-created with members of the AMOC faculty. Rather than to present an abstract academic perspective, detached from the compromises and paradoxes of consulting practice, the accounts are grounded in the actual work of faculty members, who explore their thinking and practice as work in progress, rather than to present it as a model to which others should aspire, in keeping with the nature of their contribution to AMOC.

The essays introduce the reader to a particular perspective on organisations and critically review the implications for consulting practice. They challenge the prevalent view of 'organisations as machines that can be readily manipulated by people in formal authority' and instead offer a perspective that focuses on the power of informal relationships and communication. They explore the implications of working from this alternative perspective in a world where the power of the machine metaphor is considerable.

Another dimension of the philosophical roots of this research is its connection to particular schools of sociology, psychology and social constructionism – often developed outside of the classical centres of management and organisational study in fields such as family therapy and learning theory.

The reader is introduced to the radical ideas of Gregory Bateson, philosopher, sociologist and anthropologist, some ideas and principles from Gestalt therapy, and the emerging school of relational psychology. The complexity perspective is also introduced as a major new force in the field of relational consulting, along with the inquiry movement with its request to 'inquire (and reflect) a little more and advocate a little less'. Lastly there is the dialogic perspective with its practice of suspending assumptions and seeking the wisdom which comes from thinking together rather than trading and defending individual opinions which have already been thought.

At the heart of the book are the six accounts that follow on from these framing essays. Each account examines practitioners trying to make the 'difference that makes a difference'. They do not slavishly follow an AMOC orthodoxy, rather they seek to engage with the world as they find it while also maintaining a consulting approach that has integrity for them and value for their clients.

In terms of style, these stories have not been written as post-event rationalisations, where clients are miraculously rescued by supermen or women. Nor have they been retold to fit within some pre-existent methodology or even the philosophical frame advocated at the start of the research. Learning points cannot be neatly distilled from them because each situation, each relationship and each personality gives rise to a unique way of consulting. There is a coherent philosophy at work in the stories, but there is no set of golden rules that if slavishly followed will result in consulting nirvana.

The six case studies are:

- Kevin's – who tells of a consulting experience that for him was as good as it gets. He demonstrates the tension of acting independently while being an internal consultant. He engaged with the dynamic and informal aspects of a global transformation that didn't fit another consulting firm's view on how to 'manage change'. He let the reality of not knowing emerge while not leaving people feeling powerless.

- Jon's – who parallels his recovery from a stroke with the re-establishment of his consulting practice, forcing himself to acknowledge that he is man not superman. For independent consultants everywhere he lives out the perennial challenge put by many a client, 'what would happen if you walked under a bus?' And for the more modest consultants in the world, what does it take to work with humility and doubt in a world addicted to certainty?

- Dominic and Liz's – who reveal the struggle of moving beyond simply 'doing the do'. This assignment lives through the sometimes turgid frustration of working with another consultant who is operating from a different worldview of consulting and a client team with its own tensions. To what extent do they compromise themselves?

- Francesca's – who finds herself wondering whether consultants ever make a difference. She is the ball of energy that seems to spark things in an organisation that the senior manager sees as passive and compliant, and which others see as seething with unexpressed anger and aggression. When she is there something changes. Appreciative inquiry (see Appendix 1) may or may not have been the 'right' approach, but it made a difference for a while and has certainly changed some individuals.

- Bill's – which is the story of an old Gestaltist working to change the habits of leadership in a global media company. He shares the challenge of taking a client seriously when they invite a consultancy to be innovative and different in terms of exploring a radically different notion of organisational leadership. He's not always popular with his client and sometimes puts his foot in it, but the client never loses faith in his integrity and the sense that whatever he does is being done with the client's best interests at heart.

- Iain's – Iain is a conviction consultant. He explores what it takes to wear your heart, as well as your mind, on your sleeve. Whereas AMOC would emphasise the importance of creative detachment, Iain lives and works from the perspective of creative attachment. He is also a fascinating, and successful, example of offering difference to your client while also remaining intelligible to them.

The book ends with reflections from John Higgins about his experience of the research project, and of the AMOC alumni day at which the research report was discussed and further opportunities for inquiry explored. John draws some tentative conclusions about the nature of 'relational' consulting.

References and appendices

Every chapter is followed by a section 'Further reading'. In some cases the listed works relate directly to references in the text. In other chapters, where the authors did not directly quote from a particular work, the reading gives a flavour of the theory that informs the author of the chapter. In both cases they are arranged in alphabetical order.

In the first appendix you will find a glossary of some of the recurring terms. Appendix 2 expands on the underpinning philosophy of the research. Appendix 3 shows the original research plan and a letter of invitation to contributors. The reader will notice that the original terminology has been left unchanged. Finally, Appendix 4 gives an overview of the AMOC syllabus.

Intended audience

This book will be of interest to all practising consultants. Hopefully it will inspire those consultants working for mainstream consulting organisations and independent practitioners who are interested in deepening their understanding of their established practice or are looking to develop a different approach.

The agenda of the editors

Bill Critchley is a business director of Ashridge Consulting Limited, part of Ashridge Management College. He is also founder and programme director of the Ashridge Masters in Organisation Consulting, launched in 1997 and going strong. He is an organisation consultant and in the evening transmogrifies from time to time into a Gestalt psychotherapist.

Bill is informed by social constructionism and a view that organisations are complex social processes, the latter view in turn being informed by thinking from the complexity sciences, sociology and psychology. Bill has a desire to develop a way of consulting that is founded on these philosophical beliefs. He has a passion for 'real' consulting that makes a difference. Viewing organisations as part of a social ecology, he works to overcome the obsessive tyranny of profit and shareholder value over all the other purposes that organisations serve.

John Higgins spent a number of years as a consultant chasing fads and certainties. Unaware that he was inflicting on his clients some of his personal baggage, he was still highly successful in his work for some of the world's biggest consultancies. In 1997 nagging doubts about his practice and its rewards (no job too big, no fee too large) led him to join Ashridge Consulting, where he took part in the third AMOC programme before briefly joining the faculty. However, he still found himself unable to reconcile the demands of being a father, a business developer and a proponent of minimalist consulting engagements. He gave up his formal career to become primarily a father – with a small consulting practice that fitted around his family life.

Freed from what he constructed as the hubris and greed of much of the consulting industry, as well as his own need for advocacy, he rediscovered his fascination with the craft of consulting. He became more attentive to the myriad subtleties with which insights can be shared, while understanding that 'getting it right' seemed as much a matter of chance as of effort or intelligence. Finally he came to realise that the more he engaged with the practice and theory of consulting, the more obvious and the more mysterious it became as insights from all walks of social, educational, theological and psychological study and experience came into play.

Kathleen King is also an employee of Ashridge consulting, as well as an enthusiastic member of the AMOC faculty. You can discover more about her practice and her philosophy in the chapter on relational consulting. Kathleen felt compelled to engage with the final editing when it transpired that John's close engagement with the authors and their stories made it rather difficult for him to make them sufficiently accessible to outsiders. Mindful of her own sensitivity to feedback she embarked, not without trepidation, on the potentially hazardous task of critiquing and amending John's writing. However, very quickly their 'editing meetings' turned into another enchanting round of inquiring conversations, further deepening their understanding of the research and the significance of the essays and accounts.

Whose voice is it anyway?

This is a multi-voiced piece of work, but it has been strongly influenced by Bill and John and in its latest editing by Kathleen. Ten of the twelve case studies are the result of John's conversations with graduates and faculty members, thus they are co-created. However, since John wrote the stories, it was, inevitably, his frames that determined what got noticed and recorded and what got disappeared as he tidied up the inquiry sufficiently to create coherent narratives for this report.

Others have also had their mark in terms of structure and flow. One area that led to considerable debate was how to position the graduate and faculty member stories. Would putting the faculty stories first mean that we were privileging them, giving them greater weight? In the end we agreed to acknowledge AMOC's advocacy and the fact that the graduate stories illustrate certain philosophical stances. It also allowed us to have a framework within which Bill could do an appraising response to each graduate story.

We considered it essential that faculty members' stories were told in a similar 'warts and all' voice to that of the graduate stories. This means that they also deal with the tensions of trying to work from an uncommon philosophical position while needing to remain intelligible to a world more comfortable with notions of unitary power, knowledge and high degrees of certainty. Thus we aspired to put the faculty stories at an equal level to the graduate stories, while not denying their focus on elaborating distinctive theoretical perspectives.

In every one of the stories people are working with their personal foibles and dispositions, struggling to marry the gap between espoused theories and theories in use. We hope neither faculty nor graduate stories are idealisations, leaving the reader feeling inadequate in their everyday struggles to be a good enough consultant.

The link with Middlesex University Press

MU Press is in the process of publishing a number of works around the theme of 'Reflections on Professional Practice'. The first was by Paul Barber: *Becoming a Practitioner-Researcher – A Gestalt Approach to Holistic Inquiry*. Peter Critten, from Middlesex University Business School, was involved with Paul in bringing the book to publication; but Peter is also the Link Tutor for Middlesex University on AMOC. When he saw a copy of the AMOC research report he suggested to Bill Critchley that it would fit perfectly alongside Paul Barber's book in the MU Press series. MU Press agreed and Peter has been working with Kathleen to make it more accessible to a wider audience.

SECTION 2

Advocating Some Theory

THE FACULTY PRACTITIONER PERSPECTIVE

11	**Section Introduction**
12	**Framing Bateson** Conversation with Adrian McLean and Kevin Power
23	**Short Stories about Working with a Gestalt Perspective** Conversation with Bill Critchley
31	**Towards Relational Consulting** By Kathleen King
49	**Working from a Complexity Perspective** Conversations with Caryn Vanstone (and Bill Critchley)
59	**Inquiry and Reflective Practice** Conversations with Robin Ladkin
68	**Consulting from a Dialogic Orientation** By Hugh Pidgeon

Introduction

This section contains six essays, each of which frames one particular theoretical perspective. The underpinning philosophy of Ashridge Masters in Organisation Consulting (AMOC) is social constructionism. This considers social reality to be a dynamic process, rather than a thing, in which people are active and connected agents who co-create their reality through their patterns of interaction and experiences. Within this frame, the faculty essays are expressions of professional and personal interest, particular theoretically informed areas of practice, in which each of the faculty acts as the de facto leader within the AMOC curriculum.

The six areas explored in the essays are:

- The work of Gregory Bateson and how his insights inform AMOC's particular take on the social constructionist discourse
- Gestalt psychology, its relationship to complexity thinking and the discipline of enlivening contact
- Relational psychology and the tension that exists between separateness and connectivity, agency and communion
- Complexity thinking and how it invites consultants to reframe their understanding of what a consulting intervention is
- Inquiry and reflective practice and what it takes to be both a knowing and unknowing consultant at the same time
- A dialogic orientation as a personal disposition towards seeing connectedness and working with engrained assumptions, rather than with a pre-set method.

For further details on the informing theories of AMOC see Appendix 4.

Framing Bateson

CONVERSATION WITH ADRIAN McLEAN AND KEVIN POWER

Born into a family of eminent scientists, Gregory Bateson (1904–1980) started his career as an anthropologist but went on to become one of the most important social scientists of his century, making significant contributions to a wide range of fields, including biology, psychology, psychiatry, ecology and communication. In collaboration with like-minded critical contemporaries, Bateson challenged the orthodox modernist paradigm of his era with its separation of mind and matter, asserting instead that the two are inextricably linked.

This paper concerns his influence on Adrian McLean and Kevin Power, both Bateson enthusiasts, to put it mildly. Adrian is a member of the AMOC faculty and Kevin is an alumnus. Kevin is also the main source of the references in this paper to the work of Paul Watzlawick and of the – perhaps somewhat surprising – vignettes from the world of family therapy. Watzlawick belonged to the Palo Alto group of psychotherapists, in collaboration with whom Bateson developed his theory of communication and double bind (more about which later). Kevin wrote his AMOC dissertation on Watzlawick's work and in the process became more and more interested in Bateson as a major influence on Watzlawick and his colleagues.

Puzzled by the richness of our conversations on the one hand, and my seeming inability to start writing this paper on the other, my initial sense of frustration evaporated when I realised the congruence between my sense of 'not knowing where to start' and Bateson's resistance to linear, reductionist thinking which set him apart from many of his scientific contemporaries.

Bateson's work is complex and fluid and defeats any attempts at neat summarising. He challenges our habitual way of understanding and warns us against trying to control the world we only imperfectly understand. Instead, he argues, we should aim to stay curious about it and to seek beauty rather than power. Such a warning raises all sorts of challenges and implications for consultants willing to be inspired by his work. In this paper I seek to evoke, rather than explain or summarise, some of the core concepts of this profound framework and, using Adrian and Kevin's stories, illustrate some ways in which it influences their consulting practice.

The nature of knowing

At the heart of Bateson's work is his interest in understanding processes of knowing: perception, communication, coding and translation and the relationship between the knower and the known. Ideally, according to Bateson, the relationship between the patterns of the biological world and our understanding of it should be one of *congruence*. This is a very different concept of knowing from the traditional scientific one which tends to aspire to the 'ability to predict' in experimental contexts that depend on simplification and selective attention. According to Mary Catherine Bateson, his oldest daughter, her father was deeply concerned about the effects of a reductionist paradigm and convinced that only a better epistemology would save us from irreversible disasters.

The pattern that connects

Instead of focussing on an individual or a single object, as is common practice within a reductionist paradigm, Bateson invites us to pay attention to the interconnections between phenomena and the overall form that emerges from those connections: the pattern that connects. According to Bateson, attending to that pattern, to the recurring sequences of events, the repeated interplays, adjustments and exchanges that occur between participants in any system, and understanding them, is the only way to understand how stability is achieved and how changes may occur.

Adrian became rather animated in our conversation about Bateson's concept of pattern. 'In my view' he said, 'the question "What is the pattern that connects?" is one of Bateson's great gifts to us. Social sciences have long been trapped in a methodology inherited from the traditions of physical sciences. Bateson breaks that mould and encourages us to be concerned with the living relationships that exist between phenomena and between phenomena and their environment. In my consulting practice that means I need to see whatever I am attending to in its context. In other words, I need to understand that in order to make sense of an individual's behaviours, attitudes and beliefs I need to see them as a property of the person's context as much as of the person in question. To use Bateson's terminology: I need to look for the ecology that sustains a particular pattern of relationships. For instance, in order to make sense of leadership issues in an organisation, I need to attend not just to leaders' behaviours but also to followers' behaviours, to how leaders invite certain behaviours in their followers and vice versa.'

When I asked Adrian for an example he described his work with a car manufacturer. 'Complaints about leaders in the organisation were rife. There was a strong invitation from staff to buy into their construction of the situation: our leaders are ineffective, they ought to give more direction, be clearer. However tempting it can be, I am keen not to judge or take sides. Instead I try to notice the positions various parties occupy and the symmetrical relationships that keep the situation stuck. Thus, I drew attention to the pattern I saw emerging: on the one hand staff wanted more clarity; on the other hand the leaders, having to cope with high levels of uncertainty which made strong direction impossible at that time, needed the wider organisation to trust them and be mature enough to cope with uncertainty and lack of clarity.'

In other words, Adrian's intervention consisted of drawing attention to the pattern of the relationships, the symmetrical dance of one party demanding clarity and the other party demanding enough maturity to cope with inevitable uncertainty. By surfacing this pattern he helped some staff to understand the dilemmas faced by their leaders and the extent to which they were, in their dependent stance, disempowering themselves. A key feature of Adrian's approach is his validation of the different constructions of the situation in the client organisation, in the above example those of leaders and followers. By drawing people's attention to the pattern of the relationships they are engaged in, the conversation can shift from 'you are the problem and here's what you need to do to address my needs' to 'what is possible for us given our current reality?'

'Our challenge as consultants, as I see it', said Adrian, 'is to surface the symmetrical and complementary pattern that is being played out and the extent to which it leads to people becoming stuck because they are not aware of it. The purpose of a consulting intervention is not to judge or address the situation in its current construction, but to invite people to shift the conversation to a different level.' Kevin built on this by referencing Paul Watzlawick: 'Watzlawick suggests that we should think of the family as the patient, not any one individual. In my consulting practice that means that I prefer to frame the organisation as the client, rather than the leader or whoever is my main point of contact.'

He offered an example from the world of family therapy: 'There is the classic tale of therapists working with a family with two very dysfunctional daughters. Despite their best efforts they had no success whatsoever in changing the disruptive behaviour of the girls. Eventually they gave up. Deciding they could not help the girls, they instead concentrated on improving the situation for the parents. They recommended to the parents that they go out once a week and have a good time. Not only did the parents indeed have a good time, but to the astonishment of the therapists, the behaviour of the girls changed for the better. The result was so surprising that the therapists repeated the intervention with other "stuck families" with similar success, leading the therapists to conclude that their own construction of "the children being the problem" was in some way keeping the problem in place. Once they changed their construction of the situation new possibilities emerged. It was a powerful reminder to me that the way in which we, as consultants, work with client organisations can be part of the pattern that keeps the organisation stuck.'

'Drilling up rather than down' (Bateson, 1972)

In order to shift the stuck pattern in the earlier example of the automotive manufacturer, Adrian sought to shift the level of the conversations taking place and brought together 50 leaders of projects that were felt to have a significant impact on the emerging future of the company. 'The aim of this first step was simply to enable those people to experience their interconnectedness and the complexity of what was going on within the company. I subsequently encouraged those folk to learn from each other. This next step enabled people to notice the pattern of their interactions and shifted the level of learning and conversations. When everyone is busily engaged in their individual learning journey, "Level One learning", it is very difficult to notice that interconnectedness.'

'It's what I call "drilling up"', added Kevin. 'It's an example of how, as consultants, we can help our clients to get a fleeting glimpse of the multiplicity of the different perspectives and meanings that are in play, to become aware of the previously unacknowledged pattern. Habitually we tend to "drill down", to atomise and zoom in, instead of zooming out and looking for connections.'

The pattern as evolving rather than frozen

'We think of patterns,' said Adrian, 'as if they were fixed, because it is easier for us. However, Bateson pointed out that it is more appropriate to think of the pattern that connects as constantly in motion, "a dance of interacting parts". His conceptualisation of this pattern as pulses and ripples of information flowing through the system, which migrates through its repertoire of configurations while retaining an overall characteristic identity, is very different from the static and essentially inert view of matter that underpins the scientific paradigm. Conceptualising the pattern as not static but fluid and emergent implies that it contain the possibility for novelty as well as for continuity. Getting people to think of patterns as alive is quite a challenge though.'

As an example Adrian told the story of an AMOC participant, here called Chris. 'Chris had developed some self-deprecating patterns in the course of his life. Thus he had a strong belief that behaviour that could be interpreted as aspiring to guru-status or self-glorification was wholly inappropriate. Consequently he had a tendency to discount his expertise and considerable skill in his consulting work, including his ability to bring clarity in situations others found confusing. Eventually, encouraged by his AMOC peers and myself, Chris embarked on an experiment, facilitating an appreciative inquiry with a client organisation. Now an appreciative inquiry is, by its very nature, an unpredictable process, as it is aimed at creating possibilities for newness to emerge. Chris had never really facilitated such an open-ended process before. After the event we asked him how he had conducted himself in his role as facilitator when something surprising and unplanned had occurred. Chris simply and modestly described his presence as "just normal, natural, present, real". We offered Chris a reframe: "what would it be like", we asked, "if you brought your talent for clarity to your skill at being ordinary?" In other words, we invited Chris to notice the paradox of being ordinary and special at the same time and to stay with this apparent contradiction between two characteristics Chris had always considered mutually exclusive. Bateson and his Palo Alto colleagues, such as Paul Watzlawick, considered the ability to hold two paradoxical concepts as one of the ways to disrupt and change ingrained patterns. A view borne out by the effect our reframe had on Chris.'

Towards an ecology of Mind

Bateson's assertion that things are connected (for example, that the behaviour of an individual can only be understood in the context of the setting in which they find themselves) extends beyond the connection between people to other parts of the world that we inhabit, our physical environment. He suggests that we exist as part of an ecology of relations with our surroundings and that not only do our actions have consequences for our environment, but that this in turn has consequences for us, a pattern which he called circularity. The alarming rate at which we are experiencing the effects of our exploitation of our environment is but one striking example of what Bateson meant by the concept of circularity. If we feel free to pollute a lake, the pollution will, in turn, poison us. This connectedness and circularity is a key feature of Batesonian thinking.

In *Steps to an Ecology of Mind*, Bateson traces our exploitative relationship with nature back to the way people have traditionally (in Freudian psychology) expanded the concept of the mind inwards: 'if you put God outside… you will logically and naturally see yourself as outside and against the things around you. And as you arrogate all mind to yourself you will see the world around you as mindless and therefore not entitled to moral or ethical consideration. The environment will seem to be yours to exploit' (Bateson, 1972, p.468). Instead, he suggests that the individual mind is immanent, not only in the body but also in pathways and messages outside the body. There is, he asserts, a larger Mind of which the individual mind is only a sub-system and which is immanent in the total interconnected social system and planetary ecology. He illustrates his concept of mind using the example of a blind person walking with a stick. The circuit of mind includes the blind person's hand and fingers grasping the stick, their arm and the nerves conveying information to the brain. But the stick is also part of the circuit of mind as it conveys news of difference, or information.

In the context of consulting to organisations this means that we need to pay attention to all the different forms of connectivity that exist between phenomena, including, for instance, those connections that are affective or aspirational.

The theory of logical types

Bateson was interested in various modes of experiential learning and asserted that one learns from how one learns. Pavlovian learning, for instance, sets up a learning of fatality about how events proceed. Rote learning, on the other hand, leads to seeing sequences as self-contained and complete. In each case the learning acquired from the way we learn (Pavlovian or rote) is of another, more generalised level; it is second order learning. This structure of hierarchical levels is presented by the theory of logical types, from Russell and Whitehead (1910–13, p.410), which greatly informed Bateson. Russell made a rigorous distinction between members of a class and the class itself, which is of a higher logical type, and asserted that one cannot transcend the class of which one is part. Watzlawick applied this theory in the context of family therapy and provoked some thoughts for Kevin about his consulting practice: 'If you enter an organisation on a more permanent basis, like an internal consultant, you lose your ability to notice the patterns that you have inevitably become part of. As an internal consultant I had a constant struggle to somehow stay on the margins – to keep some level of independence. I soon realised that over time my ability to notice patterns and not to collude with reciprocal behaviour gradually diminished. It was inevitable really, no matter how much I tried to stay outside of the dynamics of the organisational norms.'

'The unfortunate result', he continued, 'is that the attempted solution becomes part of the problem. The nature of the discourse and dominant ways of making sense are socially patterned. There are conditioned ways of talking about organisations and therefore the way we talk about change is informed by the same way of thinking. So when organisations want to change, their way of seeing the world ties them into certain permissible courses of action, which are framed by the same way of thinking about the world that led them to want to change in the first place.'

Adrian gave another example from everyday experience: 'When we try to explain something in English to a foreigner who fails to understand us, we often end up shouting louder in the hope that the person will understand us better. In an organisational setting this tends to take the form of the attempted change simply resulting in getting more of the same, because the organisation is still working from the same set of assumptions. As Einstein put it: you can't solve the problem with the thinking that generated the problem in the first place.'

The implication for our work as consultants is that part of our task is to help organisation members notice those hidden assumptions and perceptual frames that subtly inform how situations and problems are interpreted or constructed. Kevin and Adrian aim to support organisation members in embracing alternative assumptions and experimenting with alternative constructions or interpretations of situations. Another term for this is 'reframing'.

'Fish are the last to know about the sea'

'The advantage we have as external consultants', Adrian and Kevin concluded, 'is that we're part of the organisation and we're not part of it. Therefore, our gift is to offer what we notice and to help others notice their own thinking.'

In other words, consultants can heighten awareness of the invisible (to the client) miasma within which everything they do is steeped. The challenge for consultants, before they fall prey to hubris, is that they may also be part of that miasma – especially when they operate in a world where managers, developers and consultants are all trained (formally or informally) in a point of view that is endorsed by a common language for talking about organisational life.

Adrian developed this idea further: 'As consultants we can invite people to immerse themselves in other ways of seeing the world.' He explained how he went about this in his work with magistrates' courts. 'People often join this system of courts at a young age and stay for their entire career, with the result that they cannot conceive of the world being different from how they have experienced it over all those years. My first step was to affirm their world-view, honour their experience and be gently curious about what they did. The next step was to convene a conversation to broaden the context. Senior managers were brought in to talk about what was going on in the outside world. They were invited to see the organisation outside of their part of it and also to pay attention to the environment within which the courts operated. The staff was very attached to local ways of seeing. They saw the role of their leaders as protecting and steering them through whatever problems the organisation encountered. The fact that their leaders felt as helpless and lost as they did was a revelation to them. This was a hugely unsettling experience and I was aware that people needed time to deal with the distress and upset that this unsettling realisation engendered. Seeing the world differently can be a disturbing experience. My next step was to help staff to see that this new perspective could be interpreted as an invitation for them to participate in making changes with the leaders, to see that they didn't have to be passive victims. I laid out a line in the room with one end representing a victim role and the other that of co-creator. People were then asked to position themselves on this line, in terms of where they saw themselves now and where they would like to be. I deliberately worked in a kinaesthetic way to encourage a visceral experience of what it was like to be in one position rather than another.'

To Adrian this process represents a classic example of 'pacing and leading'. The pacing was the process of honouring their reality and helping them to express it. The leading took the form of the question as to whether they wanted to change and participate in making a difference. In this example, 90 per cent of the staff said they wanted to participate and became involved in an appreciative inquiry process. 'The process started by inviting people to inquire into what was going on when they were at their best. This provided an affirmation of strengths they were largely unaware of and also provided a paradoxical platform for change. By helping them to identify what that they wanted to keep the same, they became more open to considering how other things could be done differently. Having developed a sense of their own worth, other things seemed to shift spontaneously. People became more curious about learning from others. I asked them which other organisations embody something you can value and learn from. They identified many organisations, from The Body Shop to British Airways, focussing on what they wanted to learn. For instance, they'd ask themselves: "Who manages change really well?" We subsequently visited a number of organisations. These visits provided the opportunity for a much richer inquiry than case study work, a participation in the territory being very different from an observation of the map. I sensed that people were much more amenable to this immersion and inquiry once there had been some form of valuing and accepting their own way of working. Through the process they quite literally stepped outside of the boundaries of their thinking and immersed themselves in other cultures. The stories they brought back represented news of difference and allowed for the identification of new possibilities. This led to new conversations and ultimately fresh ideas.'

The practice of organisational immersion

In contrast to the scientific emphasis on analysis, Bateson's view was that 'to understand something you have to immerse yourself in the phenomena under scrutiny. You have to participate in something to fully understand it'. It is a view close to the anthropological position that 'anthropologists do not study villages, we study in villages.' For consultants this can be reframed as 'consultants do not study organisations, they study in organisations.' Bateson used the phrase credited to Korzybski, that 'the map is not the territory' – in other words, studying the map gives a different experience to studying in the territory. As consultants, looking at the organisation chart gives one perspective – and a very limited and reductive perspective it is – while being immersed in the experience of the exercise of authority within an organisation gives a quiet different – and more multifaceted – perspective. Thus, there is an interesting dilemma for organisation consultants: on the one hand we have the advantage of noticing patterns by having some level of detachment, on the other we need to be close enough to the organisational reality to fully understand what is really going on.

I asked Kevin and Adrian how they went about immersing themselves in organisations. Kevin referred to Patricia Shaw's notion of 'entering systems temporarily through conversation'. 'For me this means engaging with whoever you find yourself, be it in reception or in conversation with the account clerks, and then following the ebbs and flows of the organisation. That's very different from only talking to the leader, or the person who hired you. That's the first level of immersion, a process of simply being in the conversational activity of the organisation and noticing, not judging, what is going on. The second level of immersion involves looking in the mirror and noticing the patterns in the organisation you're taking part in.'

How do we participate and experience our participation in a system at the same time, I wanted to know. 'The question for me', Adrian replied, 'is how can we develop the practice of exquisite attention to ourselves encountering and participating in an organisation? This involves acknowledging that the artefacts and symbols around an office can sometimes say far more about an organisation than the conversation with the CEO. As consultants we need to attend to the quality of our experience. We need to notice our feelings, thoughts, and the conversations we find ourselves in, what we say and what others say. We need to be aware of what we are noticing and not noticing, what we are doing and not doing. This allows us to bring into our conscious awareness all sorts of data which can be configured in many different ways.'

There is a sense of mystery to working in this way, drawing as it does on our intuition and its potential for allowing us to notice connections. Adrian compared it to the activity of brass rubbing, the scrubbing of charcoal over the paper slowly revealing the image beneath. 'Each time you pass the charcoal over the paper you are getting information. One rub gives random information. Only over time is it possible to see how points connect and patterns emerge. You can think of a consultant as an instrument that notices difference in itself, notices how this particular organisation is different from another and treats this news of difference as information that can make a difference.' With the latter remark Adrian referred to Bateson's view that information is news of difference.

Noticing what we pay attention to

We developed the notion of 'awareness of what we pay attention to' further through Bateson's concept of 'punctuation'. 'The idea of punctuation challenges us to notice and realise what we pay attention to and how we order what we notice.' Adrian illustrated this by telling the story of his dog, from the days when he ran a riding stable. 'When people arrived at the stables, our dog would drop a stick at their feet. Invariably someone would pick it up and throw it. Now there are at least two distinct ways in which you can interpret this. You can think of it as people training the dog to fetch the stick or as the dog training people to throw sticks. How we look at a situation is what Bateson means by the term "punctuation". The concept confronts us with the choices we make in how we construct or interpret the world. It also allows us to experiment with alternative ways of punctuating or framing our perceptions.'

Seeing in new ways

The scientific way of thinking encourages us to look for cause and effect, to search for causal links or the root cause of a problem. In business the mindset is that careful analysis and a determined plan of action will achieve the results we desire.

Bateson suggests that this form of linear thinking ignores the context or web of factors that can often make problems stubbornly resistant to logical solutions, a perspective he developed in his work with schizophrenics and addicts. He argued that we need to learn to think and to see situations in a way that honours the ecology of factors that hold a situation in place and that these can be complex and far from common sense.

We can learn a lot from the implications of what Bateson described as 'double bind' theory, suggested Kevin. 'Leadership teams often get themselves stuck in "damned if you do, damned if you don't" scenarios. I'm reminded of my work with a global drinks business where a major change programme was way over budget with all future projections suggesting that there was no choice but to cancel any further investment in any new technology. Costs had continued to spiral upwards over a two-year period partly because every time questions were raised about the feasibility of the project the Steering Group adopted the same response: bring consultants in to diagnose the problem and make recommendations about a way forward. This "more of the same" behaviour always seemed to result in "more of the same" outcomes. More delays to the project, more complexity and more costs. The solution, in effect, was becoming part of the problem. Finally I agreed with my clients to try and run the meeting without any technical experts or external consultants in the room. We would only invite those people who had a deep knowledge of each part of the business affected (regardless of status) and the various senior executives who had a stake in the decision-making process. This group of people (some 50 in total) who represented all parts of the company had, surprisingly, never met in this context before. Everybody arrived expecting to close down the project yet we developed a number of radical options that resulted in both major cost savings and a solution that was more "fit for purpose" than before. Quite simply, the participants had taken the time out to listen, really listen, to what every one of them had to say in a different working environment. Some of the words and opinions may have been familiar but they acquired a different meaning, and led to very different conclusions, in this different context.'

What is the difference Bateson's thinking makes in Adrian and Kevin's consulting practice?

They answered the above questions as follows: 'As consultants we are participants. We are part of our clients' organisations and we use this attachment as a source of information and learning. We are responsible for the world we inhabit. We are part of the ecology and will inherit the consequences of our own actions.' Adrian added 'I'd like to emphasise the importance of our awareness of our presence, of all the ways we communicate, of the fact that we can't *not* communicate. This means that part of the practice of consulting is to develop an exquisite/heightened awareness of how we're being present, who we are with and not with, how we are with them.'

Kevin talked of being a disturbance in the system, of 'things attaching or configuring around you as you swim in the water; holding things lightly, holding the idea that you are co-creating this particular experience, that people are giving each other permission to do certain things [and not others].' He talked of 'seeing, feeling, smelling, bringing things to attention, exercising a degree of judgement and recognising the power that goes with this. All this lightness doesn't however mean that you don't advocate when that is what is needed. At the same time you must not be so attached to your advocacy that you are already wedded to a particular outcome, because if you are, you are becoming manipulative.'

An outro – stepping out of the web

By the time of our follow-up interview, Adrian and Kevin were already reworking what I'd written about our first conversation. In addition, there were certain themes, parts of the ecology of Bateson's thinking they wanted to draw attention to.

There was Bateson's take on communication theory and his broadening of what is meant by communication way beyond the transfer of information. Kevin and Adrian talked of Bateson's notion of the digital and analogue aspects of human communication, the digital being concerned with symbols such as words, while the analogue is concerned with the affective realm – the direct and sensory aspects of communication. To highlight this they told Bateson's frequently cited example of a mother confusing her son by sending out contradictory digital and analogue messages, telling her son 'I love you', but withdrawing from his embrace. This mixed message then becomes a problem because the unspoken rules of their relationship don't allow for this mixed message to be acknowledged. The implication for consultants is that they need to notice and pay attention to these mixed messages in their clients, and themselves, and make explicit what is not being spoken of or noticed.

They related the importance of this sharing of what is being noticed to another Batesonian concept, the notion of 'arcs of meaning.' It is impossible, according to Bateson, for any one person to witness or understand what is going on in a whole organisation. People can only see arcs, or parts of the whole. Rather than interpret and report meaning, a consultant needs to find ways of connecting up different 'meaning-making loops', different interpretative realms. An example would be to make available to an executive team how their intent is being interpreted in parts of the business they don't normally inquire into or get to hear about.

Consultants can sometimes feel themselves compelled to make a difference, to change patterns however insubstantial. Bateson urges people to be very respectful of patterns that sustain themselves. Maybe all we can do in our role as consultants in the face of highly resilient patterns is to heighten our clients' awareness of those patterns and raise the question 'What are these patterns in the service of?' In these situations our job is to shift the level of questioning and reflection, not to shift the particular pattern of behaviour. Paradoxically, by focusing on what is and why it is so, the potential for difference – or more of what an organisations already is – emerges.

For Adrian and Kevin, Bateson and his thinking represent an invitation to re-conceive how consultants and managers lead in organisations. It requires a shift from hubris to humility. Bateson advocates humility because as individuals we have far less power and control than we imagine. 'We need to embrace the fact that we have much less power over the whole than we tend to think we do.'

Further reading

Bateson, G (1958) *Naven: Survey of the Problems Suggested by a Composite Picture of the Culture of a New Guinea Tribe.* Stanford University Press.

Bateson, G (1972) *Steps to an Ecology of Mind.* San Francisco: Chandler.

Bateson, G (1980) *Mind and Nature.* Fontana.

Bateson, G and MC Bateson (2004) *Angels Fear: Towards an Epistemology of the Sacred.* Hampton Press.

Berman, B (1982) *Re-Enchantment of the World.* Cornell University Press.

Harries-Jones, P (1995) *A Recursive Vision: Ecological Understanding and Gregory Bateson.* University of Toronto Press.

Shaw, P (2001) *Changing Conversations in Organisations.* London: Routledge.

Watzlawick, P, JB Bavelas, et al. (1967) *Pragmatics of Human Communication. A study of interactional patterns, pathologies, and paradoxes.* New York, London: WW Norton.

Watzlawick, P, J Weakland, et al. (1974) *Change. Pinciples of Problem Formulation and Problem Resolution.* New York, London: WW Norton.

Whitehead, A and B Russell (1910–13) *Principia Mathematica* (3 vols) 2nd edition. Cambridge: Cambridge University Press.

Short Stories about Working with a Gestalt Perspective

CONVERSATION WITH BILL CRITCHLEY

An organisational story – Part I

The board of Motorpart approached Bill and a colleague with an unusual brief for a typical situation. The situation was to work on a particular change initiative; the brief was to 'come and listen to a board conversation and get to know us'. This invitation already had in itself the possibility for working from a Gestalt perspective as it invited the consultants to engage with the conversational reality of what was actually going on in a board meeting. Delighted at such a 'progressive' brief, Bill and his colleague went along and attended the meeting. Towards its end, the Scottish CEO of the division turned to Bill and said, 'You've been sitting there watching, is there anything you'd like to say?' Bill responded directly to the CEO within the relational setting of the board – and took a risk, by making rather provocative observations to a stranger. 'Well, what I've noticed,' said Bill, 'is that when occasionally someone disagrees with you, you tend to ignore or over-ride their disagreement. This has the effect of quashing it.' Bill noticed other members of the board smiling. 'Was it just me, or is this a wider experience?' asked Bill addressing the wider group. There was agreement that this was a wider experience and something of a pattern.

The CEO referred to this moment many times over the next 18 months of their collaboration and joked that Bill had taught him to be a leader. For Bill this story highlights the potency that observation of patterns of relating can have.

An organisational story – Part II

The genesis of this encounter was the board of Motorpart's decision that the company needed to become more international and behave as one virtual supplier. This would require a new organisational structure. The senior team told Bill: 'We're going to identify the main tasks and appoint groups to work on them. We want you to train people in managing change and, by the way, we want them to own the change.'

Bill asked the senior group, 'Do you think that if you make all those decisions about the tasks and groups, you are likely to create a sense of ownership? Suppose you were to invite about 50 people to come together, explain to them what you are seeking to achieve and then ask them to identify the issues that need to be addressed?' The CEO liked the idea, although one set of country managers expressed concerns: 'But suppose they come up with the wrong answer?'

Bill was challenging their directive approach to change and their assumption that if they 'sold' the changes well enough people would 'own' them. To Bill, as a Gestaltist, change happens in relationship, in the context and format within which issues are discussed and people volunteer themselves.

A therapeutic story

Recently Bill was working with a new psychotherapy client – a person he'd never met before. He noticed that the man was mumbling and muttering and looked away from Bill, to his right and down. After about twenty minutes Bill said, 'You tend to look at the floor and mumble when talking, are you aware you do this?' The man said that now that it been pointed out to him, he realised it was true. Bill continued, 'If you and I are to work together, I'm going to have to ask you to make an effort to speak to me so I can hear.' At the end of this first session, Bill asked whether the potential client wanted to continue working with him. 'Yes,' said the man, 'no-one has ever said anything about the way I speak before.'

What do these stories highlight about working from a Gestalt perspective?

- Change happens in dialogue. Bill's first intervention at Motorpart was to comment on the nature of the board's conversation in a dialogic fashion. He described it as 'a dialogic intervention commenting on the dialogue of the group'. In the second part of the Motorpart story, Bill proposes an alternative approach to change, which has at its core the conviction that 'if you want change to happen, you have to engage people in a dialogue about the issues'.
- Raise awareness. In the therapeutic story Bill brings to his patients' attention something obvious to him that the patient had not been aware of. So too with the Scottish CEO and bringing to his awareness how he squashed conflict. For Bill this awareness-raising is about 'bringing things into the open and/or talking about issues which have habitually not been talked about.'
- 'If you really want to change, focus on what *is*.' A Gestalt perspective on change can be seen as paradoxical, for it contends that by really paying attention to the here and now, what needs to change will become obvious. This attention brings with it a heightened emotional quality of awareness and therefore amplifies different views which otherwise get pushed behind a façade of agreement. This contrasts with most traditional approaches to change, which tend to focus on a detailed vision of the future – a focus which results in the alienation of those people who have created and are involved in the present.
- Follow the principle of experimentation. Change happens through experimenting, trying something out and then seeing what happens. Creative experiments can be offered to interrupt a pattern or to work with conflict. Bill gave a simple example; if two people are arguing strongly for their positions, get them to 'switch positions and argue each other's case. Invite each to take the other's perspective.'

Bill views the above four ideas as 'right-minded principles', in that they appeal to our human experience. 'We know that if we continually live in the past or the future, we waste our lives. We know that engaging in the present engenders a sensation of liveliness and that experimenting is the path to discovery.'

Heightening the contact

A core Gestalt principle is that of 'contact', which means the experience of a person coming into contact with 'the other'.

'I draw attention to the ways people make contact and invite people into a more direct contact with me.' In the service of heightening the contact that people make with others and the world around them, Bill pays attention to how people make contact with one another and invites them to do likewise in order to enable them to experience each other and the world around them more vividly. He challenges the view that encourages detachment at the point of contact and instead offers an experience of contact that is more full-blooded and present.

Contact describes the process of coming into relationship with another person and Gestaltists use the concept normatively, they talk of good contact and bad contact. Good contact is the experience of there being a full exchange between two people, where the consultant or therapist is 'shuttling between the internal and external locus of attention, where I am noticing you and noticing myself.' Good contact is 'giving full attention to this particular relational encounter in the here and now, without being distracted by thinking about the future or what happens next. This means being fully present in the here and now with one another, with eye contact and bodily resonance, where client and consultant are fully aware of what they are mutually evoking and creating in one another.'

In organisational settings, when working with groups, Bill asks questions which are experienced as more direct than most people are used to. This habit of questioning is now completely natural to him. He describes how, when with a group, he will lean forward and ask questions such as 'How do you feel when such and such happens?' Or, 'Can you say a bit more?' Thus he invites people to intensify or stay with their contact with a particular experience, rather than moving on or detaching from it.

In an action learning set recently, one of the participants kept talking about 'we' and 'us' when describing an event or a course of action. Bill kept asking him 'Where are you in this?' Thus Bill seeks to challenge people to own their actions, their part in things. He made a similar intervention when working with a couple where the man kept talking about 'the relationship', as if it was something apart and separate from him. Bill pressed him and asked, 'What do *you* do to make this relationship unhappy?' The man looked mightily irritated, and Bill is aware that people do get cross with him on occasions. In this case he pressed on. 'This may be irritating, but let me explain why I'm concentrating on seemingly minor behaviours. I'm not interested in incident themselves. What I want to know is what each of you does, what your specific contributions are to the state of your relationship. It is in these micro-interactions that change can happen.'

In this case the pattern of exchange was that the woman in this relationship relates a tale of woe, wanting her partner to listen to her. Instead he concentrates on trying to solve the problem. She feels not heard and withdraws, in reaction to which he gets angry. This pattern of interaction starts with a series of 'moves' by both parties, a pattern of gestures and responses which are subtly misunderstood, and hence leads to a predictable outcome in which both people feel confused and upset. The pattern will go on being repeated until either party changes their response so that a new possibility emerges.

Amplifying difference and hearing news of difference

Another Gestalt axiom is that change happens through amplifying difference, usually at the local level – in other words, in the midst of the nitty-gritty of day-to-day activity and interaction. This runs counter to most established management practices where the goal is to smooth differences out, and the motto seems to be 'go for agreement, align people'. Management language seeks to reduce matters to what is common; it does not look to pay attention to small differences. The Gestalt principle is that by paying attention to recurring patterns at the local level, and the different experience that people have of these patterns, a shift may occur at a larger level. To illustrate this Bill told me the story of a consulting group of which he was a senior member.

It was a small group where the men had been in post for a long time and all had the same job title. Over time, three women joined. They were all employed at the same grade, one below that of their male colleagues. They described themselves as the 'tweenies'. After a while they started to complain to the wider community that the established senior men were not noticing what it was like to be in a group of three outside of the established core. Bill reflected that the response of the established senior group could easily have been dismissive. 'We could have written off the complaints as little more than whingeing. Instead we thought "Oh sh*t. It looks like we're not leading very well."' As a consequence of paying attention to their female colleagues' different experience of the organisation, an entire re-examination of the way business was done was carried out, the management team resigned and then either re-applied for a senior position or left the organisation.

The above story highlights how change happens from within a social frame. Gregory Bateson developed a related notion that is more specifically focused on how an individual learns (changes). According to Bateson, learning – which Bill is conflating with change – happens when people hear 'news of difference' and are able to take on board a new perspective, a piece of information, which shifts their frame of reference. This cognitive/behavioural perspective supports and is supported by the Gestalt principle of amplifying difference in social contexts.

Contact in consulting situations

Bill doesn't usually go to the same depth with his organisational clients in relation to their personal stories. He does however insist on a concentration, a focus on the now, and the experience of being in contact with them. Thus he might say to a client 'At the moment I am experiencing you as a bit prickly with me. I am feeling inhibited.' His habit and discipline are to make use of his own responses to people's behaviour in his interaction with them. This frequently surprises people, as it is not what they generally expect from consultants. They will often, at a later date, comment on the way Bill relates to people. 'What we valued about you was your relationship with your colleagues, its directness, how you openly disagree with people and don't try to smooth things over.' Bill believes this frees people up to be more honest with each other.

Change takes place in relationship

This is a core belief in Gestalt (and is similar in many ways to certain precepts of complexity thinking). The consultant or therapist needs to be absolutely present in the moment, in dialogue, in people talking together. Change, in the sense of something new or novel, happens in conversation with others, but not if I stay with my established pattern of self talk. The relational context demands, or rather gives the opportunity for, an inquiry into how what I say and think is different to what the other thinks and does. It also provides a grounded situation for me to experience how what I say and think impacts the other. It is the context within which the continued negotiation between similarity and difference can take place, it confirms and disconfirms various parts of our identity. As Bill summed it up, 'If I allow myself to be slightly disturbed then I change.'

However, being in relationship is not enough in itself. In group settings, people start saying something new only if they open themselves up, make themselves vulnerable to one another, become willing to be influenced by the other, to have their sense of self challenged and/or changed, but not to the extent that the self is too disturbed.

Being present with clients – dealing with idealisation

Bill and I explored what 'being present' with the other entails. 'Ideally I'm alert', Bill explained, 'I'm not tired or preoccupied or too worried about being seen to be valuable. I am able to be really interested and willing to listen. I need to make myself available to this person or group and also simultaneously be able to think intelligently about what I'm hearing whilst I notice my own responses.'

Being present is not always as straightforward as it may seem, Bill continued: 'Of course sometimes I am preoccupied, I may not listen well. But that is not necessarily a problem, for it may lead to something interesting. A mistake, or an incompetent response may cause something to shift in the dynamic in the client–consultant relationship. Often and most importantly it can disrupt the idealised transference that occurs between client and consultant. I am not perfect – nor do I even aspire to be perfect. Of course I'm human and so are my clients. I see the opposite of idealisation as making myself vulnerable, accessible. That does not mean I think you should diminish yourself. Being vulnerable is not the same as belittling yourself. Using phrases such as "I'm not confident" is an invitation for clients to persecute you.'

Being present with clients – staying observant

'I need to be very observant, to notice if someone is looking anxious or withdrawn. It starts with an unfettered noticing and a willingness to explore what I've noticed, so if someone hasn't spoken for a while, I ask them why.' Bill explained how he shares what he notices with his clients: 'I may offer my observation by saying something like "I notice you haven't spoken for a while and I am aware that I am wondering what you are thinking."' If someone is dominating a group Bill might say, 'I notice I am finding it quite hard to interrupt you or disagree with you; I experience you as quite a dominating voice in the group.' Bill feels one of his skills is his ability to stay open to his feelings such as being impatient or anxious and then to use them to explicitly explore what is going on in a particular consulting context.

An example: running a workshop

Bill was running a workshop on Leadership in Complexity for The Thoroughgood Corporation (TTC) recently. Bill was nervous as he doesn't like programmatic workshops. He was also discomforted by three people from TTC who had asked to sit in on the session to observe him. They sat to the side of the workshop in silence.

Bill found himself speeding the group work up, cutting short the time allocated for people to do exercises and becoming increasingly aware of the three silent witnesses. He noticed that he was worried that they were getting bored and became aware that he wanted to impress them. So he went over to the silent observers and explained that he was orienting himself to their presence, rather than attending to the group. By speaking of his feelings to them, he was able to interrupt his pattern of wanting to entertain them and to refocus himself on the group for whom the workshop had been designed. 'I bring what's happening into the present, and through dialogue, I interrupt its ability to disrupt me.' The risk for Bill is that he doesn't realise how anxiety provoking this can be for others.

Emotional and intellectual presence

Gestalt privileges emotional presence over intellectual presence. 'Lose your mind and come to your senses' was the axiom of Fritz Perls, the leading proponent of Gestalt. Perls' intention was to privilege the body and to develop Gestalt as a challenge to the traditional psychoanalytic method, which was a rather heady process, focusing on the intellectual cognitive process. Perls wanted to reintroduce the importance of the body as a source of meaning making. Bill admitted that, on occasions, he probably went too far the other way and diminished the value of good thinking.

'I am interested in re-integrating thinking and feeling. I want to encourage people to think strongly and feel intelligently.' He contrasts 'thinking strongly' to a dry, desiccated habit of thinking. However, sensory engagement is not a substitute for intellectual engagement. To be at his best, Bill needs to understand enough of the content. He gave an example: 'Recently I facilitated an action learning set where the subject was around car manufacturing. I understood the content well enough to engage fully. That's really important to me.'

The intellectual engagement is not, however, in service of Bill solving his clients' problem; it is about improving the quality of his contact with his clients. It enables him to reflect back well what has been said, regarding both content and process, which he considers equally important. Bill's assertion made me wonder how long it takes to become the kind of consultant with deep emotional and intellectual skills Bill was describing here. It seemed to me that developing those deep skills and that level of awareness must take quite a long time. Bill has now been a consultant for twenty years and feels he is 'just coming into his own'. Without being too categorical, we agreed that it was unlikely that it would take less than eight to ten years to develop the necessary social, intellectual, technical and emotional capacities.

Field theory

Field theory is, in the view of its originator Kurt Lewin, not a theory, but a way of seeing. Lewin put forward the idea that in social settings everything is connected to everything else. The implications for consultants (and managers) are that an intervention made in one part of an organisation will inevitably have an effect elsewhere because of the natural interconnectedness of all things.

Bill understands Lewin's perspective as a metaphorical one, taken from the physical sciences and applied metaphorically to social systems. Consequently he questions the wisdom of taking it too literally. Instead, he finds the thinking in complexity theory more compelling because it focuses on the patterns of interaction in a more helpful way. According to complexity theory, 'we may or may not connect with each other' – connection is not inevitable. The focus is on patterns of connection, which Bill thinks is often what is meant when people talk of organisational patterns, culture or norms. 'We are connected through our interactions with each other and not through some mystical third force... and we may or may not make a difference. Sometimes effects get amplified and sometimes they get dampened.' What Bill is introducing is a more explicit agency at work in organisational connections than is suggested by Lewin.

In both complexity theory and field theory, the focus is taken away from the individual and shifted to mutual interactions between people. For Bill this is about reframing our understanding of what it means to be an individual who exists as part of a community. It is about seeing the dynamic coexistence of the sense of 'I' and the sense of 'we': 'We can't be a community without individuals or an individual without community.' He further exemplified this belief with reference to Mead's comment, 'The individual is the singular and the group is the plural of the same social phenomena.' For a consultant, this presents a necessity to move beyond the notion of simplistic individual agency.

An example: collective accountability and field theory in a firm of design engineers

Bill is currently working with a firm of design engineers that serves as a potential example of this. The firm has a very intelligent managing partner, who works extremely hard and is getting very stressed by the situation. His presenting problem is that individual parts of the business are doing their own thing whereas he is convinced that the firm needs a strategy for the business as a whole.

As Bill talked to him, it became apparent that everyone left the management of the business to the managing partner. The senior partners did not feel accountable for the business. They did their own thing and abrogated their responsibility for the management of the business as a whole.

Bill arranged a meeting of the senior partners where they discussed the issue of accountability. Bill used the opportunity to raise the theme of 'collective' accountability. Owning his observation Bill said, 'It seems to me that what is really needed is a leadership team that has a shared sense of collective responsibility. Currently you leave issues of collective responsibility for the business to the managing partner, who is willing to take on this responsibility. You need to change your pattern.'

The tough consultant

Bill has worked with this firm of design engineers for over three years. During the early days, when working with the partners to develop a better sense of strategy, he was described as being very tough on them – which was just what they needed.

Because they experienced Bill as exceedingly challenging they chose to continue to work with one of his more emollient colleagues. However, three years later they came back to Bill: 'It's your toughness we need now.'

'Being tough' is a Gestalt quality. It involves a willingness to name things that are unnamed, to offer a provocation that makes a difference. This doesn't mean you'll always get the recognition that you feel you deserve. Whilst the design engineering story has a happy ending, Bill's work for another company doesn't. The client's finished product was put forward for an award for the quality of its design. Bill's role in this design was crucial – something confirmed by the chief client – and yet he was not invited to the award ceremony. Being tough (and effective) doesn't necessarily mean you're loved.

Further reading

Beisser, AR (1970) 'The Paradoxical Theory of Change' in J Fagan and LL Shepard (eds) *Gestalt Therapy Now*. New York: Science and Behaviour Books.

Clarkson, P (2004) *Gestalt Counselling in Action*. London: Sage.

Lewin, K (1997) *Resolving Social Conflicts and Field Theory in Social Science*. Washington DC: American Psychological Association.

Mead, G (2002 – originally published Chicago: Open Court, 1932) *The Philosophy of the Present*. New York: Prometheus Books.

Nevis, C (1987) *Organisational Consulting. A Gestalt Approach*. New York: Gardiner Press.

Perls, F, R Hefferline and P Goodman (1951) *Gestalt Therapy: Excitement and growth in the human personality*. New York: Julian Press.

Stacey, RD (2001) *Complex Responsive Processes in Organisations. Learning and Knowledge Creation*. London: Routledge.

Stacey, R (ed.) (2005) *Experiencing Emergence in Organisations: local interaction and the emergence of global pattern*. London: Routledge.

Towards Relational Consulting

BY KATHLEEN KING

I have long been puzzled by our apparent inability in organisations to live values of democracy, interdependence and mutual support. Although I and others espouse those values we continue to behave in individualistic, controlling and competitive ways. Clients too seem distressed, or at least mystified, by their ongoing difficulties with changing the way they work. Management literature provides numerous recipes for going about changing an organisational culture; yet to me, much of this appears to amount to little more than prescriptions that, whilst they may have worked in one context, would be difficult to apply to another. Some of the methodologies appear to be post-hoc rationalisations that simplify a complex and intractable process.

In this chapter I aim to share the journey that led me to my current sense-making of this paradox – the outcome of an action research project in pursuit of a PhD at the University of Bath – and its influence on my practice as a consultant.

My first tentative steps as an internal consultant

During my first attempts at supporting organisations through significant changes, I had placed high hopes on the 'learning organisation' literature. I remember the excitement with which I discovered *The Fifth Discipline* (Senge, 1994) as a budding organisational development (OD) consultant in 1995. Here, I thought, was a brilliant recipe for my new role. In my enthusiasm I may have paid insufficient heed to Senge's warning that his proposed approach would require sustained effort and profound culture shifts, away from wanting to be in control, having answers, and forcefully advocating one's views to get others' buy-in. I energetically set about applying Senge's tools, oblivious to the contradictions between my behaviour (advocating *the* answer, trying to control others or at least getting their buy-in) and the nature of the values underpinning the framework that informed my interventions. Needless to say I was not very successful. First of all I bumped up against conflicting values and visions in the organisation, and powerful players pulling in different directions. Moreover, the suggested discipline of exploring one's mental models, values and fundamental aims in life was not something my clients sought to engage in. Finally, the discipline of seeing patterns rather than thinking in terms of linear cause-and-effect chains, although valuable, was in my experience a technical and potentially rather mechanistic exercise in its own right.

Reflecting on my failure to effect significant changes in the culture of the organisation, I became increasingly aware of the tension between the values emblazoned in our mission statement, and espoused by all but the most cynical of us, and the reality of our daily struggles for recognition, resources and power in the pursuit of our own and the organisation's objectives. Most difficult to digest was the realisation that I too, frustrated and disappointed as I was with my colleagues, was caught in this paradox.

Searching for answers to my conundrum, for new and better recipes, I came across the work of Chris Argyris (Argyris, 1990). Argyris too was interested in understanding why organisations or individuals seem to choose to act in ways contrary to their best interest and to the values they espouse. Based on extensive research in organisations, Argyris formed the conclusion that there is a gap between our espoused theory of how to act in organisations and our theory-in-use. This is the theory that actually informs our actions and that values winning over losing, saving face (our own and that of others) and unilateral control. Argyris argues that our theory-in-use is reinforced by social values such as respect for others, which leads us to defer to others and to avoid confronting their reasoning or actions; and integrity, which encourages us to stick to our principles and beliefs. This results in what Argyris calls Model 1 behaviour, the typical pattern of which is: start with caring, support and respect in the pursuit of your goals. If this does not work, use strength and integrity, stick to your guns and exert pressure. Under those conditions individuals who have most power or who can outtalk others will have the last word and the potential for genuine dialogue and organisational effectiveness is eroded. Argyris advocates that OD practitioners should help clients by surfacing, through intensive cycles of inquiry, their tacit maps, in order to discover what really informs their actions, instead of what they assume informs them, so that they may learn to re-design those maps and produce more effective actions.

It is impossible to do justice to Argyris' fascinating body of work in this chapter. I recognised so much of what was described and started to explore my own mental maps using Argyris' two column analysis, writing down on one side what was said, on the other the inferences I had made, noting how my unchecked inferences influenced my subsequent interventions. As a result I began to take a more inquiring stance, checking out my assumptions more frequently and learning in the process how often my initial assumptions had been wide of the mark. I also began to use Argyris' action inquiry method in my work with clients. On a couple of occasions the result of the inquiry process was dramatic. One team especially, ready and keen to engage in deep reflection, began to see how their need to avoid the discomfort of anxiety-provoking situations, combined with their drive to achieve their objectives, led to ineffective routines of conflict avoidance, procrastination or manipulation, unilateral control and splitting of the team – to name but a few. The degree of honesty the team members brought to the inquiry generated a heady atmosphere of renewed energy and optimism. It was an exhilarating experience for all of us. But within a matter of months the team had, perhaps partly as a result of increased pressure to produce results and of imminent redundancies, reverted to its old dysfunctional patterns.

I was disappointed. This had been my A-team. I hadn't even attempted to work with teams where the ability and willingness to reflect and question one's motives and behaviour was much less in evidence. Clearly this was not going to work for me as my new OD recipe.

Much later I came to agree with Stacey and colleagues who critique Argyris for devaluing human spontaneity and unpredictability and for dismissing the *communicative* nature of our changing sense of self-in-the-world, viewing it instead as individual minds intentionally choosing to change through insight into their own mental patterns. But at that time in my career I was interested in exploring the nature of the anxiety that seemed to drive my 'A-team' to revert to the old patterns of behaviour they had been so keen to leave behind. It was the beginning of an enduring inquiry into the role of emotions in organisational life. Around that time I left my employer to start a new phase in my career.

On becoming an Ashridge consultant

Perhaps most clouds do have a silver lining. Certainly, in my experience, profound learning often happens in times of discomfort and uncertainty. Joining Ashridge Consulting Limited (ACL) was one of those uncomfortable times for me for a number of reasons: I struggled to make the transition from internal to external consulting; coming from a highly structured and rule-bound environment, the organic nature of the ACL community disoriented me; and I struggled to develop a sense of belonging in an organisation where relationships and connection mainly grow in the context of client teams, which I could not yet join. As my anxiety rose, I was increasingly at risk of constructing myself as needy and difficult, further reducing my chances of building rapport with my colleagues. In those early months my action research group at the University of Bath provided a source of connection, moral support, and perhaps most importantly, offered valuable frameworks from which to explore my discomfort, pointing me in the direction of the literature on emotion in organisations.

My initial exploration brought me into contact with Arlie Hochschild's work. In *The Managed Heart: Commercialization of Human Feeling* (1983) Hochschild shows how much work, especially providing a face-to-face service, involves having to present the 'right' (that is, managerially prescribed) emotional appearance to the client, which requires real labour on the employee's part. Although managing feelings is fundamental to civilised living, emotional labour, according to Hochschild, comes at a personal cost: if we fake a particular feeling we end up feeling dishonest; if on the other hand we work hard at feeling the emotion we are expected to display (for example, confident instead of anxious and unsure of ourselves) we are at risk of losing the signal function of our genuine feelings. Both generate stress in the long term. How do we know what kind of emotional display is expected? Feeling rules, a cultural prescription of how one ought to feel in a particular circumstance, set out what is owed in gestures of exchange between people. We recognise a feeling rule 'by inspecting how we assess our feelings, how other people assess our emotional display, and by sanctions from ourselves and from them' (ibid. p.57). Hochschild's work opened up a rich vein of inquiry with colleagues. In the first instance we focussed on our experience of joining and establishing ourselves in ACL. Did it require emotional labour – or in other words, were we expected to display emotions that covered up how we were really feeling? What were the feeling rules in our community and how did we recognise them? We soon became interested in the value of this concept for our consulting practice: did we experience consulting as requiring emotional labour and, if so, in what circumstances? What were the feeling rules in our relationship with our clients? Was emotional labour required from our clients in their organisations? At what cost?

Despite the appeal of the concepts 'emotional labour' and 'feeling rules', and despite the fact that we thought they did feature sometimes in our consulting practice – and in our experience of belonging to the ACL community – we decided that there was a significant difference in the role of emotions in consulting from their role in the work of the flight attendants described by Hochschild. Perhaps 'emotional labour' was a highly appropriate concept in expert consulting, where the consultant is expected to be self-assured, in control and confident, even if her true feelings are quite different. In our process-oriented consulting practice, on the contrary, feelings seemed to play a more complex role. From authors such as Schein (1999) and Block (1999), we had learned the importance of being aware of our feelings so that we could use them as a valuable source of information about what might be going on for the client and in the relationship with the client. Furthermore, Block encouraged us to be authentic in our consulting practice by 'putting into words what you are experiencing with the client as you work', which he considered the 'most powerful thing you can do to have the leverage you are looking for and to build client commitment'.

Personally, I was left with more questions than answers. First of all I objected to Schein's rationalist-realist – as opposed to social constructionist – and mechanistic view that underpins his work, as illustrated by terminology such as : 'Unfreezing, Changing Through Cognitive Restructuring, Refreezing' and 'Intrapsychic Processes' (1987, XII). According to Schein, the consultant needs to be a skilled observer of human interaction, always maintaining the role of audience, with the clients in the role of actors in the 'Drama of Human Exchange' (1987, p.82). In my consulting practice I had began to doubt the possibility or desirability of 'staying in the role of audience'. Even if I saw myself in a different role from that of my clients, I did not experience it as, nor aspired to it being, that of a rational detached observer. Nor did I agree with Schein's construction of emotions as getting in the way of rational behaviour and decision making. Was the presupposition that it was possible and desirable to minimise the emotional aspect of human behaviour not deeply flawed in itself?

I share an entry on the issue from my reflective diary, an important aspect of my inquiry process:

> November 2004
>
> The idea that emotions interfere with rationality is certainly still prevalent in much management thinking. Last week a client, a senior manager in a global oil company, told me the most valuable learning he had obtained from his relationship with his mentor, a board member in the same company, was the imperative to take all emotion out of decision making. I invited my client to think of a recent business decision. Had it been solely based on facts and figures? Had some data appeared more convincing than others?
>
> I suggested we need to collapse the rational–emotional distinction (Fineman, 2000) and quoted research that shows how decision making becomes impossible for individuals who have had the emotional side of the brain impaired. To illustrate my case I gave an example from Ricardo Semler's "The Seven-Day Weekend" (2003), in which he describes how the planning manager of a major oil company succeeded in predicting the price of crude oil five years into the future

> much more accurately than the 110 employees and the bank of computers that support the official projections of the company. My client was intrigued, but not convinced.

Secondly, I found myself asking questions about the complex nature of the seemingly straightforward concept 'authenticity'. It seemed to suggest a core, stable sense of self which does not take into account the malleable and multifaceted sense of identity that emerges in different roles and relationships. I further doubted the feasibility and even desirability of 'being authentic' at all times. In my experience the expression of feelings with clients and colleagues is contingent upon many variables: will it help my client if I express how I feel (for example, would I tell a deeply depressed client that our conversation is dragging me down too?); is my feeling related to what is going on in my relationship with this client, or does it originate in a different sphere of my life? If I am outraged by the behaviour of my client, do I share me sense of fury, or do I modify my language so that my client can hear the message?

Perhaps most of all, I was interested in the instrumental approach to feelings in the consulting literature: feelings are interesting because they give us information. Recognising and managing one's feelings can help us to deal with situations more effectively. In my consulting relationships I experience a range of emotions, from delight and elation, to distress and trauma. It seemed as if I was expected to rise above these, process them, and move on. How I could do that processing, and with whom, did not appear to be a question worth addressing, except in the psychodynamic literature on consulting, which suggests that consultants seek supervision, much as psychotherapists do.

In contrast to the supervision process advocated in the psychodynamic literature, in which the relationship between supervisor and client does not really feature, colleagues and I found that good relationships with colleagues, either within or outside a client team, were truly important for the quality of our work and our personal sense of confidence, wellbeing and wholeness. I had experienced a similar need to connect with others in those difficult first months of joining ACL. Bowlby (1989) calls the urgent desire for comfort and support in adversity 'attachment behaviour' and, rather than seeing it as childish or regressive, he regards the capacity to make intimate emotional bonds with others, sometimes in the care-seeking role and sometimes in the care-giving role, as a principal feature of effective personality functioning and mental health. He further states that healthy adults can display attachment behaviour when they feel under stress and that this display is to be seen as a healthy response to a difficult situation. I really appreciated the reframe. From feeling needy and dependent, I could now begin to think of my need to establish connections with others as a positive and healthy response to anxiety-provoking situations. Most of my consulting work triggers some level of anxiety, so it is hardly surprising that I feel the need to establish good relationships with colleagues in order to flourish in my work. All the more interesting, I thought, that this need for connecting does not feature in the mainstream consulting literature.

The following diary extract is an illustration of processing difficult work amongst colleagues:

> *January 2003*
>
> *Three colleagues and I are engaged in a consulting engagement with the board of a high profile organisation. Following two successful events, we have just emerged from a traumatic experience in which two of my colleagues were subjected to behaviour that ranged from passive to explicit aggression. All of us were reeling from the experience. We have spent a considerable amount of time trying to make sense of what happened, and supporting each other in a process of restoration and healing. We emerged from our conversations feeling stronger, both individually and as a team.*

I noticed a similar pattern with my clients: in times of organisational turbulence there seemed to be a significant rise in the need for and frequency of water cooler conversations, impromptu meetings in the pub and more formal get-togethers. And, not unusually, staff who did not feel the pressure in quite the same way, tended to feel impatient with this desire to connect and experienced it as neediness and dependence.

If seeking connections is a healthy response to turbulence and stress – of which there is plenty in the current business environment – and if both clients and scholars stress the need for more team work and collaboration and for dismantling hierarchical and functional boundaries in order to survive in their competitive environment, why does it remain so very difficult for people in organisations to do so, I wondered. I had come full circle, returning to my question of why we aspire to one set of values, one way of working, and appear so incapable of achieving it.

Inspiration from left field

I brought my question to my PhD learning group at the University of Bath. 'Well', said one of my colleagues, 'you may find feminist psychologists have some interesting views on this'. I cringed. I had resisted all writings feminist in the previous years as a result of some ill-formed, and even less well-founded, prejudices against feminist literature. I had some very unhappy memories of working in a feminist context in Belgium and, although I had found value in feminist writings at the time, I had maintained a strong enough prejudice against feminist groups to avoid associating myself with them. Underlying my avoidance was, I admit, the fear of being constructed by colleagues or clients as a feminist, and the rejection I expected would be the inevitable result.

Nevertheless, I had come across some interesting looking references in my reading of the 'emotions in organisations' literature, and eventually obtained a copy of Jean Miller's much praised work *Towards a new psychology of women* (1986). It was compelling reading. Together with her colleagues at the Stone Center, the author, a practising psychoanalyst, developed relational psychology, a feminist poststructuralist critique of prevailing models of psychological development. While it is obvious, according to Miller, that all of living and development takes place in relationships – a notion congruent with a participatory and social constructionist paradigm – our theories of development seem to be based on a notion of development as a process of separation from others. Psychologists use terms such as fusion and dependency to characterise a child's early relationship with its mother, and terms such as independence, separation and autonomy to describe the end point of development, maturity. In our Western culture men, but not women, have been encouraged to pursue this ideal of autonomy and separation, whilst the work of tending to relationships, especially relationships that foster development, has been assigned to women. Miller further argues that because of women's subordination, relational work has been relegated to the private sphere and consistently devalued by both men and women and that the emphasis on 'male qualities' in the public sphere, such as autonomy, domination and competition, has been oppressive to both men and women and detrimental to our society at large:

> All social structures that male society has built so far have included within them the suppression of other men. In other ways, too, all of our society's advances are still a very mixed blessing. …Technologically advanced society has led to vast improvements for a small group of men and some improvements for a somewhat larger group – at the expense of misery for many and the destruction of whole cultures for others. (Ibid. pp.77–8)

Well, much food for thought. Miller's arguments did seem to hold water: values and characteristics associated with masculine role stereotypes, such as control, competition rationality and objectivity dominate our Western world. Our organisations are rife with them. Our exploitative relationship with our very world is testimony to our inability to comprehend our deep interdependence with our environment, as current publications in the press, documenting the alarming deterioration of our planet, illustrate.

Was our inability to change our organisational behaviour from competitive, controlling and domineering to interdependent, collaborative and dialogic, really based on age-old gender patterning? Was the devaluing of the latter really related to the fact that we had for centuries relegated it to the private sphere and thought of it as women's work?

I was confused. In my experience the gender divide didn't seem quite so clear cut. Some of my male colleagues and clients were more caring, more interested in developing others, more interdependent in their approach than some of my female clients and colleagues. Some of my most ambitious, driven, autocratic clients were women. In my tentative exploratory conversations with colleagues I bumped up against similar protestations. Nevertheless, taking inter-individual differences out of the equation, the argument seemed to hold. Wasn't much of the nurturing, relational work in organisations traditionally taken on by women? The management literature too was rife with articles about the 'feminisation' of the workplace, 'feminisation' being shorthand for turning the workplace into a more caring, nurturing place.

Are women really, in their very nature, more oriented towards relationship and connection, and men more driven towards self-fulfilment and autonomy? Why would that be so? Carol Gilligan's (1993) research explored that very question. According to Gilligan the interpersonal dynamics of gender identity formation are different for boys and girls because the primary caregiver for both sexes in the first three years is typically female. Female identity formation takes place in a context of ongoing relationships, and girls consequently – experiencing themselves as like their mothers – fuse the experience of attachment with the process of identity formation. In contrast, boys, in defining themselves as masculine, separate themselves from their mothers, curtailing their sense of empathic ties. Male development therefore entails a more emphatic individuation and a more defensive firming of experienced ego boundaries. Difference is often interpreted in terms of 'better' or 'worse' and, according to Gilligan, this difference in development has been interpreted traditionally as 'women having weaker ego boundaries than men' rather than as 'girls have a basis of empathy built into their primary definition of self in a way that boys do not'. Consequently, our conception of adulthood favours separation, autonomy and individuation. The difference in the process of identity formation has implications for men and women's moral development. The moral imperative emerging in interviews with women in Gilligan's studies, is an injunction to care, a responsibility to alleviate the troubles of this world. For men, the moral imperative appears as an injunction to respect the rights of others and thus to protect from interference the rights to life and self-fulfilment. Gilligan sees development for both sexes as a process of integrating rights and responsibilities through the discovery of the complementarity of both moral perspectives.

Gilligan's argument for integration of a masculine and feminine perspective on morality had in fact been proffered many years earlier by Bakan (1966) who distinguishes two fundamental modalities in the existence of living beings, which he calls 'agency' and 'communion'. Agency is an expression of independence, and manifests itself in self-protection, self-assertion, self-expansion and in the formation of separations. Communion is the sense of 'being at one' with other organisms, and manifests itself in contact, openness, lack of separation and fusion. Bakan considers agency and communion as strategies for coping with anxiety and uncertainty in life. Agency seeks to reduce anxiety by controlling the world around the individual, by 'doing', activity, entering into 'contracts', achieving; whilst communion seeks union and non-contractual co-operation, is based on tolerance and trust, showing forgiveness rather than retribution, by 'being', rather than 'doing'. He associates agency with maleness and communion with femaleness, and maturity with an integration of the two modalities. Bakan develops the argument that the agency feature has been dominant in prevailing life strategies, with mixed blessings: 'Our so-called affluent society is evidence of the success of the agentic strategy. But… there is a rising sense of emptiness, meaninglessness, and absurdity', and that 'the villain is unmitigated agency'. The moral imperative, according to Bakan, is to mitigate agency with communion.

I began to reflect on my client work from the above perspectives. Working my way through my reflective diary notes, part of my research process, I began to notice patterns: the degenerative quality of imbalance between agency and communion stared me in the face, page after page. If Bakan was right, and both agency and communion were coping strategies in situations of increased anxiety, then it would figure that, in turbulent organisational situations, we notice an increase in both agentic and connective behaviour. Bakan's terms, although associated with gender, made it easier for me to look across the gender divide. I found unmitigated agency in controlling, autocratic and exploitative behaviour and in pressure for *action*, leading to organisational distress and ultimately poor performance by the people subjected to it. Unmitigated communion I saw in lack of assertion, rescuing behaviour, an inability to act, prioritise or delegate, and leading to resentment, stress, and once again, to underachievement of individuals and teams. I came to think of agency and communion as mutually dependent and reinforcing behaviours – a kind of yin–yang pattern. If I lack agency I cannot establish healthy relationships: since I disappear myself, my needs and my abilities, I create imbalanced and ultimately ineffective, unsustainable or unhealthy connections. If, on the other hand, I am too agentic, I disappear the other. Relating then requires me to balance my agency with that of the other, requires me to see, hear the other as a person, and be seen and heard by her. Was that what Bohm (1996) had in mind when he developed his concept of dialogue?

I started to explore the value of relational psychology with colleagues and agreed, not without apprehension, to introduce it on the Ashridge Masters in Organisation Consulting (AMOC). I quote from my diary:

> June 2004
>
> Relational psychology is now on the AMOC curriculum. Last week I introduced the framework to my colleagues on the AMOC faculty, feminist origins included. Colleagues were interested but voiced some scepticism about the feminist connection. I pointed out that, in the past, we had adopted a prescriptive developmental framework, oblivious to the fact that it had its origins in the study of the male half of the population, and that feminist scholars were at least explicit about their research being grounded in women's experience. Conversations will continue, no doubt, as we start to examine the implications for our lives, our practice as consultants, colleagues and members of faculty.
>
> I am glad to have crossed this bridge and am aware that it is an ongoing challenge.

AMOC, I thought, would be a litmus test. What would a group of experienced consultants, and by no means a fluffy brigade, make of this? I have a vivid memory of the growing excitement in the large circle of participants on an AMOC workshop. After an initial bristling (perhaps only a figment of my imagination) at the mention of the feminist origins of relational psychology, I found an unexpected degree of interest and recognition. At the end of the workshop one of the participants, an OD consultant in a large pharmaceutical company, said he could finally make sense of much of what was going on in his organisation: how senior women operate and how they are constructed; the tension between the need for team work and collaboration on the one hand and the pull towards autonomy and individual achievement on the other.

We talked at length about the difficulty of introducing relational practice in organisations with masculine cultures. We had more questions than answers, and I did admit that I do despair sometimes.

Taking relational psychology into organisations

Joyce Fletcher took the work of Miller and Gilligan into the organisational arena. Fletcher started from the premise that current, common-sense definitions of work implicitly valued certain (masculine) aspects of work and the people (mostly men) who tended to work this way, while making invisible other, arguably as important (feminine) aspects of work and devaluing the people (mostly women) who tended to work this way. In her study of working practices of female engineers, she sought to surface those invisible aspects of work by detailing a way of working that was rooted in a relational or stereotypical feminine value system, which she called relational practice.

She defines relational practice as 'a way of working that reflects a relational logic of effectiveness and requires a number of relational skills such as empathy, mutuality, reciprocity, and a sensitivity to emotional contexts' (1999, p.84). Below, I describe the four categories of activity that constitute relational practice, which Fletcher developed as a result of her research, and offer some reflections and examples from my practice.

Preserving: focus on the task

This category covers a range of activities in order to preserve 'the life and wellbeing' of the project, including activities outside one's direct responsibility, with an attitude of 'doing whatever it takes' to ensure the success of the project, even if it means putting aside one's personal agenda, placing project needs ahead of individual career concerns, or sacrificing some symbols of status.

'Preserving', as described by Fletcher, is not without its risks. The 'willingness to do what it takes' to deliver to deadlines and expectations, is open to abuse and exploitation if not carefully balanced with an assertive negotiating and guarding of boundaries with colleagues and clients. Asserting boundaries in my engagement with clients is, in my experience, particularly important because the way clients relate to me is usually indicative of patterns in the organisation. Power plays, overly hierarchical behaviour (pulling rank), blaming others for failure, abdicating responsibility are some examples. This is often borne out in patterns such as repeated last minute cancellations without apparent good reason, clients having exaggerated expectations – often in the form of expecting me to do the relational work in their place – and inappropriate high status behaviour – for example, put downs, derogatory remarks and inappropriate challenging of my expertise. Asserting boundaries, whilst naming the pattern I observe, and contrasting it with the espoused values of the client or the organisation, can help clients to become more aware of the extent to which they contribute to precisely the organisational pattern they claim to want to change.

My work with a 'charitable trust' offers an example of my challenge to the chair of the board, in a way that surfaced his pattern of relating whilst allowing us to work well together during the extra-ordinary board meeting. I quote from my diary:

> I had been warned. An intense man. Doesn't suffer fools gladly. Flown in from abroad and will not want to waste time. Cut to the chase.
>
> I did get questioned on my credentials and seemed to pass. Past experience, qualifications, etc. We had talked about his business a little when he sprung a surprise: "Let me tell you something. If this was my company I would not have you, nothing against you personally, but I wouldn't have a facilitator for this kind of meeting." "I understand." "I don't think you do." "Can I test my understanding?" "Go ahead." "My understanding is that you are used to being in control, that you like it and that you do not gladly hand it over to an external facilitator." Long and intense look. "Right. I must tell you that most trustees are of the same feeling." "I see." So another surprise. I had known that the CEO had had his doubts, but as far as I could see now I was not very much wanted. I explained the purpose of having an external facilitator: freeing the chair up to take part in the meeting. Not that I thought for a minute that being in the chair would have stopped him from doing that. Au contraire.
>
> We talked more about my work, my role in this meeting ('And you will produce notes'), and his experience in his business and on the board of a global company, and I felt we parted on good enough terms.

Mutual empowering: focus on other

'Mutual empowering' refers to behaviours intended to enable others' achievement and contribution. Fletcher explains that she chose the term 'empowering', rather than more commonly used terms such as nurturing or helping, to highlight the fact that behaviours in this category are intended to enhance others' powers and abilities. She distinguishes it from the more standard use of the term which treats power as something that is given to the employee, internalised by the employee and given back to the organisation in the form of increased performance. The qualifier 'mutual' refers to the respectful commitment by all to work on the self-development of all individuals in the relationship and indicates the underlying belief that to contribute to another's growth is to allow that person to contribute to your own emotional, relational or intellectual growth.

I experience this as the most important aspect of relational practice. It is, I think, the most disruptive of the conventional organisational discourse. Establishing a mutually empowering relationship with clients is not always easy. An instrumental orientation from my client often shows itself in the call for expertise: 'I pay you; you tell me what to do and how to do it'. The temptation to demonstrate my expertise is often strong, and not always appropriate. However, engaging my client in thinking about his (more often than hers; I have more male clients) future or that of the organisation, from the basis of a more *mutual* relationship, tends to generate a sense of personal power for the client, and a willingness to tap his own resources in taking responsibility for future action. Once clients overcome their initial reluctance, they are often enthused and invigorated in the process, as I hope the following vignette demonstrates:

> In May 2004 I was running a workshop, part of a large, ongoing programme, for a group of about forty clients: 'Organisational metaphors'. The workshop was designed by a colleague, in collaboration with the client organisation, and I was given a PowerPoint presentation and handouts. Instead of running an interactive workshop, I decided to start from the experience of the clients in the room, gradually building up various metaphors with them. In my opening lines I explained that I expected all the expertise and knowledge to be already in the room, and that it was my intention to work with the group to conceptualise what they knew experientially and to learn from their expertise. I closed the workshop sharing what I had learned from the experience. We had a great time together. Many clients came to see me at the end to express their surprise and joy at discovering their own expertise or their (hitherto underestimated) ability to engage with concepts and models.

Of course it can be wholly appropriate to explain, make suggestions or give advice. On those occasions I try to do so in a mutually empowering way: explaining the steps in my thinking, adjusting my status play, sometimes explaining how I have come to learn what I know about the matter at hand.

Self-achieving: focus on self

'Self-achieving' refers to using relational skills to enhance one's own professional growth and effectiveness. It is based on the belief that relationships are important to personal efficacy and that the long-term benefits of maintaining and nurturing affiliations with others are worth the effort. Fletcher distinguishes three types of self-achieving activities: making an effort to repair potential or perceived breaks in connections, reflecting and relational asking. I experience all three as attended to with care in the Ashridge Consulting community, where asking for help comes easy to me: the risk that I will be constructed as ineffectual is small, unlike in organisations where the emphasis is strongly on autonomy and independence. Seeking out relationally oriented colleagues, I find a readiness to offer help, without concern for being 'taken advantage of', a willingness to do 'whatever it takes' (preserving) for the benefit of the whole, and a 'mutual empowering' – those colleagues will offer help in a way that enables me to develop my own knowledge and skill, whilst articulating what they learnt or found interesting in our conversation. If needing help is seen not as an individual deficiency, but as a universal human condition, then asking for help is not something to be avoided, but an opportunity to practise calling forth 'enabling' behaviour in others (Fletcher, 1999). I will often seek out my mentees when asking for help, thus further establishing a relationship of mutuality, outside the context of mentoring conversations.

In this enabling climate I believe I have learnt more in five years than in the rest of my professional career.

Creating team: focus on team

'Creating team' covers a range of activities intended to foster group life. It differs from what is generally thought of as team building, because it is concerned with creating the background conditions in which group life can flourish, rather than with the task of creating a team identity. Fletcher distinguishes two types of activities: those focussed on individuals within the collective and those focused on the collective itself.

The examples in Fletcher's study include sending verbal and non-verbal affirming messages, listening and responding with empathy to non-work related information and listening to feelings. The engineers comment on how their male colleagues will seek out female colleagues when they want to discuss personal issues. They experience it as a serious responsibility, and construct it as 'work'. It does, in my view, not equate with emotional labour, in which feelings are treated instrumentally and as commodities (Hochschild, 1983), but is the result of a conscious strategy to enhance team spirit. Relational theory suggests that being aware of feelings is important to team effectiveness and that individuals who feel understood and accepted are more likely to be accepting of others, leading to what Miller and Stiver (1997) call 'a zest for interaction and connection'. Constructing attention to others' feelings as 'work' helps to open a space for a relational discourse and avoid the underlying intention being misinterpreted as an expression of personal attributes. I offer an illustration from my diary.

> 12 March 2004
>
> Much food for thought after an interesting conversation with Guido today. We met for a drink after a period of little contact. After swapping stories about our lives, our families and our work, the large XX client project, talk of the day in ACL, arose in the conversation. Because my colleague and co-director Paul had sent an email to the ACL community inviting expressions of interest, I had been in the difficult position of explaining to many colleagues why they had not been invited onto the team. I spent a considerable amount of energy crafting a carefully worded email. The email had struck Guido as an example of the extent to which I 'need to be liked'. Overcoming an initial sense of irritation, I explained how I saw that email as an illustration of my relational practice: a purposeful, choiceful action, with the intent of sustaining good relationships with colleagues. I used the opportunity to explore the differences in our ways of working (Guido's and mine) from a relational perspective, and hence my reason for not inviting Guido on my teams in the last year. It was a difficult conversation, but we agreed it had been enlightening. We parted on good terms.

Attending to the collective also entails creating conditions *among* people in order to create an environment that fosters collaboration and co-operation, including using one's interpersonal skills to absorb stress or reduce conflict, and creating structural practices that encourage relational ways of working.

Examples of relational activities focussed on individuals' needs and on the conditions among team members include creating moments for the team to reconnect in the midst of a client engagement, absorbing stress by supporting colleagues in difficult assignments and reducing conflict by working it through or diffusing it.

It is not possible to do justice to Fletcher's work here. In *Disappearing Acts: Gender, Power, and Relational Practice at Work* (1999) she explores the above categories in detail and offers many lively examples.

Fletcher argues that relational skills are not commonly associated with everyday effectiveness in the way one works in organisations, and that their potential transformational power is lost because they are incorporated in management conversations and literature according to the rules of the old discourse, which privilege instrumentality over relationality. Thus, within the old paradigm the only way relational skills 'make sense' is to conceptualise them as instrumentally useful. In order to recapture the feminine challenge to instrumentality, she argues, we need to make the power of relational activity more visible.

The potentially transformative quality of relational activity, according to Fletcher, lies in what Miller and others have called 'mutual growth-in-connection'. The notion that relational work can be an occasion for growth for both partners in the relationship is precisely what is disappeared when relational attributes of vulnerability, empathy and emotionality are conceptualised as useful in addressing currently defined organisational issues, in other words, if they are co-opted in an instrumental approach.

In other words, Fletcher makes a fundamental distinction between using relational skills to achieve instrumental goals and using relational skills to *relate* and then making instrumental decisions based on that interaction. Using relational skills to engage in growth in connection not only alters the process, it offers the possibility of outcomes that were previously unknowable. If both partners exit an interaction influenced by it in some way, the context in which future decisions are made is also changed, new factors may be considered and new framings of old questions may be suggested. That, according to Fletcher, is the truly transformational potential of feminine, relational skills, which is invisible in the current representation of the female advantage.

The possibility of change not in a preordained, shared vision approach, but change that is emergent and unpredictable, and may require the manager or change agent to respond in new ways, is eminently congruent with Stacey's perspective on organisations as complex responsive processes of relating, and with social constructionism. It is, in my experience, a powerful challenge to the prevailing organisational discourse and exceedingly difficult to embrace, for clients and, still on many occasions, for myself. An instrumental approach allows us to operate within a familiar discourse, and leaves us with at least an illusion of being in control.

I have started to use Fletcher's framework as a tool for explicitly claiming strategic intent and agency in my relational practice (as the diary extract of my conversation with Guido illustrates). At the same time, I continue to pay increasing attention to the way and extent to which relational activities are at risk of being disappeared in ACL and in client organisations, and seek to develop a vocabulary and strategies to surface such activities and to frame them as contributing to the espoused values of the organisation.

It's not all moonshine and roses

I intuitively – or as Miller (1986) would say, as a result of my psychological development process and socialisation – aspire to work relationally. My current inquiry focus is on the extent to which I can sustain a relational approach with clients and challenge the organisational discourse. As I have explained, many of our clients are seeking to change their practices in the direction of relational working (although they would not frame it in that way). Taking a consulting approach that models what they aspire to, at least at an espoused level, is important to me, not in the least because it is also congruent with my own values.

However, relationships inside the client organisation and with consultants are often formal and instrumental and clients can be suspicious of any attempts to establish connections beyond the boundaries of formal meetings and PowerPoint presentations.

Taking a relational approach in a corporation with a traditional, hierarchical and instrumental culture is not without its pitfalls (Meyerson and Fletcher, 2000). In a witty and sharp address 'Wives – of the organisation' to the Women and Organisation conference, Anne Huff (1990) warns us that, as women rise in the professional ranks, they appear to be taking over, and even generating, a disproportionate share of relational activities, and that, almost without exception, their careers suffer. Women, according to Huff, are uniquely vulnerable to 'relational claims', while men are much less responsive to them, because of the following forces:

1. The desire to live in ways that connect them to others
2. A 'radar' that continually alerts them to the needs of others and the tasks that need to be done
3. The tendency of both men and women to adopt familiar social roles when they are uncomfortable with women in professional roles
4. The growing need for relational skills in organisations
5. The tendency of groups to institutionalise useful supportive behaviours and treat them as assumed routines.

Huff's personal strategy for resisting the role of organisation wife, which she recommends to her audience, consists of learning to say no to secondary activities, relinquish the standard setting that leads to over-responding to things she notices (such as rickety furniture that needs replacing), sharing the relational tasks, expecting more from male colleagues and less from female colleagues, and learning to focus: 'to sacrifice a dozen worthy causes for that one monumental task that can be accomplished'. The examples from her personal experience and the specific advice are both helpful and compelling, and have been useful reminders for putting boundaries around my own relational work, so that, for one thing, I have managed to create time and energy to complete the task of writing this chapter. They are also good pointers in my work with relationally oriented clients.

Judi Marshall (1989) offers a similar note of caution: just as agency can degenerate into over-control, destruction of the environment, and repression of uncertainty and all but manageable emotions; communion can lead to over-adaptation, lack of boundaries and can be moved by external forces, with no voice or direction of its own. Maturity means integrating the two tendencies in a way that maintains the distinctiveness of each. Or, as Gilligan (1993) puts it: balancing the 'felt duty to care' with 'the right to care', 'to act responsively toward self and others and thus to sustain connection'.

I have started to develop a number of coping strategies, some of which have been informed by Fletcher's suggested strategies for 'getting beyond' disappearing (1999). Recognising and valuing my own relational work as a result of choice and strategic intent help me to remain discerning and choiceful, rather than to default thoughtlessly to generating or accepting relational work – exhausting myself in the process on occasions.

Growing-in-connection with colleagues and with some of my clients is the aspect of my consulting practice I value most as a means to re-energise and to work through difficult or challenging episodes in my consulting practice. Finding a good balance in my life between work-fun and outside-work-fun is also an important aspect of looking after myself, and one in which I have still quite a bit to learn.

In conclusion

Clients, then, don't often enter into a relationship with a consultant from a place of mutuality, and most might well express surprise at the thought that they could. However, with encouragement and a sustained relational approach, it is possible to develop a more mutual relationship. In my experience clients can actually come to cherish a sense of growth-in-connection, and the feeling that they offer me learning and growth too. One example comes to mind of a coaching client.

> I first met Clive when his organisation was going through turbulent times. Our first meetings took place in an office in London, but as the pressure increased and Clive became more stressed, I insisted we meet in Ashridge and start with lunch. During lunch we talked about our families, lives and interests outside work. We continued our meandering conversation during a walk in the beautiful gardens, and spent the rest of the afternoon cooped up in a coaching room, doing some difficult work. Our coaching relationship is ongoing, and we now meet regularly at Ashridge, despite the tremendous pressure of Clive's job. An Ashridge meeting always starts with lunch and, weather permitting, a walk. But even when we meet in the formal London office we make time for reconnecting. We have discussed the impact of the quality of our relationship on the quality of our

> *coaching meetings and agree it has made a big difference. We also continue to share what we learn from our meetings; it is a small but important acknowledgement of their reciprocal quality.*

However, mutuality does remain a challenging concept in the context of relationships with clients. I cannot demand that clients engage in an 'other than instrumental' relationship with me. But I can, and aim to, enter into a relationship with a client from a relational perspective. I expect to be changed in some way by our interaction. Sometimes mutuality can only develop after addressing conflict and/or some difficult surfacing of differences between what my client espouses and his actions. Such encounters can be taxing. I continue to try, and to reflect in my diary on the potential cost and the outcome. When appropriate I will share some of my reflections with my client(s) when we next meet.

Before I go

In this chapter I have sought to offer you some food for thought by painting a picture of how my practice as a consultant is developing and by sharing some of the thinking that has informed that development. If you had the impression that I offer a new consulting recipe, I have somehow failed you. I arrived at my current thinking and practice in the course of a very personal journey. I expect your journey is a very different one, and I do hope I can leave you inspired to pursue it with some fresh perspectives.

Further reading

Argyris, C (1990) *Overcoming Organisational Defences. Facilitating Organisational Learning*. Englewood Cliffs: Prentice Hall.

Bakan, D (1966) *The Duality of Human Existence*. Boston MA: Beakon Press.

Block, P (1999) *Flawless Consulting, A Guide to Getting your Expertise Used*. San Francisco: Jossey-Bass.

Bohm, D (1996) *On Dialogue*. London: Routledge.

Bowlby, J (1989) *A Secure Base. Clinical Applications of Attachment Theory*. London: Routledge.

Fineman, S (ed.) (2000) *Emotion in Organisations*. London: Sage.

Fletcher, JK (1999) Disappearing Acts: *Gender, Power, and Relational Practice at Work*. Cambridge MA: MIT Press.

Gilligan, C (1993) *In a Different Voice. Psychological Theory and Women's Development*. Cambridge MA: Harvard University Press.

Hochschild, A (1983) *The Managed Heart: Commercialization of Human Feeling*. Berkeley: University of California Press.

Huff, A (1990) 'Wives – of the organisation', paper given to the Women and Work conference, Arlington TX.

Marshall, J (1989) 'Re-visioning career concepts: a feminist invitation' in M Arthur, D Hall and B Lawrence, *Handbook of Career Theory*. Cambridge: Cambridge University Press, pp.275–91.

Meyerson, DE and JK Fletcher (2000) 'A Modest Manifesto for Shattering the Glass Ceiling', *Harvard Business Review*, January–February 2000, pp.127–35.

Miller, JB (1986) *Toward a new psychology of women*. Boston MA: Beacon Press.

Miller, JB and I Stiver (1997) *The Healing Connection*. Boston MA: Beacon Press.

Schein, EH (1987) *Process Consultation, Vol. 2. Lessons for Managers and Consultants*. Reading MA: Addison-Wesley.

Schein, EH (1999) *Process Consultation Revisited. Building the Helping Relationship*. Harlow, England: Addison-Wesley.

Semler, R (2003) *The Seven-Day Weekend. A better way to work in the 21st Century*. London.

Senge, P (1994) *The Fifth Discipline. The Art and Practice of the Learning Organisation*. New York: Currency Doubleday.

Working from a Complexity Perspective

CONVERSATIONS WITH CARYN VANSTONE (AND BILL CRITCHLEY)

This essay has been constructed in three phases. Firstly, I had a conversation with Caryn about her practice and wrote a text based on our conversation. Secondly, Caryn reviewed my text and added her comments. In order to keep some of the unpolished quality of the material, and to avoid presenting herself too slickly, Caryn inserted her comments into my text in indented format, as you will notice below. Thirdly, Bill decided to expand upon specific theoretical frames and draw attention to certain points he believes to be of importance for consultants working from a complexity perspective.

Introduction

In my write-up of our conversation I quoted Caryn: 'I can feel the perspective; I understand it intellectually and yet I can find myself still wanting to "bring someone round" to a certain way of making sense of what they are experiencing – often my way.' Caryn, noticing her discomfort upon reading my draft added:

> Reading this, my immediate desire is to delete it – to present myself more 'perfectly' than this. I know that trying to 'bring people round' to my point of view is not entirely congruent with the inter-subjective and emergent perspectives of complexity theory. Then I remind myself that the complexity perspective, as I think about it, is not a prescriptive theory which asserts 'if this... then that', but a descriptive perspective on the nature of organising processes, which invites us to make sense of the processes of communicative interaction in a way which is fundamentally different from systems theory, and other positivist perspectives on organisations. Nevertheless I continue to notice my desire to control your sense of me through my perfect articulation of complexity theory. But I know I can't – although, being human, I shall no doubt continue to try!

Caryn is a business director of Ashridge Consulting (ACL) and a member of the AMOC faculty. Before taking part in the first AMOC programme in 1997–8, she worked in the utility sector where she was one of the few senior women in the organisation. She also experienced the questionable effects of working with many consultants who worked from the conventional, instrumental position of most of the consulting trade.

> So many of those consultants were simply not ethical. It seemed to me that even when they were working with vaguely participative methods they had already predetermined their sense of the right answer, and manipulated the group to achieve it. Maybe this was their sense of the value they were adding? Anyway – it mostly led to paralysis and the diminishing self-worth of the people in the organisation left behind afterwards.

Caryn locates the theory of complex social processes in the broad philosophical field of social constructionism, which asserts the absence of any objective 'truth' in social relationships. It draws attention to the emergence over time of dominant themes and discourses through the operation of power in social relating and hence to the socially constructed nature of values and norms. This explains her equivocal relationship with notions of control. Working at her best she has let go of the need, the fantasy, that she can dictate how someone else will receive and respond to the words and 'gestures' she makes. Indeed she goes further, and would say that, at her best, she is positively relieved that she no longer needs to take responsibility for other people's responses to her.

But she finds herself repeatedly invited into relationships with her clients whose expectation of predictive agency is imbued with a traditional set of assumptions about how organisations are and how external advisers can make a difference. Indeed she still finds herself being drawn into a comfortable collusion with these assumptions. A significant amount of consulting work is performed from a mechanistic view of organisations, a belief that they are bounded systems where relatively simple relationships of cause and effect operate between relatively sovereign individuals. The consultant is invited into the role of mechanic or architect where sound diagnosis followed by rational design will lead inevitably to 'right' action.

The complexity perspective on the other hand offers a fundamentally different conception of organisational dynamics, where cause and effect are largely unknowable, where the main 'currency' of organising is the communicative interactions as people 'go on' together. From this perspective, the basic contract that exists between client and consultant is a willingness to step together into the experience of not knowing, to have good faith that something interesting and valuable will come of working together and inquiring into the multiplicity of experiences that inform organisational dynamics. This is a world away from contracts for specific deliverables and guaranteed outcomes.

> Reading this now, I am wondering 'what would clients make of this?' And I am immediately reminded that this is a huge step for someone to take who feels 'accountable' and responsible for outcomes in their business. I am currently experiencing myself as a leader (of a large-scale project) and therefore 'managing' others and 'managing' the performance of the whole – and I am feeling for the first time in years, the difficulty that this frame of reference presents to those 'in charge'.

A fundamental shift in how we think about organisations

Seeing organisations as 'complex social processes' is a definition developed by Ralph Stacey and his colleagues at Hertfordshire University, who in Caryn's view have done the most useful work in taking a theory which evolved in the natural sciences and then thinking rigorously about its relevance for organisations. They do not make a simple translation from the natural sciences to social phenomena as many populists of this emerging field are wont to do. Instead they have drawn heavily on the work of two sociologists, George Mead and Norbert Elias, and the emerging inter-subjective and relational streams of psychological theory, and have combined these with the core insights of complexity science. The focus of this theoretical integration is on how humans simultaneously form, and are formed by, organisations in an ongoing process of gesture and response, which can be neither controlled nor predicted – a process of communicative interaction that is fundamentally social in nature. This perspective contrasts with much conventional psychological thinking which locates meaning-making and identity formation within the individual, rather than emerging in the interactions between people.

What emerges from this synthesis is a coherent perspective on organisations which, while profoundly challenging traditional thinking, resonates strongly with Caryn's lived experience of what actually happens in them.

The traditional view, often referred to as the Newtonian or mechanistic perspective, sees change in organisations as located in individuals or parts of the organisation. This is the view that Caryn experienced in the HR department of the utility for which she used to work. The focus is on individual units within the organisation, and within these units the individual competency of people. The solutions, a popular word among many traditional consulting firms, tend to be based in individual training to address skills deficiencies, performance measurement systems to address problems of organisational alignment or ways of incentivising appropriate behaviour. As Caryn summarises it, the underlying belief is that by ensuring that all the parts work, that they all fit together into a structure which is fit for purpose, then the whole 'machine' should work effectively.

This view is often referred to as Taylorism, or 'scientific management', and evolved from a primary focus on parts of a system, to a focus on the whole system. 'Systems thinking' became the new mantra of organisation theorists, and the term 'system' continued to be used by the first wave of complexity theorists, which has clouded and confused some of the unique insights from complexity thinking. The early complexity writers spoke of organisations as complex-adaptive systems. My sense is that confusion arose because both Newtonian- and complexity-informed practitioners made use of the word 'system' but actually meant quite different things. When Caryn was a client in her days as a utility manager, the consulting company she had to work with was a typical practitioner in the field of business process re-engineering, which focused on how the actions of individual parts fitted together to make up a whole 'system'. It was still at heart a machine-metaphor-informed perspective on how organisations operate. This way of working assumed that there was a whole that could be known and understood from some privileged position of detached observation.

In the late 90s this perspective became associated with 'getting the whole system in the room'. Organisations were put through a particular method of working with large groups, with a focus on 'seeing the patterns in the system' and predicated upon the assumption of 'a knowable system of parts' with the ambition of 'fixing the whole'. To Caryn, the notion of a knowable 'whole', with boundaries that denote 'what's on the inside and what's on the outside' is rather bizarre, but it was the underlying assumption of systems thinking in the late nineties.

Complexity thinkers challenge this reification of organisations, in which an organisation is a thought of as a 'thing' existing in a bounded physical space. Instead, they propose a temporal view, which understands organisations as an ongoing *process* of communicative interaction which cannot be 'seen' by a detached observer as an object occupying a space. They assert that we are all participants in this process; that there is no such thing as 'the system' as there are no physical boundaries, only the ones we construct in our heads; there is no clear definition of inside and outside, or where an organisation begins or ends. To ground this theory Caryn takes the example of ACL and asks, 'If ACL is a system, are the clients on the inside or the outside? And if these clients go home and talk with their kids and gain a piece of insight which they apply at work, are their kids then on the inside or outside of the "system"?'

Her alternative framing is that organisations are patterns of interaction without boundaries. The complex responsive processes that make up human interaction are mutually influencing, but this is not the same as being a system. They are a dynamic and ever-changing series of new and not-new experiences. Her final challenge to the systems thinkers comes with the problem of explaining novelty. From a systems perspective, everything that has the potential to unfold must be enfolded to begin with; therefore there is no potential for novelty to happen in a bounded system.

> ...and yet I still often work with large groups with my clients – using appreciative inquiry summits, open space and a variety of blends of other approaches. Why does it work if I don't think I am working with the 'whole system'? I think I am working with large groups without the assumption of 'wholeness'. By bringing together a large group I assume that I am providing the opportunity for diverse new connections to be made, from which emerges new possibilities and fresh sense-making – in effect, a shift in the discourse patterns arising from difference meeting familiarity.

Being freed by letting go of the systems perspective

Caryn finds the complexity perspective liberating, whereas she found systems thinking paralysing. She has had experience of working with, and seeing people working with, the National Health Service (NHS) and finds the idea that the whole NHS system can be worked with quite ludicrous. If the system as a whole has to be worked with then more and more people would have to be involved, which eventually makes it impossible to get started anywhere. After all, what is the 'whole' NHS? Does one include pharmaceutical companies? Families? Government?

> So I see organisations paralysed by wanting to work with 'the whole', because they don't know how to do this; how to get started. What they often come up with are highly elaborate, over-engineered and hugely expensive change programmes to be 'driven through' the whole organisation. Those programmes take a very long time, cause a lot of distress, dislocation and frustration, because they go 'off track', don't achieve full 'buy in', get overtaken by events and do not produce the intended results.

The liberation comes from the focus that complexity thinking places on relationships, patterns of communication and how people go on together at the local level. It abandons the hubris of believing that a group of consultants can, by applying sophisticated change models and programmes, move a whole organisation from an unsatisfactory place to a more desirable one. Universal recipes designed in one part of an organisation do not translate into uniform behavioural change in the variety of local contexts and settings. We all know this from our experience. Complexity thinking speaks instead of the possibility of changing patterns of communication at the local level, which may amplify into a shift in pattern at a larger scale. Caryn finds herself now free to start anywhere in her work with her clients, whenever and however she meets with people.

I am therefore making a different assumption to that made when working with a distinct part of a 'system'. I work at a local level with a particular department, or group of people interested in some issue or change. My challenge to my clients is to start to notice how the relationships and connections extend beyond their supposed boundaries. By extending and noticing connectivity, small shifts in one area can (but may not) result in new patterns that spread in an unpredictable way into the organisation. On many occasions in my work I have noticed how something started in one place, seemed to go underground and then popped up somewhere completely different. This is a good example of the liveliness and potency of informal relationships that most change perspectives either deny or try to overcome. At first I thought clients might resist this approach, but in the main I find that people respond intuitively from a deep experience of their lives in organisations and say 'yes – of course it makes sense to develop new and interesting relationships, and not just engage the usual suspects'.

A short story about trying to assert control through a 'values' programme

Caryn has been working for a number of years with ATech, a company in the communications/technology sector. When she first started talking with them, they expressed their desire to revitalise the corporate values. They talked about values as if they were a 'thing' that people had lost, or never acquired, rather than implicit 'rules' that emerged in the way people interacted with each other. Therefore the view was that individuals (as distinct entities) would need a training programme to learn to enact the behaviours that the values required.

Caryn started by musing on the way of thinking that gives rise to this kind of brief, which is not at all uncommon. It seemed worthwhile to unpack some of the underlying assumptions. First of all it presupposes that there is one set of rules which, if consistently applied will lead to consistently desirable behaviour. Secondly it assumes that it is possible to identify this set of rules which can then be generalised and applied in any situation regardless of local context.

It further assumes that this set of rules can readily be conceptualised a priori; in other words, the lessons of past experience can be applied to future situations, so that nothing novel or unpredictable is expected to occur. However, by definition these rules are either not self-evident, or not in everyone's interest to follow. So a further assumption is being made, that a very rational group of leaders can identify this one set of rules and require the rest of the organisation to comply with them.

When these assumptions are made visible, it becomes apparent that the project was misconceived. The first ideas about taking a different approach emerged in informal conversations between Caryn and a personal friend working for ATech. Caryn saw herself as participating in the ATech process of communicative interaction, asking provocative questions which then stimulated different discourses between her friend and other senior managers in the organisation. Caryn describes this as working in the 'betweenness', interrupting a pattern of thinking through a series of conversations. In this case her intervention resulted in corporate HR having a different conversation with the board, which then took a different view as to what was needed in the organisation. As we can see, Caryn was not working in the formal system, which is the domain of most consulting interventions. She was engaging with the informal processes. The fact that the board developed a different perspective on corporate values and how to engage with them was the consequence of all sorts of small shifts in conversations happening in all sorts of relationships – none of which were predictable at the time of the informal 'chats'.

Beyond training programmes to inquiring into the present reality

Rather than considering values as missing and to be learnt, ATech decided to inquire into how values were already manifest in current behaviour. This developed into experimenting with a large group gathering (over 200 highly diverse employees) which seeded a wide variety of 'out of control' change conversations, experiments and shifts in the organisation around the world.

> Catching up with some of the people involved in this, I have been surprised by the range and number of different ways in which people have made sense of this experience – leading to very different enactments of what they learnt at the gathering, back in their own cultures and settings. This feels wonderfully rich and alive to me – and particularly suited to a technology company for whom singular thinking and alignment would probably be the kiss of death.

The more one inquires into the implications of approaching the world this way, the more radical it becomes. Interaction and conversation are seen as the main currency of the organisation, the prime focus of managers and consultants being on the conversations that are taking place in ATech and in the world that ATech exists in and creates. Intervention becomes a matter of noticing what is being talked about, amplifying certain conversations; talking differently.

One of the leading practitioners working from this perspective, Patricia Shaw, is a significant influence on Caryn's work. Caryn understands Patricia's consulting practice as being focused on working with clients in the 'now', the living present. This contrasts with much consulting which assumes there is somewhere else to be and that the consultant is the one who knows about a 'somewhere other than the present' destination – and will take the client there. As Caryn interprets Patricia's practice, the consultant intervenes by noticing and drawing attention to conversational patterns and this sparks the potential for novelty. To borrow from Gregory Bateson, the consultant tries to 'be the difference that makes a difference.'

> Despite this, I can find myself with a clear mental picture of some destination that the organisation should move towards – and this can unfortunately colour my work with them. I struggle to stay with what is, rather than working as if there was something to become that is different. The more I get drawn into some 'other place/other future' orientation, the less I am able to notice the patterns, or spark novelty in the present. I think it is this tendency that undermines so many change efforts.

Caryn does not believe that she has the power to bring about specific reactions, responses and changes in her clients and organisations as a result of her intentional interventions. She knows that she does not have the capacity for 'predictive agency'. This does not, however, equate to a sense of powerlessness. Managers, leaders and consultants exercise power through the intentions they bring into their interactions and conversations and through what they try to amplify and dampen in the pattern of conversation. Their interactions and relationships may be louder than other peoples', but they are nevertheless participants in the messy process of communicative interaction along with everyone else.

So what does 'working from a complexity perspective' mean?

Caryn sees herself working from a complexity perspective, a perspective that is figural in her consulting philosophy and that of her organisation. But what does this mean?

Organising is conversing and an organisation is patterns of conversation. As active creators and participants in these patterns, people negotiate how to go on together, getting work done and paying attention to how work gets done. Norbert Elias points out that power is inherent in this process of negotiation, because in engaging in joint action people are inevitably constrained by one another's needs, intentions and concerns as well as by formal power differentials. This shifting power dynamic creates, sustains, or undermines particular patterns of relationship.

Within this context there is no such thing as an autonomous individual because individual characters and identities only exist in relationship with others. Formal ways of structuring conversations are designed in the form of organisational charts, rules, procedures and so forth, but they are mediated, sometimes subverted, by the informal social networks and emergent ways of people going on together. Hence changes to structures and procedures are only a small part of a change process. The real work lies in engaging with the informal processes, the way that people come together and go about their business in a variety of non-prescribed and unpredictable ways.

In Caryn's work, therefore, the focus of the inquiry and the intervention is on the interactions, stories and patterns that arise from people's experience, for it is in these that culture lives.

> I can imagine a client reading this and saying to themselves 'this sounds as though there is no formal structure; is it just about turning up and making it up as you go along?' – and being a bit worried by that!

Caryn finds herself not only influenced by the work of other complexity academics such as Stacey and Shaw, but also by improvisation artists such as Frank Barrett (jazz pianist) and Neil Mullarkey (The Comedy Store). All of them point to the importance of minimal structure whilst creating conditions for innovation and surprise. The structure in these cases enables interaction and conversation (between players for example) but does not attempt to predetermine outcome. Frank Barrett talks about a good piece of jazz being four people on a quest to create order. This order does not pre-exist, it isn't 'discovered' in that sense, it is a pattern that emerges and is co-created through their every interaction.

Some informing principles of working from a complexity perspective

(a) Structure

An absence of structure tends to heighten anxiety and inhibit innovation. The problem is that many organisations like to maximise structure in order to produce alignment and predictability, which people have learnt to equate with safety. It is also the case that when managers are highly anxious they try and reduce their anxiety by imposing structure. But an over-engineered structure has a perverse effect. The more people try to contain human sense making by providing proceduralised interpretations and rules, the less likely it is that people will work flexibly and intelligently within the structure. They are more likely to comply with the rules than to improvise in response to the exigencies of the moment.

Structure and novelty coexist and enable each other. Procedures are needed to support core organisational processes, but paradoxically leaders need to both uphold and challenge procedures at the same time, especially the informing habits and assumptions in which the processes and procedures are grounded.

Without this continuous and intelligent review of structure, organisations are likely to indulge in frequent, convulsive and often unsuccessful restructuring or re-engineering.

I remember attending an evening talk by Ralph Stacey to a local branch of the Strategic Planning Society in 1998. Many jaws hit the floor when he announced that the role of leaders was to be 'a good enough mother'. He was drawing from the notion that good enough parenting is about just enough structure to create just enough safety, and just enough freedom and lack of control to allow for mistakes and experiments – scraped knees as well as successfully climbed trees. This facilitates learningful play – a concept often lost on the world of organisations, but deeply relevant in my view.

(b) Connectivity

When working in organisations Caryn seeks to help people foster connectivity. If people are not well connected, and are stuck in a set of repetitive conversations involving the same players, then the organisation is likely to be stuck in a situation of high stability and low novelty. As a consultant, the goal is to try and find ways of connecting people who do not usually meet, so that something new may happen. Change emerges from, as Bateson put it, 'news of difference'. Fostering connectivity also relies on a certain level of redundancy in organisation, the slack that has been so often driven out by the organisational orthodoxy of efficiency at all costs. Such redundancy allows for some hanging out, finding out what each other are up to, sharing ideas, making meaning, challenging each other – as Hewlett Packard are reputed to have done in their halcyon early days.

(c) Power differentials

When an excessive differential in power is exercised, initiative, disagreement, experimentation and so forth are inhibited; conformity and compliance are safer and hence novelty or innovation does not emerge. If high power is used by one organisational grouping to suppress the views of others, one frame of reference becomes dominant, thus disallowing the flow of information, experiments and initiatives which might challenge it. Even when the high power group espouses the need for diversity, a pattern of power relations may suppress it. The high power group may say 'we can be different', but the social experience carries with it the message that 'you can best survive by being like us', by coming up with 'the right answer.'

In order to stimulate a rich mix of relationships, both formal and informal, Caryn has had to work in a particular way. Typically external consultants are well connected into the formal aspects of an organisation; after all, they are usually invited in by someone of high status within the organisation. However, external consultants are rarely well connected into the informal aspects of organisational life (the reverse may well be the case for internal consultants). To address this, Caryn spends a lot of time just hanging out in organisations. This has given her a relational presence that allows her to be present differently (or to 'do different stuff' as she originally put it), to 'hang out' in the corridors and engage in conversations that may or may not be the difference that makes a difference.

Caryn hasn't always been able to charge money for this time, because 'hanging out' is not usually seen as a legitimate billable activity, whereas working in the formal arena, such as running workshops, large group events, and attending formal management meetings, is. Patricia Shaw on the other hand, in her book *Changing the Conversation in Organisations*, describes how in her practice she formally contracts for engaging with informal processes in a series of emerging conversations.

(d) Diversity

In her work Caryn challenges the conventional emphasis on the virtue of alignment and harmonisation. She agrees with people such as Mintzberg who have argued that when it comes to organisational strategy the weeds are as important (if not more so) than the carefully nurtured tomatoes fostered by the formal corporate system. Novelty emerges from some messiness and contention; hence her consulting questions run along these lines:

- How do you notice difference round here?
- How do you bring it to life?
- How do you allow different perspectives?

And the hardest thing is to encourage and support intellectual diversity.

Why does living with a complexity perspective matter to Caryn?

> I would like to experience organisations as communities, arenas of human sense making. This must assume that I don't always experience them this way, which on face value seems to contradict everything I have just said about what organisations are. I guess what I mean here is that I don't always experience organisations as generative communities, flourishing arenas of sense making.

Caryn sees the need to move away from a worldview built around the notions of individualism, efficiency and alignment. She has a physical memory behind her ribcage of what it was like to consult and work in an organisation where the frame of reference was constructed around those three orthodoxies. This negative memory is fuelled by what this meant for the human relationships she was part of. She experienced the application of these three principles as destructive of the web of conversations and relationships that were the lifeblood of the place.

Her attraction to the complexity perspective comes from her experience of the reactions of some people at the media company she has been working for over the last few years. She and people within the organisation have noticed that they are connecting differently with their colleagues and with themselves. 'It is the humanity of it', that attracts her to the effects of working in the way she does. She feels enriched when she sees and is part of people being in conversation with each other. It is not a matter of people being swept along in some happy-clappy evangelical experience; it is something much more ordinary and real than that.

For Caryn, the complexity perspective validates a personal need to engage with people in the reality of their current situation, set within the context of the relationships and conversations that they both inform and are informed by. A complexity perspective is a life-affirming perspective, one that allows her to be fully present and a voice in the pattern of interaction that informs how organisational processes work and change.

In short, working in this way exposes me. It creates the need to embrace a world which is both messy and ordered, stable and novel, ordinary and extraordinary. It is a world that is an expression of all that human beings are – which fundamentally reconnects me with my own sense of being human – flaws and all.

Further reading

Barrett, F (2000) 'Cultivating an Aesthetic of Unfolding: Jazz improvisation as a Self-organising System' in S Lindstead and HJ Hopfl, *The Aesthetics of Organisations*. London: Sage.

Bateson, G (2000) *Steps to an Ecology of Mind*. Chicago: University of Chicago Press.

Elias, N (1991) *The society of individuals*. Oxford: Blackwells.

Mead, G (1967) *Mind, Self and Society, from the Standpoint of a Social Behaviorist*. London: The University of Chicago Press.

Mintzberg, H (1998) *Strategy Safari – A guided tour through the wilds of strategic management*. New York: Simon and Schuster.

Shaw, P (2001) *Changing Conversations in Organisations*. London: Routledge.

Shaw, P and R Stacey (eds) *Experiencing Spontaneity, Risk and Improvisation in Organisational Life*. Working Live, London: Routledge.

Stacey, RD (2001) *Complex Responsive Processes in Organisations. Learning and Knowledge Creation*. London: Routledge.

Stacey, RD (2003) *Complexity and Group Processes*. Hove: Brunner-Routledge.

Stacey, RD, D Griffin, et al. (2000) *Complexity and Management*.

Inquiry and Reflective Practice

CONVERSATIONS WITH ROBIN LADKIN

This essay was written in two phases: I wrote out the notes from my conversation with Robin, and he then shared them with a number of his clients and colleagues, to get their thoughts and responses. I have called that text 'Round 1'. In 'Round 2' I share our reflections that resulted from the feedback Robin received from clients and colleagues.

ROUND 1

> 'When I imagine my experience is more useful than my inquiring I am useless...
> When I deny my experience I'm not effective.'

Robin's practice, as teacher and as consultant, is informed by a deep attachment to the discipline of inquiry, of supporting and being with his clients as together they pay closer attention to what is going on in the outer world, as well as within themselves. At the same time he does not deny his clients' or his own expertise.

Working with the experience of knowing and not knowing at the same time

'I bring a wealth of business content into my consulting. It is a significant aspect of my practice. Much of my credibility is based on my knowledge of the psychology of organisations and people. I have a thorough understanding of strategy and when necessary, I can even do a pretty good job of quantifying things.'

In my conversations with Robin I was struck most forcibly by his view that taking an inquiring approach to consulting does not mean 'turning up with a blank canvas'. Rather, it is about arriving with an orientation to inquire while also owning and putting to use his expertise in leading and managing in organisational contexts. Robin illustrated that view with an example: 'I am currently coaching the Chief Operating Officer of Ambient Design, a likely successor to the CEO. I was working with him as he crafted a strategy paper. I was listening attentively and, at the same time, I was examining the rigour of his argument and making judgements about the quality of it. In other words, I have expertise in strategising and I want to honour that expertise; however, it can never be a substitute for the discipline of deeply attentive inquiry. When I find myself with clients or colleagues who do not share my expertise in a relevant area, I seek to make that expertise available to them in a way that does not leave them feeling overwhelmed or less able, nor do I pretend it to be anything other than limited or partial. When I imagine my experience is more useful than my inquiring, I'm useless. When I deny my experience I'm not effective.'

The challenge for Robin, as I understand it, is to ensure that inquiry and knowing are not split, that the experience of knowing and not knowing are always simultaneously present.

Inquiry as a social activity

Robin talks of staying 'interested and curious' when inquiring with colleagues or clients. 'I know what it feels like to see something with fresh eyes. So many times I have experienced a wonderful revelatory conversation with a friend or colleague, who is seeing a place I know well for the first time and whose fresh impression enables me to see it afresh too.'

The risk I associate with bringing prior expertise or insight to bear on a situation is that this prior knowledge diminishes my capacity to remain intrigued about the situation, to notice what may be different from my preconceived ideas and expectations. Robin challenged me to both acknowledge my prior insights, while at the same time staying open to a new perspective emerging in the moment. Indeed the practice of inquiry seems to demand that capacity for seeing the world afresh, while being aware of the history that is brought to the encounter.

The theme of 'keeping a fresh pair of eyes' also ran through Robin's accounts of his collaboration with colleagues in their work for Ambient Design. 'I love working with one or more colleagues and the quality of inquiry that can bring to our consulting practice. It really helps me to sustain my ability to inquire well. In consulting to Ambient Design I was working with Sarah, Rory and Anthony. We used to make those forays out into the organisation. Our conversations when we reconvened really refreshed me. Since I had worked with the organisation on and off for ten years or so, the ability to freshen up and stay open was of great importance. It was also what we aspired to, and saw, in our conversations with managers.'

Given the relational dimension of his consulting philosophy, I understood Robin's experience of that 'freshening up' as mutual and not simply a matter of him receiving a gift from someone else.

Slowing down

Robin repeatedly talked about 'staying with the data, the sensations and perceptions for long enough rather than leaping into some form of explanation or implication.' This practice of staying with the data, quantitative and qualitative, interior and exterior, opens up possibilities for bringing more material into the conversation. This material includes 'more people, more incidents, more richness' and enables a wider range of explanations to become available.

In much of our management discourse I see a habit of excessive reductionism, of running away from diversity and an overly eager exploration of the similar. We, people brought up in this tradition, know how to seek out and work with the congruent and the limited. The practice of seeking out more, diverse data is a significant challenge to traditional consulting epistemologies – or ways of knowing. The requirement is to find a technique for working with, rather than eliminating or masking, diversity and difference.

One of the requirements for allowing more, different data into the conversation is to allow more time – to slow down. Slowing down is not easy for Robin. 'There is considerable pressure on managers and leaders to be increasingly quick in processing information, reaching conclusions and identifying consequences. I have a tendency for speeding too. My colleague Sarah has an ability to slow me right down, drawing me back into paying attention to what's going on, rather than jumping to conclusions about what needs to be done. It's an enormously valuable quality and, not surprisingly, it can really upset and frustrate me.'

Slowing down, giving the inquiry process due time, is difficult for two reasons. Firstly, consultants tend to work at a fast pace. Robin and many of his colleagues are doing too much work and find it difficult to take the extra time that a slower-paced inquiry requires. Secondly, consultants frequently work in a fast-paced world. Much of the rhetoric concerns 'the ever-increasing speed of change' and the focus tends to be on solving problems so that the next challenge, speeding towards us over the horizon, can be faced. According to Robin 'challenging the pace at which we, our clients and the world at large are working, is one of the benefits inquiring consultants can bring. If the pace remains unchallenged, patterns tend to remain unchallenged and organisations and their people are at risk of endlessly repeating the same cycle. Slowing down the inquiry process can help to surface resiliently recurring patterns, and hence provide an opportunity to see the world differently. Of course a quick response may be wholly appropriate on occasions, but a response that follows a thoughtful inquiry is likely to be more thoughtful and choice-ful.'

Slowing down is a challenge to everyone involved – the client, the consultant and those who have a stake in the consulting process and its organisational impact.

Changing the way we discover and share

The employee satisfaction survey in Ambient Design had caused some real concern. Rather than accepting the results at face value, the consulting team sought to inquire into the stories behind the results and to have a large number of people included in the process. 'We spent a considerable amount of time working with focus groups. Participants were asked to express their thoughts and feelings in drawings, which were then presented to the Executive Committee. The effect was really powerful.'

Making use of media other than surveys and reports is a striking aspect of Robin's practice. He uses creative devices not as a substitute for traditional inquiry techniques, but as a means to enrich the data that is available to both client and consultant. 'Drawings', for instance, 'allow people to express their experience differently, in this case in a way that really spoke to the Executive Committee and enriched their understanding of what was going on in the organisation.'

Another aspect of slowing down the inquiry was the way in which a management development programme was constructed. 'It was clear that managers in the organisation needed to develop some basic skills, but rather than just designing a programme and inviting the managers to it, colleagues and I wanted to try and engage the potential participants in an inquiry process. By supporting managers in inquiring into each others' experience of management in their organisation, they might start to see the world differently and hence to work differently, without the need for a management development programme. Alternatively, by involving managers in the inquiry, the programme content was more likely to reflect their needs as they had expressed them, rather than as someone else had dictated. Through inquiry and co-creation new insights and ownership for a course of action could be developed.'

This also fits, for me, with Robin's belief that he must work with an explicit acknowledgement of his own expertise. I sense that embedded within that belief is an implicit assumption that the expertise of the client must also be acknowledged and worked with. People have much more wisdom about their predicament than is traditionally allowed for in more paternalistic managerial and consulting discourses – a belief that is at the heart of the Reg Revans inspired action learning movement.

I was intrigued with how Robin had managed to convince the client of the value of this, slower than usual pace, inquiry. What about budgetary constraints, I wondered? And how would I feel as a manager, presenting dire survey results to a consultant and being told that 'we need to explore this in more depth before we decide on a course of action'?

'We were fortunate', Robin explained. 'The HR director in Ambient Design was familiar with the processes of inquiry and engagement, and convinced of their value. He was also confident that he had the necessary credibility to persuade his colleagues to participate.' For me this highlights the relational aspects of expertise in a consulting situation. The opportunity to work differently was only possible because of the expertise in both Robin and his client, their capacity to hear each other and their ability to engage with a wider population.

Paying attention to the overall inquiry process

'In our work with Ambient Design we learned the hard way how important it is to frame an inquiry with great care. That's just another way of saying the inquiry failed to a considerable extent. Although we worked successfully with the Executive Committee, the work with the Operational Managers in the summer didn't go well. Colleagues and I are now going through a process of anguished reflection, asking ourselves what we failed to see and where we got manoeuvred into a way of working we did not want.'

'I can see that I was pursuing a very strong agenda', Robin admitted. 'I wanted to get the clients to see that they needed to manage in different ways at different levels. It was my initial ambition to get the Operational Managers to talk to the Executive Committee members, with both groups asking of each other that they attend to their own jobs rather than trying to do each others'. However, for all sorts of logistical reasons, it didn't pan out this way and that meeting never happened. When we all came together, without any opportunity to prepare the ground, colleagues and I failed to frame clearly what was expected from operational and executive leaders. We wanted those groups to explain what they needed from one another, but somehow we didn't manage to make that sufficiently explicit. In the absence of a clear frame the Operational Managers became very pissed off. They felt excluded from strategic conversations and did not accept their responsibility for managing at operational levels.'

Three themes present themselves to me in this story. Firstly, the work with the Operational Managers does not seem to have been an inquiry, since Robin admitted to pursuing an agenda. It seems important to me to be clear whether we are inquiring or whether we are proposing. Secondly, there are moments when proposing can be wholly appropriate; times when our experience tells us that our agenda is valid. In those moments we can still incorporate an element of inquiry into our advocacy by remaining genuinely open to the response our advocacy is evoking. Thirdly, there is the important question of pace, the speed with which an issue is presented. In Robin's story about Ambient I get a sense of something being landed on the Operational Managers – a fait accompli which excluded inquiry.

Underpinning Robin's work is the assumption that we operate in a world of multiple realities and possibilities; that we are actively involved in an ongoing process of constructing our experience of the world and the experiences we believe are possible. 'It is important', Robin explained, 'that we notice both the constructing process and the construction. I am interested in how people describe themselves and how they construct this description. We failed in our work with the Operational Managers because we didn't engage enough people in the process of inquiry. In contrast, we did an inquiry with the Executive Committee. We spent two days with them, recreating the history of their strategy over the last three years. They had maps of the world over the walls and populated it with data streams, looking for inter-dependencies between their various business activities. As a result of their own work, they could see the business they had been running, and came to the realisation that it was in fact three businesses rather than one. We didn't do this with the Operational Managers group. Instead we were seduced into meeting a request to "please teach us the things we need to learn in an interesting way".'

I am struck by two things. Firstly, that it was the senior group that was treated seriously with regard to the inquiry. I do wonder how much this reflects the habit of paying more attention to the 'top' of the organisation than to any other parts. Secondly, I notice how easy it can be not to challenge a request to be taught – and not to pay attention to the constructing process that believes teaching is what is needed.

The discipline of formulating a framing question

Following our conversation about the difficulty Robin and his colleagues encountered in Ambient Design, we explored the issue of framing further. 'You don't just announce: "we're going to inquire". It is your job as a consultant to provide a particular focus, and to ensure that your frame is not "bogus", i.e. already wedded to a particular outcome.'

Robin illustrated his proposition with an example from his work with the Paperspot Company. 'The consulting team had been asked to put together a one week leadership programme. Colleagues and I did an inquiry with managers, including board members, as a result of which it became clear that we needed to address some specific content, especially "acquisitions" and "the impact of digital technology". The framing question we offered the group when they arrived was "What makes Paperspot a great company?"'

I remember thinking during our conversation, 'Well a pretty workmanlike question, nothing too spectacular or sophisticated there.' But then Robin started to explain to me the very careful thinking underpinning this framing question: 'It opens up two new questions: what do we mean by "great" and to whom and/or what does this "greatness" refer? Colleagues and I considered the latter as a really valuable provocation as we were trying to help people surface what they saw as the organisation's purpose, so we decided to stay with our rather open-ended question. Had we made the question more specific we would have pre-empted some of the thinking for them. An appropriate balance between sufficient openness and enough clarity is at the heart of good inquiry questions. It can be really tempting for consultants to err on the side of clarity. I was glad we managed to resist the temptation in our work with Paperspot.'

Much inquiry and development work suffers from consultants pre-empting the thinking of their clients, taking on some of the work that is much better done by the clients themselves. The Operational Managers at Ambient Design were implicitly asking the consulting team to 'please teach us what we need to know', thus putting the onus of the responsibility to do the work on the consulting team. Expecting others to tell them what to do may well have been a recurring pattern for them. Robin and colleagues colluded with this familiar and frustrating pattern.

Inquiry as provocation

'You are inquiring into language', said Robin, 'into how people make meaning. By choosing particular words when asking a question, you can invite a charged response. Thus, we had made an implicit judgement that asking people at Paperspot to work with the word "great" would be challenging for them. Our question had a frisson to it. Were we asking people to boast, to exaggerate, to celebrate, to compare or what?'

This frisson, inviting a charged response, is related to the belief that an inquiry should contain a provocation, have some energy associated with it and have the potential to disturb people. Robin elaborated: 'With "disturbing" the client I mean that we seek to disrupt a pattern of readily available responses, pat answers. We want to invite our clients to be really thoughtful in their answers. That invitation is not always well received. Some clients don't really want people to think for themselves.'

Robin calls this a 'provocative inquiry', one that is framed to challenge both constructions and the process of constructing. 'It does not leave an organisation unmoved, because once clients engage in a provocative inquiry, the genie is out of the bottle and cannot easily be put back. If nothing else, it surfaces what is and isn't allowed to be named. It shows the nature of the power relations in an organisation. In the case of Ambient Design, it surfaced the extent to which Operational Managers were directed by the Executive Committee.'

The relationship between inquiry, reflective practice and choice

'In my role as a teacher, I seek to encourage people to find ways and means to acquire a reflective distance from themselves as people and practitioners, so that they can develop a perspective of themselves that offers difference. The point of inquiry is to open up a quality of curiosity... to notice differently. Educating consultant inquirers is all about enabling them to become skilled at knowing how to notice difference so others can notice it too. The task of the skilled provocative inquirer is to identify "how can I get people to hear themselves differently?" To put it more succinctly: if you accept the responsibility of recognising you choose how you think, then the question becomes "Why do you choose to think the way you do?" That question, and the assumption of choicefulness, leads to considerations such as: So is this an appropriate way to think? Might I think differently? Do I want to think like this? What might become possible if I changed the way I think?'

Change as a result of choosing to see the world differently

According to Robin, many organisations seek confirmation of established patterns and would be pleased to 'get everyone thinking in the same way'. This is rarely, if ever, a healthy ambition and probably unattainable anyway. Challenging established patterns, getting people to see anew is vital to the health of any organisation or individual.

At Ambient Design the longstanding CEO is not prepared to let go of his need for detailed control of the whole organisation. He now refuses to work with Robin. 'I'm now working with the non-Executives who say that it is time for him to go'. The well known adage, 'if you can't change the people, change the people', came to mind.

Robin leads a module on AMOC called Contextual Perspectives, which is a heartfelt invitation 'to be aware that we can see the world differently'. This passion is core to Robin's sense of how to bring about change. 'I hesitate to say that change is inevitable if people see the world differently, but I believe it is pretty likely – although I have to confess I do challenge my own assumption on occasions!'

At the heart of wanting to work with provocative inquiry is Robin's sense of personal mission. 'My mission is to help people make clear and conscious choices, and that includes the choice to stay happily as they are. Thus, if Ambient Design continues to constrain its business by basing it on its singular consulting business view, then that's fine. What's more they'll probably be better off for having made the choice consciously.'

'Inquiry is in the pursuit of choice, not change per se.' This relationship between inquiry and choice is a matter of personal belief for Robin. 'I could try and justify it, but I don't have a good justification. At some level this is a meaning I make. I want to provoke people in as generative way as possible to open up choice. I believe that we are more likely to make good choices, rather than bad ones, if we are individually and collectively aware of the choices we make.'

ROUND 2 – DWELLING

Inquiry and reflection are not one-off activities; they are ongoing processes that can be engaged with on a shallow or deep level. The written responses Robin received on the text from our first interview were not, to us, terribly inspiring. However, the conversations Robin had were highly informative and energising. For Robin and this group of people, inquiry and reflection are served by a mixture of writing and conversation, with the most lively work taking place in conversation.

Advocating well

In our follow up meeting we started a conversation about balancing inquiry and advocacy. Robin shared the feedback from the Chief Operating Officer of Ambient Design, who said: 'Yes you are opinionated, but two things make this okay. Firstly your opinions are quite interesting and secondly they come from a position of appreciation. I enjoy engaging with you because I believe that you are fundamentally in the service of what we're trying to do around here.' In other words, Robin's advocacy could be experienced as pushing and challenging but with a good and respectful intent.

Inquiry, authenticity and appreciation

Sharing this 'inquiry into inquiry' with Sarah resulted in a profound reframe of what might be going on in their relationship with Ambient Design. The two of them are now planning to meet with their coaching supervisor/shadow consultant for the work, with the question 'How do we work with an "alcoholic" organisation?'

In her conversation with Robin, Sarah identified a slippery quality in their engagement with Ambient Design. They looked at how the work was going from their consulting perspective, considering the balance between advocacy and inquiry and the extent to which Sarah's capacity for maintaining an open and inquiring stance was being disabled by Robin's opinions. They then decided to consider what other hypotheses, what other frames could be used to examine their experience. Over time they came to notice that a number of the senior people were alcoholic, very skilled social drinkers. The challenge when working with people addicted to drinking is that you never know if you're working with the alcohol or the person, hence the slippery quality to any conversations, insights or commitments.

What is instructive for Robin is not the outcome – although that may be interesting in terms of the work at Ambient Design – but how he and Sarah deepened their inquiry and reflection into what may have been going on. They took the obvious, but often truncated, step of taking time out to have a conversation. They spent two and a half hours reflecting together rather than concentrating on what to do next. By doing this they noticed that they 'were at a bit of a loss', a sensation that traditional, fast-paced management and consulting avoids.

The grace of the ordinary

In my conversations with Robin, I was struck by how easy it is to intellectualise about what it takes to inquire well, to reflect thoughtfully, to act in a timely fashion and advocate in a way that can be heard. At the same time I felt that maybe, just maybe, there is a real simplicity to the whole process.

I believe thoughtful reflection is about the quality of engagement between client and consultant, and having appreciative respect for the clients you work with. But human beings have as innate a capacity to understand each other and what the other person needs as they do to misunderstand.

If we pay attention to, and work with, our capacity for connecting and understanding, while being mindful of our potential inability to do so, we can engage readily in a provocative inquiry. But we need to go with our self-aware instincts and avoid the trap of separating out the experiences of knowing and not knowing. Advocacy, the experience of knowing and being knowledgeable, must always take place with an inquiring attitude – an attitude that invites curiosity, both about our certainties and uncertainties. I would also like to emphasise the relational context of an inquiring attitude – a consultant can only be in an inquiring relationship if this attitude is shared with the client. If inquiry is not mutual, then clients may undermine the inquiry by demanding a focus on advocated certainty – the thoughtless comfort of familiar answers to familiar questions.

Understanding our cognitive limitations

The most dangerous hubris then concerns the extent to which we believe in our unlimited ability to understand the world. Robin explained: 'We differentiate ourselves from other creatures because of our greater cognitive capacity, but often fail to recognise that it is limited. However much we may think we know, we have to work with the reality of how much we don't know – hence the need for knowing and inquiry to coexist.'

'In my consulting practice, this confronts me with the question "how much do we need to know before we act?" I notice that I tend to be drawn to "fire, ready, aim" consulting. I'm very good at pushing people into experimentation. I often prefer the option "let's have a go and learn", to "let's think about it some more". This is not about being reckless however: before "having a go" I do always ask myself whether we have enough to go on.'

Consulting from a Dialogic Orientation

BY HUGH PIDGEON

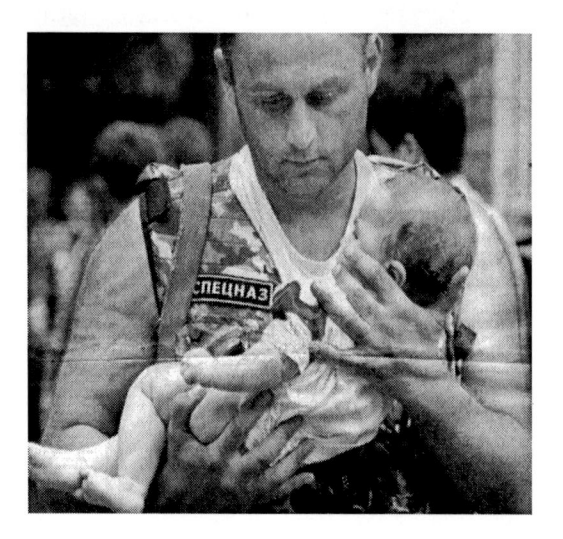

It was the picture on the front page of the newspaper that first caught my attention. The soft, curled form of a baby held incongruously against a military flak-jacket within the large, spread-fingered hands of a Russian police officer. The detail was so vivid one could see the fine hair on the officer's arms, the expression on his face utterly sombre.

The child was one of a desperately small number of children and women to be released by what Nick Paton Walsh had described the day before – the first day of the AMOC workshop I was running – as '17 Islamist extremists, well-versed in Russian siege tactics, ready to die, and demanding the unacceptable, the withdrawal of Russian troops from Chechnya' (Paton Walsh, 2004). In fact there were 35 of them and all but one of them were to die, their demands unmet, along with more than 330 of those they had herded into the bomb-strung gymnasium of Beslan Middle School Number One, in an awful disintegration of smoke and panic as one and then another of the bombs were detonated, probably accidentally. Of those who died that Friday in unimaginably terrifying circumstances, held for three days with neither food nor water, 156 were children.

In all the notes I have made since, as I began to consider what I might write in this chapter on consulting from a dialogic orientation, I notice most how many arrows there are connecting one thought with another, one event with another, one piece of writing in one field suggesting another in a different field, until much of the writing itself has become smudged in the welter of cross-referencing. The declaration of martial law in Nepal is there, so is Condoleezza Rice; the draining of the Aral Sea is there too, and the collapse of the coral reefs in the face of rising temperatures in the Pacific. But that Saturday morning as we assembled for the third day of the workshop to address the subject of dialogue, I took no notes at all, nor as we sat together considering what everyone now knew of what had unfolded in that far-away corner of the Caucasus, did anyone else.

As one participant wrote in her assignment later, 'Individuals began to speak, one after the other, making sense of what had happened there. It was not planned, there was no outcome prescribed or agenda set but... I had a real sense that a bigger meaning began to emerge... a sense that we were all interconnected. I felt this moment most when Hugh was moved to read a commentary from the *Guardian*... He became tearful, and others (including myself) did too.'

What happened that week in Beslan cannot be understood as the politics of a local primary school, or of the far-off annexed corner of Russia we now know as North Ossetia – any more than the killing of Robert McCartney was a Northern Ireland problem. On the Sunday of that weekend, Nick Paton Walsh wrote in the *Observer* of a fearsome anger being added to the response of incredulity and grief in the town, with threats of vengeance and reprisal. But Chechnya is not 'against' Ossettia or its other neighbouring region, Ingushetia. As Simon Tisdall put it in the piece I had brought to the group that morning, 'like Czechoslovakia in a different time, the Caucasian lands of Chechnya, North and South Ossetia, Ingushetia and Dagestan cannot be dismissed as distant countries of which we know little and care less. What happens there matters here' (Tisdall, 2004).

And yes, I was tearful. I was again when I read the same passage out to John Higgins some weeks later, as we talked about what might usefully be said about this subject of dialogue. For what Simon wrote reminded us that morning of our own common humanity. He reached the father in me, for sure. And he reached that part in me that can be entirely daunted by the very interconnectedness that such an event as this reveals – reminding us of what we already knew, have always known, that we are all inextricably entangled.

This was the passage I read out that morning:

> Who in these torrid days of random, global violence has not become accustomed, even inured, to the suicide bombings in Iraq or a host of other trouble spots? Yet who, anywhere in the world is not touched, angered or frightened – or all three – by the thought of young kids traumatised by masked killers wearing bomb-belts?
>
> When the victims are children, the sort of horror on show in Beslan, real or threatened, represents the adult world's ultimate betrayal of innocence, it's final failure to nurture and protect. Here is a shared disgrace, borne of a universal grief. Here is an international crying shame, beseeching an urgent remedy. (Tisdall, 2004)

Something of Simon's evocation of the universal settled amongst us. I don't remember much of what followed. There was no direction to the conversation, no sense of time. We began to understand 'Chechnya' as a construction, as a construction like other constructions of ethnicity and nationhood with which we too could identify, borne of our need to belong. We also understood that in the process of belonging, we create 'other' – not us. The innocence of membership – the children all wore the school uniform and carried balloons – in another context becomes the basis for rivalry, in another context again for claims of privilege and the posturing of moral righteousness. That too we could identify with, feel uncomfortable with, and shift uneasily in our seats.

I remember being disconcerted most by learning that two of the extremist group with bomb-belts tied around them had been women, mothers of children themselves. I don't know why I didn't have the same thought about those men who were also fathers. Somehow the fact that these women had given birth to children of their own was more shocking. Finally, the silence held amongst us deepened to the point where no-one had anything else to say. I checked, and then after another minute or so, we broke for coffee.

So what of any of that was dialogic in its orientation? Well for me, this most of all: we were attending to what David Bohm in his writing – from which I've learned the vocabulary even to ask this question – calls the 'totality' of things. We were confronted first with the fact that we only knew of these events, and felt touched by them, through the media for whom they were enacted. In other words, we were already not outside the events as observers but were implicated in the causes of them. The women who formed part of the extremist group were 'black widows' – women who themselves had lost their children in the systematic brutalisation of Chechnya by Russian troops over years, now conveniently grouped under the umbrella of the war against terror and largely unchallenged by the West – not least because of our dependence on oil.

David Bohm is uncompromising in his analysis. As one of the foremost scientific thinkers and distinguished theoretical physicists of his generation, his main concern, as he put it, was with 'understanding the nature of reality in general, and of consciousness in particular, as a coherent whole, which is never static or complete, but which is an unending process of movement and unfoldment'. He noted that for every evolutionary advance associated with our capacity to separate out, divide up and analyse – at first conceptually and then in practice to separate ourselves from our environment – there has been a corresponding set of negative and destructive results across all the spheres of human activity.

He might almost have been commenting on the events that were to preoccupy us that morning on 4 September 2004: 'There has developed a widespread feeling of helplessness and despair in the face of what seems to be an overwhelming mass of disparate social forces, going beyond the control and even the comprehension of the human beings who are caught up in it' (Bohm, 1980, p.2). He is equally clear that the forces derive not from the events themselves but from the way we think about them. In a limited context, differentiation, analysis and division into parts is convenient and useful, but then we forget that reality is not to be so easily divided; we think of our environment, as Bohm put it, 'as an aggregate of separately existent parts, to be exploited by different groups of people', our world as constituted of separate fragments. 'The notion that all these fragments are separately existent is evidently an illusion, and this illusion cannot do other than lead to endless conflict and confusion.'

That morning we experienced – albeit at several removes – some of the consequences of that conflict and that confusion. We became clear how it made no sense at all to speak of the extremist group as 'the beasts of Beslan' as a caption in that day's *Daily Mail* had called them, as if that explained anything. We could see how their attachment to an ideal had created both the conviction that sustained them and the obduracy with which they refused all offers of food and water for the children, all communication save acceptance of their terms. We could see how the violence they employed in their cause only served to perpetuate the violence they themselves had suffered.

We were by no means of one mind, nor did we all feel the same way about the experience we had shared before we broke for coffee. As one person was to write later, that was an assumption she resented a bit: 'I remember thinking that it was a terrible atrocity but I can't say I felt sad or particularly moved. I did not empathise in the way that parents in the room did as I don't have children myself… I was in a different place'. She went on to wonder whether the grief she was witnessing was a form of transference, in origin having very little to do with the circumstances in Beslan.

But that was also part of the totality of our understanding – in this case, coming out two workshops further on as I invited a sub-set of the group to meet with me while we were at Schumacher College. We spoke then of how I might now understand their experience of that morning, and of how in a sense the dialogue had continued, certainly into the writing of the assignments and was now part of the group's ongoing reference and exchange.

These insights came by way of looking at the totality of the situation, of understanding that, for example, every action we take speaks to a wider context that we will never entirely understand. As we learned from another part of Bohm's work, the intentions we have derive their meaning from a wider significance whose origins we are rarely aware of. I remember reading this passage out later that day: 'Intentions are commonly thought to be conscious and deliberate. But you really have very little ability to choose your intentions. Deeper intentions generally arise out of the total significance (of the situation) in ways of which one is not aware, and over which one has little or no control' (Nichol, 2003, p.167).

After coffee I had invited the group to go off in pairs to recall an occasion where the outcome was not as they had intended, and they had come back with stories mostly of awkwardness and personal embarrassment at things not working out as they had planned, with a strong sense of not being as much in control of the situation as they had thought. The embarrassment was always felt as an individual limitation, hard to acknowledge, as if our lives should always match our aspirations (the assumption, implicit in the inference usually taken from Chris Argyris' work, that our theory-in-use should match our espoused theory) – when in fact, what we actually end up doing will always be more complicated than we had anticipated. Not least because we are relational beings, not least because the sheer complexity of the variables involved makes it highly unlikely we will simply 'deliver' on what we promised ourselves.

As Ralph Stacey observed in a reading we studied in parallel, 'intention is no longer an attribute of an individual… it emerges in conversational relationships (what David Bohm would have called *reciprocal relationships*) only to be articulated by an individual'. It was not Juliet's *intention* that Romeo should kill himself. It was not Andrew Gilligan's that the inexorable, complex patterning of events initiated by the Foreign Affairs Committee should lead to the chemical weapons expert David Kelly taking his own life. It was almost certainly not the direct intention of the extremist group in Beslan that so many would die so shockingly that morning on 3 September in Beslan Middle School Number One. And yet the possibilities were already implicate, each within their own entangled histories.

There is a lot of misunderstanding of what David Bohm meant by implicate. Ralph Stacey particularly has challenged the whole notion, as he understands it from Bohm's work, of an 'implicate order' already present at any one moment, waiting only to unfold as events take their course. One of the participants, in his assignment that followed the workshop, also questioned the existence of an 'invisible reality' in some way 'under' our experience. For me, as I wrote in my commentary back to him some four or five weeks later, the implicate order is not pointing to some invariant but otherwise invisible reality, that would unfold in the sense of being revealed.

I understand it in the same way I understand that nothing disappears but simply changes its form; in the same way I understand that, from the very beginning of the universe, the number of atoms that make up life on Earth have remained the same – but in infinitely more evolved a form, in terms of the sheer variety of their combination. In that sense, the current forms of order are implicate in the physical context from which they arise. But that's very different from saying that they are already 'there' but invisible. Which is why I've always liked Gary Hamel's conviction that 'it makes no sense trying to predict the future', and that '...it's more a question of identifying the revolutionary portent of changes which have already occurred.'

So as a consultant, working with a client group, I would always be interested in the legacies of the group's history, the broader context in which they were seeking to operate, in what was already happening that they hadn't given credence to. I would assume that everything said thus far, by its very nature, would have been partial. I would notice the consequences of anyone becoming over-attached to a particular outcome, which of itself would ensure that the understanding developing in the group would be partial. I would notice how far the opinions being expressed were held individually, notice what seemed to be at stake in their defence. I would attend to what had not been said but was implicit – seek to tease out the underlying assumptions contained even in the very language and structuring of the argument being put forward, noticing the consequences of it being positioned in the first place as an argument, for or against.

So, for example, when Condoleezza Rice gave a press conference recently in London, she said that the fact that 'the Iranian people wanted a democratic future' was 'something that those of us who happen to be on the right side of freedom's divide have got to speak about' (MacAskill, 2005). What I notice is not that she is for or against – although she was pretty adamant about the Iranian government being 'loathed', as she put it – but that her interest is entirely invested in upholding one side of a divide. The divide in itself is entirely a construction of thought, over against another: one side – confidently, without blush or hesitation – being 'right'.

I turn again to read David Bohm's words: 'It is especially important to consider this question today, for fragmentation is now very widespread, not only throughout society, but also in each individual; and this is leading to a kind of general confusion of the mind, which creates an endless series of problems and interferes with our clarity of perception so seriously as to prevent us from being able to solve most of them' (Bohm, 1980, p.1).

But then I notice that my observations have adopted something of the very same tone of self-righteousness which I have read into the US Secretary of State's words; and that I cannot claim sanctuary behind David Bohm. If I were ever to work for Condoleezza Rice as a consultant, I would have to do better than that.

There is something else that I think is needed, if I am to claim a dialogic orientation as a consultant. Because I don't think it is enough to have insights such as these, hugely influential as they have been on my life. They inform my work, they influence how I respond, but there's more to it than that.

In many respects they are not very far removed from the excellent summary that Margaret Wheatley has in her book *Leadership and the New Science*. The chapter which starts with the most wonderful evocation of almost every consultant's experience – and most companies' experience of most consultants: 'the room adrift in flipchart paper – clouds of lists, issues, schedules, plans, accountabilities – crudely taped to the wall....' That one. She concludes at the end of the chapter that her growing sensibility of a quantum universe – the same universe studied by David Bohm – has affected her organisational life in several ways:

> First, I try hard to discipline myself to remain aware of the whole and to resist my well-trained desire to analyze the parts to death.... Second, I know I am wasting time whenever I draw straight arrows between two variables in a cause-and-effect diagram, or positions things as polarities.... Third, I no longer argue with anyone about what is real. Fourth, the time I formerly spent on detailed planning and analysis I now use to look at the structures that might facilitate relationships.

Pretty well as succinct a summary as you'll find of the practical implications for a consultant of seeing the world this way. For a long while I used to carry it around with me – but then I carried a lot of notes around with me in those days.

Many of the insights in David Bohm's teachings are carried equally succinctly in the models that came out of the extensive research done by Bill Isaacs and his colleagues at the Massachusetts Institute of Technology in Harvard, and these too I have carried around with me for a number of years now, and have fallen back on many times. He is particularly clear on the perils of the kind of shared ideals that led in the end to the catastrophe in Beslan. Over the 10-year period of the research, he developed an entire typology of principles and capabilities that maps the mutual interdependence of seemingly opposing qualities and attributes, and suggests how one might both understand and respond appropriately to the corrosive and (ultimately) degenerative effects of fragmentation, violence, and idolatry – and the certainty with which all three are sometimes sustained. We see in David Kantor's insightful work (Kantor and Lehr, 1975) that Bill has drawn into the net of his own cross-referencing, how a virtue can turn in on itself and become its opposite; how one can become stuck with the very qualities that a group might otherwise most benefit from.

One of the difficulties with models, as I discovered once more only a few weeks ago, is that their very elegance and succinctness can be turned to the service of bringing something about: they acquire a potential instrumentality, in other words, which fosters an attachment to an outcome, albeit one of conviviality, or participative relationship, or collective intelligence. I had agreed to support a day in which all three were called for, working with the senior academic team of a distinguished college of art in the UK. I met with the new principal the week before and discovered he knew of David Bohm's work through his interest in Coleridge's distinction between 'primary imagination' and 'fancy', which Bohm wrote about in his book *On Creativity*. We spent an entirely delightful morning walking in the fields near his home talking of the potential of the college to evolve beyond its present state, which he described as a network of privatised practice.

Beyond a few headings on the back of an envelope, neither of us held any particular agenda for the morning. We talked of the college's latent potential, of what was implicate in its unique heritage and traditions – and recognised that if we were going to stay with the ecological reference, that evolution offered no guarantees. The potential of which he spoke could germinate, could stay dormant, or rot. It felt like a single conversation to which each of us contributed. I left feeling full of optimism and excitement for the day I was to spend with them all the following week.

And then, when it came to it, I found myself over-attached to fulfilling the promise of our conversation. I have to confess I was even planning how I might use the day as a case study on dialogic insight for this chapter! I was thinking too hard. The principal was to start the morning talking informally about the aspirations he held for them all, and I ended up speaking first. At one point I became over-exercised over how the group might perceive their intention in their behaviour; and wondered where the best place might be to slip in a model I'd brought with me which I thought might go down well. All very clever stuff, but it was not what was needed. Bill Isaacs quotes a friend as defining dialogue as a state out of which we are continually falling. I certainly fell quite a way that day, although I hope nobody noticed too much. It was what one might call an ok day, but I was not in any kind of reciprocal relationship with the group; I was ahead of them.

Models also carry a potential for orthodoxy which, as I discovered in several assignments that came in over the weeks following the workshop, invites their own resistance. One spoke of the 'ideology feel' he found in some of Bill Isaacs' writing: 'I noticed myself wondering many times "how does he know that?"' Another wrote: 'I felt I could not question the efficacy of the theory within the workshop; that there must be something wrong with me if I could not see what others could see...'; and she wondered how many of her colleagues were 'colluding [in the general approbation being accorded to the three days of the workshop] to maintain the official ideology of AMOC'.

That was hard to read. Every definition we attempt has the potential to exclude. Every statement of belief has within it the seeds of alienation. I think there is a constant challenge to stay passionate in one's advocacy within a programme of this nature, offering skills with some level of authority, without letting this slide into forceful persuasion and to remain mindful of the subtle coercion of the individual by a group excited with its own process of learning. Every attempt to codify and formalise the procedural arrangements associated with an idea will always acquire a life of its own, a claim to legitimacy.

But when it comes to dialogue, I don't think extraordinary settings are required, as one participant had put it; nor, as it happens, do I think there is any particular virtue, beyond a certain symbolic value, in sitting in a circle. And I ventured the view, in one of the assignment commentaries I returned, that David Bohm didn't set out to recommend groups of 20 to 40. I know the recommendation is in his published writing, but I don't think it's intrinsic to his informing scientific insights and philosophy. My picture is that people around him at the time got excited at the possibility of determining a means of re-creating the experience they themselves were having at that moment, and that he went along with it, since for him group process was quite a new territory.

As part of my preparation for writing this chapter I went back to a book I've had on my shelf for some time, Guy Claxton's *Hare Brain, Tortoise Mind*. I remembered he had something interesting to say about thinking in 'd-mode', and quite a lot to say about wisdom. I thought I knew the book well, but there was an account that I discovered I had entirely missed. Coming to it now so many years later was a complete revelation. He describes the late Robin Skynner, author with the comedian John Cleese of the two 'survival' books *Families and How to Survive Them* and *Life and How to Survive It*, in discussion with Fritjof Capra at Schumacher College in June 1992. Even with more than forty years' experience, it regularly happens, he says, that a few minutes into the first consultation with a new group or a new family he is to work with, he feels lost. 'Suddenly his accumulated knowledge and skill appear to desert him. It seems as if he has no precedents on which to draw. He may wonder what he is doing there, or may even feel fraudulent. Nothing wise occurs to him to say or do.' Yet, Robin says, one of the major benefits of the experience he has accumulated over the years is the courage not to flee from this barren state.

This is such a familiar experience to me, he might as well have been describing my own. It is a place I have found not to be susceptible either to notes or to models. I have only recently acquired Robin's courage. Even now it will fail me sometimes, and it takes real discipline not to resort to that old habit of imagining that the notes I might make by way of preparation, or that useful sequence of slides I've got somewhere will be useful to me when it comes to the actual encounter. In a curious way I think I knew even then that what needed to be said would emerge out of the encounter itself; but my apprehension of the very same barren state Robin Skynner describes would lead to preparation so extensive and at the same time so disorderly that at the very last minute the carefully prepared patterning of the thoughts I had with me, would disintegrate in a blur of too-hard-to-follow cross-referencing, forcing a return to this elemental space of not knowing. It is a tough place to be.

I have experienced it again in writing this piece: the same slightly desperate accumulation of notes, the same sense of confusion as the connectedness of one thought to another proliferates into a multi-headed monster mocking my reputation (at least within the modest confines of the AMOC) for scholarship. And yet the ability to stay in this desert place with the courage of which Robin speaks is probably for me at the heart of what I have to say about working from a dialogic orientation. It is a quality that Guy Claxton speaks of as 'daring to wait'; the 'something else that was needed' of which I wrote earlier in this chapter, over and beyond dialogic insight.

It speaks more to dialogue as a disposition, a state of personal orientation, rather than a particular set of techniques, or even a particular way of understanding. As Guy writes in *Hare Brain, Tortoise Mind*, 'knowing emerges from, and is a response to, not-knowing. Learning – the process of coming to know – emerges from uncertainty.' This is John Keats' 'negative capability' that produces the Man of Achievement, 'when a man is capable of being in uncertainties, mysteries, doubts, without any irritable reaching after fact and reason.'

As Guy Claxton comments, to wait in this way requires a kind of inner security. Because from a consulting perspective it requires you 'to attend to a whole range of situations patiently and *without comprehension*; to resist the temptation to foreclose on what that experience may have to teach' (my italics). It is the quality of intimacy involving no mediation of thought that Martin Buber, himself writing on dialogue, called I-Thou, in contrast to the instrumentality associated with I-It. But it's still a tough call.

The remainder of Guy's fascinating book is given over to demonstrating that this 'slow way of knowing' – what Heidegger called meditative thinking, by way of contrast with calculative thinking – is better suited to dealing with hard cases than 'd-mode' (standing for the deliberative mode of the intellect otherwise dominant in our culture). Hard cases he describes as 'complex and ambiguous situations in which conventional or egocentric thinking only results in heightened polarisation, antagonism and impasse... where important decisions have to be made on the basis of insufficient data... where meaning and interpretation are unclear and conjectural... where many variables interact in intricate ways'. Yes, each of these we saw playing out in Beslan over the three days of our workshop. Each typifies most of the consulting engagements that come our way, if not in the presenting histories, certainly in the background.

Let me quote David Bohm one last time, in what I take to be a profoundly challenging paragraph to us as practitioners:

> The question of fragmentation and wholeness is a subtle and difficult one, more subtle and difficult than those which lead to fundamentally new discoveries in science. To ask how to end fragmentation and to expect an answer in a few minutes makes even less sense than to ask how to develop a theory as new as Einstein's was when he was working on it, and to expect to be told what to do in terms of some programme, expressed in terms of formulae and recipes. (Bohm, 1980, p.22)

I recall Ralph Stacey facing a similar dilemma as he attempted a radical reframing of what it might mean to act from the perspective of understanding organisations as complex responsive processes – that the theory would do the opposite of what it is proposing if it were to be pressed into offering applications and prescriptions. What he was proposing was neither to apply nor prescribe but to *refocus attention*. I think it is a brilliant chapter (Chapter 17 in Stacey, 2000) and a significant contribution to the literature in a field that more generally remains wrapped in obscure and speculative applications of theories that didn't have their origin in the study of human behaviour. I notice that he confesses he found the chapter the hardest to write. I have found this equally hard to write, and it is with considerable apprehension I would like to make a similarly disarming proposition.

David Bohm's work itself radically refocuses our attention – or attempts to restore what in some sense we have always known and in our preoccupations have become blinded to. At the core of his thesis – as he spelled it out initially in the field of quantum mechanics and then more widely in his examination of widespread social, economic and ecological disorder – was the view that the fragmentation he observed was in the process of our thinking. So I propose that at least from a consulting perspective, the most suitable dialogic orientation would be to develop the capacity to suspend thinking itself.

I know this as the place of creative indifference. In another language from a different discipline it would be called compassionate non-attachment. Its nearest cousin would be mindfulness. It was the place the college principal and I took with us on our walk, and which I then lost sight of for a while when I met his team. The notion comes from the work of the early twentieth-century German philosopher Sigmund Friedlaender, who introduced Fritz Perls, the founder of Gestalt psychotherapy, to the idea that opposites define each other and that there is a resting point in the middle – the point of creative indifference – which embraces both polarities. Some would argue with the use of the term 'indifference' with its English connotation of lack of investment, but personally I rather like the shock value of the juxtaposition of the two words as they are.

The essentially Aristotelian contrast he sought to make was to the Judeo-Christian model of 'good' and 'bad' as separate absolutes which so informed the debate over Beslan that we saw unfolding each day in our newspapers. And this was Perls' summary of what he took from Friedlander: 'that every event is related to a zero-point from which a differentiation into opposites takes place. These opposites show in their specific context a great affinity to each other. *By remaining alert in the centre, we can acquire the creative ability of seeing both sides of an occurrence and completing an incomplete "half".*' (Perls, 1974 – my italics) Over the years I have found these words a constant source of inspiration and reference. I knew of them long before I had heard of David Bohm. But it is this idea of alertness at the centre without comprehension I find at the very heart of what it means to me to work from a dialogic orientation. I may never get the call from Condoleezza Rice. But I'll be ready.

> You do not need to leave your room. Remain sitting at your table and listen. Do not even listen, simply wait. Do not even wait, be quite still and solitary. The world will freely offer itself to you to be unmasked, it has no choice, it will roll in ecstasy at your feet.
>
> F. Kafka, *Reflections* (cited in Scott, 1969)

Further reading

Bion, W (1970) *Attention and Interpretation*. Brunner-Routledge. (Keats' use of the term 'negative capability' is taken from a letter to his brothers in 1817, and quoted in this work.)

Bohm, D (1980) *Wholeness and the Implicate Order*. Routledge.

Buber, M (1987) *I and Thou*. Edinburgh: T&T Clark.

Claxton, G (1997) *Hare Brain, Tortoise Mind, why intelligence increases when you think less*. London: Fourth Estate.

Hamel, G (1997) 'The dirty little secret of strategy', *Financial Times*, 24 April 1997.

Isaacs, W (1999) *Dialogue, and the art of thinking together*. Currency Doubleday.

Kantor, D and W Lehr (1975) *In the family*. San Francisco: Jossey-Bass.

MacAskill, E (2005) 'Rice lavishes praise on Britain – but attacks "loathed" Iran', *Guardian*, 5 February 2005.

Paton Walsh, N (2004) 'New breed of extremist turns fight for independence into unrelenting holy war: Putin faces critical test to save pupils as Chechen conflict spreads', *Guardian*, 2 September 2004.

Perls, F (1974) *Ego, Hunger and Aggression: The beginning of Gestalt Therapy*. Allen and Unwin.

Nichol, L (2003) *The essential David Bohm*. Routledge.

Scott, N (1969) *Negative Capability: Studies in the New Literature and the Religious Situation*. New Haven CT: Yale University Press.

Stacey, R (2000) *Strategic Management and Organisational Dynamics, the Challenge of Complexity*. Pitman.

Tisdall, S (2004) 'A terrible lesson from a classroom in Beslan: The west can no longer ignore the violence and killings in Chechnya', *Guardian*, Comment and Analysis, 3 September 2004.

Wheatley, M (1999) *Leadership and the New Science*. Berrett-Koehler.

SECTION 3

Inquiring Into Practice

THE GRADUATE PRACTITIONER PERSPECTIVE

   81   Section Introduction – The Inquiry Process

   83   Kevin – As Good as it Gets
   97   Bill's Postscript to Kevin's Story –
          Looking through Six Theoretical Frames

100   Jon – Man not Superman
111   Bill's Postscript to Jon's Story –
         Looking through Six Theoretical Frames

114   Dominic and Liz – Not Just Doing the Do
126   Bill's Postscript to Dominic and Liz's Story –
         Looking through Six Theoretical Frames

129   Francesca – Do Consultants Make a Difference?
139   Bill's Postscript to Francesca's Story –
         Looking through Six Theoretical Frames

142   Bill – The Old Gestaltist and the Global Media Company
153   Bill's Postscript to Bill's Story –
         Looking through Six Theoretical Frames

155   Iain – Consulting with Conviction
164   Bill's Postscript to Iain's Story –
         Looking through Six Theoretical Frames

Introduction

This section introduces six stories. Five of these concern the experience of AMOC graduates who responded to Bill's formal invitation (See Appendix 2) to about 20 AMOC alumni, all practising consultants with a reputation for sound reflective ability. Bill volunteered to contribute a story in order to enable us to test out our proposed inquiry process.

The inquiry process

John met with each of the consultants and invited them to talk about a current or recent assignment or set of relationships. All six people talked freely about what had gone on, or was happening. Within the frame of concentrating on actual consulting work, John simply allowed the story to unfold, probing occasionally as he sought to understand what was going on and why things were unfolding as they were from the consultant's perspective. The four questions referenced in Appendix 3 were the only structure John brought to the interviews, and even those were held lightly. However, he concluded each of the first interviews with a reflective question, asking his co-inquirers what theoretical frames they thought were underpinning their work.

The inquiry seemed to go according to plan, with the caveat that not every one of the storytellers was staying with the initial intention to concentrate on a single current project. One person was keen to use this inquiry as an opportunity to make sense of a past assignment; another, Jon, wanted to reflect on two current projects to discover how one informed the other. The latter was a highly emotionally charged inquiry as it coincided with Jon having a stroke. The inquiry tracked his professional recovery as his physical recovery progressed.

Everyone agreed that John would write up their story and then share it with them. The editing/rewriting process was, however, different in each case. Some people edited their own stories; others spoke with partners and then made handwritten amendments or made suggestions to John over the phone. In two cases (including one story that had to be sadly abandoned at a late stage because of concerns about confidentiality and loss of organisational face), John met with his co-inquirer repeatedly in order to get the story to a state where the storyteller was happy, while John remained satisfied that the story stayed sufficiently fresh and authentic. John had concerns about extensive editing. Firstly the stories were at risk of becoming sanitised, with the language being toned down and the off-the-cuff remarks replaced with something a little more 'profound'. Secondly, as most of the inquiries concerned live projects, the stories and the critical incidents kept changing, which made writing up exceedingly difficult, choosing the appropriate tense being one of the issues.

If John had expected a neat process of inquiry cycles, with the next phase involving meeting the consultants with their clients to discuss the story agreed in the previous cycle, reality proved to be considerably more messy. In only one case did the meeting with the client go according to plan. One client admitted not having read the text when he met with John. However, in the conversation, he still broadly validated the story as told by the consultant, while also highlighting differences in priority and perception. The reflective process seemed to John to spiral out of control, with not only clients but also other consultants involved in the various projects providing extensive written responses, while John also embarked on difficult Transatlantic conference calls with people who hadn't seen any text and arrived with other issues at the front of their mind.

In the final cycle John went back to the storytellers and, as originally envisaged, focussed the reflection on the text and how the various third parties had responded. But people's lives don't compartmentalise that easily. In most cases other projects or developments coloured or overwhelmed the final reflective round of the inquiry. One of the participants had just found out some friends had been murdered; another was going on from his meeting with John to negotiate a redundancy settlement with the firm he had joined at the start of the inquiry process.

At this point the stories were developing into huge tomes and John found himself attached to keeping the text true to what had been said originally. Feedback from Bill and others suggested that the reflective tale was wagging the narrative body of the research into incoherence and tedious repetition. Finally John agreed to be the author of the reflective cycle of each of the narratives, sharing what he had noticed and what it brought to his mind with regard to the business and craft of consulting.

Kevin – As Good as it Gets

This story is about Kevin's experience of working with, and within, a major programme of change in a global company. Kevin was involved over a period of three years. The transformation is still ongoing and may never be complete.

Our story concentrates on a snapshot from the first year: a five-day workshop during which the top 120 people in the company were engaged in a difficult process of agreeing a new way of working that would dramatically interfere with deeply ingrained patterns and power dynamics. It is retrospective, told with the benefit of hindsight. It is incomplete: one person's perspective, based on prominent memories of a period of turbulence and intensity, which almost took over his life. Kevin, the consultant moth drawn to the flame of the beguiling project.

My meetings with Kevin during the preparation of this paper often had an intense quality that seemed to mirror the intensity of his work with this organisation. I found myself drawn into the dramatic events, the suspense of it all. There were also many moments of reflection, stepping back, making sense and drawing connections with the frameworks that inform Kevin's practice – accounts of which I have given a prominent place in this paper.

Prologue – setting the scene

Kevin wanted me to offer some context before we get into the story. Firstly, I need to say something about the company: Sugarbrand has been around for what seems like forever, producing and selling some very popular snack brands. Its heritage of ethical business practice was one of the reasons Kevin felt drawn to working with this company. Secondly, the transformation programme involved changes in business processes, organisation and behaviours, and the technology platform for its worldwide operations. Thirdly, the project at the heart of our story was effectively a pilot for the new ways of working in the Asia Pacific region (AsiaPac), and affected fourteen sites spread across the continent of Australia.

The project team itself consisted of an ever-changing group: two hundred and fifty Sugarbrand employees from different countries and independent consultants, such as Kevin, along with people from one of the world's large, established consultancies (which I will call Solutions Inc.) involved in the IT redesign and implementation aspects. As often happens in large change projects, the IT aspects of it proved to be difficult and controversial on a number of fronts. To add to the complexity, the project group was geographically split between Australia and the UK – 10,000 miles apart!

Lastly, I'd like to introduce our other protagonists: Gary was the regional MD of the Australian and AsiaPac business, an expatriate American. At the time of writing, Gary leads the Americas business and is now a member of the executive leadership team of the Global plc. Steven, the overall Programme Director, was the person Kevin was effectively reporting to and the most unconventional leader he had come across in a corporate setting. Rick was the Global Process Director with accountability for the integrity of the project and its implementation across the world. Kevin worked closely with Rick who was, in effect, both a client and a close colleague.

Finally, a little background about Kevin. He was invited to work with Sugarbrand for an initial 12-month period as an external consultant by an old colleague, the head of Group Organisational Effectiveness, who had known him for many years. Up to this point, Kevin had worked in different roles in the consumer goods and retail sectors; including line and project management, finance and organisation development. As the project got underway Kevin was asked to become a Sugarbrand employee. Somewhat ambivalent about rejoining corporate life, he eventually agreed to a running fixed-term contract. But more about that later.

A tall order

The integration of the various strands to this project represented a mountainous task in itself. The new blueprint also required the consolidation of supply chains and support functions across different states or countries and a closer relationship between sales, marketing and their customers. However, unlike many of its competitors, Sugarbrand had always sought to protect the sanctity of the local business unit. For some, the heritage of the company was inextricably linked to the local identity of the brands in each of its markets – for example, many Australians assumed that Sugarbrand was an Australian company!

One notable feature of the organisation's culture was the consensual approach to decision making which Kevin, usually an active proponent of dialogue and inclusion, paradoxically experienced in this project as slowing down progress and regeneration.

From the outset the people leading the project were intent on 'doing this the right way' by learning from the experiences of others who had attempted similar major change initiatives.

Scaling heights

Kevin thinks of the Australian and AsiaPac project pilot as one of the most formative experiences in his career to date. 'I was doing work I loved. I was responsible for contracting pieces of change work, supporting stakeholder relationships in the various business units, as well as being an advisor and coach to my colleagues on the programme board. I also had to establish a team of internal change consultants to support each of the various implementations in each of the regions. With Rick, I had to keep an ongoing dialogue with those Business Units in Europe and the US who were nervously watching how things were working out in Australia. As time went on, I sensed I was being drawn deeper and deeper into the project whilst I was trying to maintain a degree of independence and detachment.'

Kevin talks vividly about how exciting it was to be in an organisation in such a state of flux, where there was no sense of old and new anymore and where his relationships simultaneously spanned the spectrum of colleague, client, adviser, confidante and friend. He describes the work as like being in a constant pressure cooker.

'The stakes were very high and I was working with people who were often at a heightened state of anxiety but also at a high level of receptivity to new ideas.

It felt like we were designing stuff on the hoof but it was exhilarating – if somewhat hit and miss at times, especially as timescales and priorities were shifting constantly. At certain times I felt that no progress was being made, although with hindsight I can see we were making all the progress we could. I learnt that sometimes you have to stay with the feelings of stuckness and confusion in order to make greater leaps forward.'

Chemistry

With all these roles and perspectives in play, Kevin felt compelled to work in a completely transparent way, to be above suspicion. It was not easy to keep this perception of integrity intact in such a climate of substantial change. 'The politics of the situation could be highly charged at times, so you had to behave with absolute authenticity even if you were deeply attached to the success of the project.'

In his role of regional MD, Gary was the key stakeholder in the Asia Pacific business. At the start Gary was inevitably nervous. He felt exposed and concerned about the impression the main board was developing of him – especially as in his first year as MD he had been frustrated by the limited pace of change that had been achieved within the Australian operations. Another concern was the probable performance dip that usually occurs during a period of major organisational change – a dip that few organisations are willing to acknowledge and factor into their planning. Whatever Gary's concerns about Kevin and how the project would affect him, he gave Kevin the benefit of the doubt and a relationship developed which Kevin describes as unique: 'There was this amazing connection between us; the most intuitive I've ever had with a senior leader. Gary's trust in me was such that he allowed me to take significant risks in my work with his team, despite the incredibly high stakes. I had this strong sense of mutual chemistry, of being on the same wavelength, of a shared respect that allowed us to work in an open and effective way from the start.'

From a contracting point of view, Rick would be responsible for the overall implementation of the new blueprint and Kevin, as Director of Change Integration, would focus on putting the best possible change process in place. There was also a mutual interdependence between Gary and Steven, the Global Programme leader. Gary needed the project to help deliver the expected performance improvement, while Steven needed Gary's active support to pilot the new ways of working before they could be introduced on a global scale.

Appreciating what you bring to the party

Kevin's diverse experiences of working in a variety of line roles as well as other change projects turned out to be the perfect ingredients for the job. 'Up until this point I'd felt that I'd jumped around. I wasn't able to put a label on what it was I did and people do try to identify you with something familiar. Now I began to realise that this could become an asset rather than a liability, giving me a freedom to operate that otherwise might not have been available to me.'

In his work with Sugarbrand, Kevin felt able to draw on everything he had learned on AMOC, where he had inquired into and reflected deeply on how to help himself and others work through situations of ambiguity and complexity.

From the start of the work he felt an empathy with the people trying to make sense of the proposed changes. 'I was familiar with what they were experiencing. I've been in the position myself of having to introduce or respond to highly challenging changes. There also seemed to be a parallel process going on where, as the organisation was trying to learn about the new way of doing business, I was trying to ground and integrate what I had learned on AMOC into my day-to-day practice.'

The pace of the work was relentless. In one year Kevin and his colleagues made five trips to Australia, having to do all the preparations necessary ahead of time so that after landing on a Sunday they would be able to hit the ground running on the Monday morning for two weeks of workshops and related activity – we will look at one of those trips in more detail shortly. With hindsight Kevin wonders whether he should have moved to Australia for that period.

Personal dilemmas – 'I don't want a career here'

When Kevin was invited to join Sugarbrand and to go back into the corporate world, he was torn. 'On the one hand I felt I was betraying my sense of purpose and the freedom I had experienced as an independent consultant – freedom from rituals, norms and structures that I had come to associate with being a member of a corporate system. On the other hand I felt an almost spiritual connection to the organisation and its roots. I greatly valued the deep bond that kept this particular community together and felt a duty of care.'

When Kevin decided to join for a fixed term he chose to report to Steven, the overall Programme Leader. Although he was given the opportunity to be part of a central, group-level function, he chose not to join this. He believed that he would be at risk of being sucked into organisational politics, being seen as 'the man who would report back' and thus never being able or allowed to fully join the programme leadership team.

In the early days with Steven he found himself invited into playing a subordinate role: 'Steven had a way of provoking a certain reaction in me which I realised later was his way of testing my personal loyalty to him'. Kevin carefully avoided a submissive or aggressive response. Instead he set about reconstructing his role by telling Steven, 'I want to help you to be successful. I think I can best contribute to your success in a consulting relationship with you, rather than as your subordinate. I am passionate, caring and curious about this work, but I want to establish my credibility as a consultant not as an employee.' He reassured Steven that he did not want a career in Sugarbrand, a mantra he often found himself repeating when times got tough. Kevin is convinced that the way he constructed his role made it possible for him to rise above issues that might otherwise have drawn him in and compromised his sense of integrity.

He wanted no less than the best of both worlds: to be part of something and be apart from it at the same time, to feel both a sense of attachment and detachment. 'If I had put myself completely outside of the programme I would have felt like a distant cousin; instead I felt like an exotic sibling. I was able to experience the exhilaration of what we were achieving together and feel the growing pains of an organisation that was trying to transform itself... while remaining sufficiently apart to notice patterns and be curious about them.'

Upon reading the above paragraph Kevin stressed its importance to him: 'Those few lines capture the essence of what it was like for me to perform this role. It also hints at the inner turmoil I experienced around inclusion and exclusion as a consultant.'

With hindsight, Kevin thinks of his re-entry into the corporate world as both a backward and a forward move: 'I re-engaged from a different place, as a different human being. I felt less of a need to play a role, more able to be myself, more experimental, more grounded and more powerful. I believe that my sense of personal power came from letting go of my need to achieve and climb the corporate ladder, I refused to be judged against that yardstick any longer.'

Kevin – man of mystery

A South African colleague gave Kevin the affectionate nickname of 'Man of Mystery' because he was fascinated by Kevin's unusual responses to different situations and the way he seemed to keep popping up in all sorts of unexpected places. 'I preferred to follow the ebbs and flows rather than the formalities of organisational life. Nothing was settled and roles were constantly shifting so I would often follow my nose which meant working against the grain at times. Had I stayed in one place things would have passed me by; I had to forage and follow scents, rather than wait for issues to arrive on my desk.'

With the work in a constant state of flux, Kevin sought to follow the spontaneous movements in the system, guided by the tides and points of attraction in the organisation. Rather than feeling out of control or at the mercy of events, Kevin describes feeling incredibly grounded when working in this way: 'I learned to understand what was important, to watch myself and others as conductors of energy. I felt slightly disembodied and untouched by the stresses generated by the turmoil of the work. The stress I did experience came from my own patterns, my habit of trying to do too much; to do the best job I can do at all times, to squeeze as much as possible out of every hour. The ambiguity of situations and the politics associated with this sort of corporate upheaval didn't cause me anxiety. My anxiety came from my desire to be true to what I believed in so that I could work with integrity and a degree of independence.'

Language and reframing – problems are normal and healthy

Kevin's views about the nature of change are informed by the following quotation from Jung:

> All the greatest and most important problems of life are fundamentally insoluble… They can never be solved only outgrown. This 'outgrowing' proves on further investigation to require a new level of consciousness. Some higher or wider interest appeared on the horizon and through this broadening of outlook the insoluble problem lost its urgency. It was not solved logically in its own terms but faded when confronted with a new and stronger life urge. (Jung, 1964)

Kevin is acutely aware of the role language and context can play in shifting attention and reframing a situation so that new possibilities can emerge. In Sugarbrand he went about this by gently subverting the view that a problem was always something that had to be fixed or dwelt upon. This helped his colleagues to reflect on how they constructed issues as figural or were overreacting to tensions or ambiguity. 'I found that new possibilities could arise when people felt able to acknowledge that "the problem" is actually part of the healthy experience of working with what is. Organisations are constantly trying to resolve problems. In some cases they need to get beyond them, or find a way of looking at them from a different perspective.'

Informed by his AMOC experience

Kevin's motivation to continually invite people to find new ways of framing their problem/situation, and to find alternative courses of action dates from his time on AMOC, where he became fascinated by the work of Watzlawick and his notion of constructivism: 'I became highly sensitised to the way in which we constantly co-construct our realities through the language and frames of reference we use. I began increasingly to pay attention to the multiple realities being constructed around me and to the extent to which we often create stressful conditions for ourselves and others. As a result I developed a habit of looking for different and more resourceful ways of framing situations.'

His AMOC experience also encouraged Kevin to work with the chaos rather than to fight against it. 'I found that the more chaotic the work got, the more interesting it became. By the last year of the project when there was much more order about, I found it less fulfilling. AMOC helped me to see chaos as a positive force. By chaos I mean the experience of working in a context where people don't know what's happening beyond next week, where there are few stakes in the ground, where roles and responsibilities are ambiguous, where you're trying to help shape new ways of working whilst others are fighting to keep things as they are.'

The image that best described Kevin's experience came from the Nick Park animation of Wallace and Gromit in *The Wrong Trousers*, where the railway track is being laid in front of the train as the train speeds through the living room. 'We were in a creative process without the luxury of knowing the next step.'

From AMOC Kevin also learnt the importance of pacing, of working with and respecting the language frames that people use, of not judging them or saying that they must adopt one way of talking about the world rather than another. However, that doesn't mean he simply accepts what people say, their construction of reality: 'I am curious about the words people use and invite them to be curious too about the consequences of talking about the world in one way rather than another. I try to subvert through curiosity and inquiry rather than advocacy, although that's not always easy. AMOC has helped me to be aware of those moments when I'm advocating through the guise of inquiry. I know I have to work very hard to keep to a spirit of inquiry. I believe the ability to inquire skilfully is terribly important because in my view change comes from inquiry and awareness rather than from advocacy. It is often a gentle, invisible process rather than a visible jolt or an explicit point of departure.'

Part of Kevin's role was to develop organisation design, and different ways of travelling and different routes to follow. It was a useful way of exploring and generating options in the first instance. Once choices had been made, it provided a framework for thinking about how to move the organisation on. The process resulted in a variety of scenarios and helped to identify potential bifurcation points where significant choices needed to be made or would arise in the future. 'A key feature of this process was that it helped us to embrace uncertainty and ambiguity and let go of our need for order, control or predictability.'

'We need to acknowledge that the world is changing at a rate of knots and that the amount of control and predictability is relatively small. Businesses get sold, acquired and merged. New competitors and initiatives come and go; markets bloom unexpectedly while others go belly up.' The nearest Kevin gets to some guiding principles comes from the analogy drawn from the Columbus story: 'don't over-prescribe and don't over-predict, but do plan and prepare for change', an injunction which is both appropriate and paradoxical.

The tip of the change iceberg: the workshop in Australia

When Gary and Kevin first met, they were about to embark on a five-day series of conferences and workshops with the various leadership teams in the AsiaPac region. The intention was to explore new ways of working, the configuration of the new computer system and what this meant for their current organisation model. The scale of the change envisaged was enormous and people were comparing it to 'asking a country to shift from driving on the left to driving on the right hand side of the road'.

Gary, who had been wary of the scale of change required and worried about the opinion of those watching around the world, now began to see the project as an opportunity to reorganise not only Australia but his entire region. His aspirations to support a step change in business growth in the region involved getting more people out on the road, face to face with customers and working with new leading-edge technology. However, he was still smarting from his prior experience of trying to change things, particularly in the regional heartland of Australia. Hence his first words to Kevin were: 'You don't know what you are letting yourself in for. I've been here 18 months and we keep talking about making these kinds of changes happen. These guys have been running this place pretty successfully for the last 20 odd years so what's in it for them to do anything differently?' Over time, Gary began to trust that together with people like Rick and Kevin he could bring about the vision he aspired to in AsiaPac. However, this did not mean that he was always comfortable with Kevin's style and approach.

Over the five days, 120 people from the region – business leaders, process experts and managers, representing each different function and geographical area – discussed the extent to which the nature of the business environment was changing and the wide-ranging implications for their ways of working. In various configurations, working with colleagues across functional and country boundaries, the Sugarbrand managers began to develop a sense of how they would need to start looking beyond the narrow confines of their function or geographical area if the business was to thrive in a fast changing marketplace.

Kevin talked passionately about the palpable challenge in the room: 'Basically, we were holding up a mirror to these people, inviting them to look at how their current business model and management style were creating real constraints to their ability to grow in the longer term. I think they realised it was easier said than done as their recurring patterns and behaviours were deeply rooted and there were enormous implications at stake for the existing power structures. This was a long established and comfortable hierarchy with a number of interdependent and vested interests… and it all started with the regional board structures. There was no place to hide and what was interesting about the process was the extent to which so many people were involved in a variety of experiences which helped them to inquire into the change implications from each functional perspective. Over the first three days they were examining the whole as well as the parts. There were plenty of diversion tactics being used but we did not allow these usual avoidance behaviours to divert us.'

On day four, the AsiaPac and Australian board members, 18 senior managers in all, met to discuss the outcomes and proposals that were emerging. Kevin started the conversation with an invitation to 'reflect on what you consider to be your most dynamic and successful business achievements and how we could use that expertise to make these changes a reality'. The group began to consider more and more far-reaching ideas, many based on the feedback they had received from the rest of the organisation. The public nature of the debate in the previous days meant that the board stayed with the evolving ideas longer than they would have traditionally done. After all they had been part of the process themselves so they couldn't separate themselves from the suggestions being made… in many cases they had contributed to them.

The rest of the organisation had also presented them with a serious challenge: 'If you expect us to change the way we work and behave, we expect the same from you.' Not changing was no longer an option for the board. In the anxiety of the moment Gary had an emotional outburst: 'Kevin, this is taking us too far – I'm not sure I signed up to this', projecting onto Kevin the pressure they had in fact inflicted on themselves. After the event, Gary explained that his outburst was a result of the realisation that he did not consider it feasible to deliver what was necessary with the people in the room, his colleagues on the board.

As the conversation got stickier and closer to deep and pertinent issues and the level of uncertainty in the room rose, Rick, the Global Process Director, felt a growing sense of anxiety, and whispered in Kevin's ear: 'You're losing them – Where's this going?' Kevin however remained comfortable with what was going on, feeling quite capable of working with the fear and vulnerability people were experiencing at the edge of chaos. 'I believe', he told me, 'that moments of truth are often preceded by that momentary feeling that everything is going to go pear shaped. Indeed it is in these moments that I can feel most grounded. I owe that to the times I discovered the extremes of my own vulnerability through AMOC.'

As they were reaching the end of the fifth day, it seemed that the group had genuinely moved to a different place; and that decisions had been made about how the new organisation needed to look and what the new roles and responsibilities were to be. Gary took advantage of this decisive moment and read out an announcement that would go out to the whole organisation that evening. There was to be no opportunity for backtracking or for the decision to be reopened and unpicked in endless conversations. Even though there were enormous implications for each person in the meeting, everyone knew that this had to be the way ahead.

At the end of the workshop Gary and Kevin's relationship changed significantly. Until then Kevin had remained in his facilitator role, but as things drew to a close Gary asked him to help script some closing words, which they duly did.

A turning point

The reaction to the work, the tension and the impactful decisions that had been made and widely announced was dramatic for many of the people involved. In the days that followed the workshop a number of the longer-serving senior managers came to see Gary to explain that they did not feel they were the right people to lead the newly emerging organisation; that perhaps the time had come for them to move on.

Shortly afterwards, Kevin himself went through a kind of cathartic reaction to the tension – unexpressed and out of his awareness at the time – that comes with taking a group into difficult places and conversations, and holding them in that discomfort. But it soon passed and, as the members of the group began to react to the consequences of their crumbling power structures, he realised the full significance of what had been achieved: 'Although it was one week during a three-year change programme, in retrospect it was a real turning point for Sugarbrand especially as the Asia Pacific model was adopted by every regional business eventually.'

Changing the pattern

Attempts to 'unblock Australia' had been going on for years. This time something really did shift. How did that change come about? Kevin considers that the way Gary lead his team, his emotional intelligence and the group's respect for him, were significant contributing factors. Over the two days Gary modelled both vulnerability and decisiveness. He was able to stay with the process through all the ambiguity and the uncertainty about the result; although nobody could guarantee a valuable outcome, he persisted in the face of enormous anxiety.

But there were of course other factors at play. In the first three days of the workshop a compelling case for change had been made and the consequences of a new way of working clearly identified. All the rational angles had been covered and all the 'ah buts' addressed. In this wider setting, the voices of those who wished to embrace the new ways of working were amplified, made more powerful by the process. In the two-day board event and subsequently, senior people embraced the personal and emotional consequences of having to lead differently. People began to see the how, what and when of an incredibly complex change. Previously the inability to get a handle on the practicalities of making things happen had prevented many from making changes. It was this seeming impossibility to see the wood for the trees, rather than a denial that change needed to happen, that had prevented many people from taking any change initiatives.

Further, a significant amount of time, effort and thought had gone into designing the workshop. For instance, some structured dialogue work was included to help people gradually express their feelings about the changes associated with the new ways of working. Open space and plenary work was alternated with small groups of varying configurations, so that people had the opportunity to connect with colleagues from different parts of the organisation.

There was also the way that Kevin chose to facilitate proceedings. 'When facilitating groups', he explained, 'I try not to allow the baggage and the history of the group I'm working with to invade my consciousness... I concentrate on working only with what is going on in the room. This means politely ignoring much of the helpful advice that people try to give me about watching out for this person or being sensitive to that issue. All such sensitivity can do is lock the group into its already well-established defensive patterns.' In other words, the only reality of interest to Kevin is the reality of the group in the room. He is not interested in colluding with other constructions. In his experience, working in this way helps him to remain calm when a group gets into a highly emotional state – although he admits that he tends do his own 'flapping', usually in the lead up to a workshop, worrying about design and logistics and about how to ensure full participation.

According to Kevin all the information he needs as a facilitator is available to him in the here and now. Thus, in the two-day workshop with Gary and the other senior managers, he named what he perceived was going on in the room. He brought attention to the language which seemed to be all about demarcation and territory. He made comments such as 'I notice that you get very passionate about this [particular aspect of] change', and 'the way you talk about this sounds as if it will never happen'. More than anything he seeks to stay with the business in hand and pays attention to typical avoidance tactics. As Kevin puts it 'I'll hold it... hold it for as long as it takes. I let the group stay with the discomfort and don't let it move onto an easier subject. As a consultant I try to articulate what I see and hear, as I experience it... at face value. Holding a mirror up, if you like. I also try to create the space for people to say what they see and what they think without interruption or constraint. I want them to hear, really hear, each other. Too often we consultants collude with our clients by suppressing what is really going on... the elephant in the room, if you like. It's an uneasy balance though and there will always be time constraints and the pressure to keep moving the conversation forward towards action.'

Lessons in working with difference

The change team established by Kevin brought a diverse group of individuals together with many different perspectives and levels of experience in the field. Some reverted to detailed planning and structured approaches; others were more intuitive. Kevin was responsible for enabling this group to work together. He sought to lead his team by standing alongside them, to find a way for the personal differences to be a source of positive tension. He demanded self-reliance from his colleagues (whatever their philosophical perspective) and refused to create the hierarchical structures that some wanted. 'There was generally a good spirit in the team but when we were trying to grapple with a complex or thorny challenge we would often end up grappling [intellectually] with each other.'

Kevin described vividly how the way he led this team was very different to the approach he would have taken before his time out of the corporate world: 'I felt much more human, more expressive, more real. I didn't try to fake or hide my feelings, for instance I talked quite openly about my sense of anxiety. The team experienced me as quite messy and vague at times – I prefer to do my thinking in the moment with my colleagues. This was probably not always helpful, as I know a lot of people look for certainty and decisiveness in their leaders especially during times of high ambiguity.'

Throughout our conversations, and upon rereading my notes, I have been struck by Kevin's ability to engage with the world in its diversity; to remain curious about the way people around him frame their world; and to put himself into their shoes. The essence of his approach is, I think, represented by the intranet site at Sugarbrand, which records details of many change tools and techniques which were developed throughout the various projects and initiatives during Kevin's time there. For AMOC purists, like me, this may smack of a simplistic engineering mindset. Doesn't this kind of website support the belief that change strategies can be captured in an instruction manual? We purists would want to emphasise how it is only in multiple narratives and stories that change can begin to be understood. Kevin simply expresses the belief that both approaches can coexist and can support each other well, as long as people's intention is to help start a dialogue rather than to provide an answer: 'I think you have to acknowledge the fact that people like to have reference materials which provide a form of security blanket. Of course we know that tools and frameworks don't create change. However, for me and others who had developed all these insights over that period, the alternative was to walk away from the business taking all that learning with us. We did run a number of workshops which were based on these reference materials, which were great conversation starters, as a way of tapping into what people already know. It was a pragmatic attempt to "capture" what we thought potentially helpful in the form of real life case studies – but we were well aware that the written word or an intellectual understanding is not a panacea for knowledge, experience and learning.'

Epilogue

It would be no surprise to learn that the overall change programme didn't continue exactly according to the original plans. However, the organisation transformation work in Australia did become the 'blueprint' for the rest of the Sugarbrand business. As so often happens, some aspects of the technology failed initially and the lessons from this costly experience informed the way subsequent projects were managed in other parts of the world.

Two years into the transformation journey, Sugarbrand made the largest acquisition in its history and the change work became a vehicle for integrating the newly acquired company and for establishing a new regional structure based on core processes and technology. Kevin found himself working within this new business focus and having to give up some of the original, embedded and carefully negotiated principles underpinning the previous programme of work. Not only did the priorities have to change, the scale of complexity involved in the change increased as the new programme had to address the challenges involved in trying to integrate two different organisational cultures.

Making sense following further reflective inquiry

Getting confirmation of Kevin's story proved challenging. The two senior executives, Rick and Gary, are now based in the US and neither of them got around to reading the full story I'd created with Kevin. Nevertheless we did manage to speak to both of them and they added their perspective on the story told in the previous pages. From those conversations, and from my subsequent conversations with Kevin, the following themes stood out:

- The nature of trust in the relationship between consultant and client
- Working with the tension of difference
- Being a free consultant.

I elaborate my thoughts on these themes.

The nature of trust in the relationship between consultant and client

Sometimes we can choose to establish a relationship based on trust; sometimes the situation forces our hand. In Kevin's work with Sugarbrand, trust seemed to be demanded by the situation. Gary did not really have anyone else to turn to and Rick and Kevin were thrown together even though they perhaps had conflicting philosophies and approaches. This involuntary trust seemed to blossom as both Gary and Rick discovered that Kevin could support them in a way no-one else could. Their relationship also seemed to bear out the truism that 'there's nothing like achievement to cement a relationship'. Right until the first workshop in Australia both Gary and Rick were unsure as to what difference Kevin's approach could make. Following that first workshop they had evidence that his approach worked, regardless of what they thought of it. I sense that their attitude towards Kevin shifted from equivocal to genuine respect.

Kevin also had a genuine respect for the talents of these men and for what they were trying to achieve. He seems able to combine a heartfelt appreciation for the tough calls senior leaders make without becoming passive or in awe. His challenge of Gary was sufficiently robust for Gary to feel that he would have considered it unacceptable if they had been working in a more formal peer or subordinate relationship.

Working with the tension of difference

Kevin, Gary and Rick had to engage with a highly predetermined implementation strategy as designed by Solutions Inc., whilst having to find a way of making this idealised approach actually work in the local Australian culture. This was a continued source of tension. In this difficult work Kevin's capacity to work with local cultures, to both hear and be heard by people out in the field and at all levels of the organisation stood out for his clients.

I was also struck by Kevin's ability to surface different perspectives and to hold them so that people could really appreciate the differences, rather than feel compelled to convert people to one view or another. What is more, Kevin is able to work with this difference in a way that allows new insights to emerge, insights that were not present in any one of the particular perspectives that he had asked people to hold on to.

Kevin also took his demand that difference be taken seriously to his own heart. Thus he learned to work together with Rick in a genuinely respectful way, blending

Rick's impatience to get things done with his own more reflective, 'touchy-feely' approach (to quote Rick). Metaphorically speaking, a 'buttoned-down corporate player' established a more productive partnership with Columbo, the detective played by Peter Falk in the 1970s, than with the Sherlock Holmes rational consulting model.

On being a free consultant

Throughout our conversations I was struck by the extent to which Kevin was able to speak the unspeakable in his work with Sugarbrand, and to draw attention to patterns of behaviour and language in the organisation. Whilst he has a very well developed consulting philosophy, his practice is often quite spontaneous and intuitive. He tends to respond to what needs to be done in the moment as matters are unfolding, rather than trying to force-fit what is happening to a pre-designed plan or methodology. This means that he sometimes experiences his consulting practice as quite messy – hence the Columbo reference earlier – and ill-fitting with any of the neatly packaged consulting stances described by consulting gurus such as Block or Schein. However, Kevin does value prescriptions, only he does not follow them slavishly. He knows that to do his best work he needs to draw on everything he *is*. I did, on occasions, sense an inner critic in Kevin who tells him to be neater, less messy – despite the fact that he knows he would be colluding with a buttoned-down world, and not at his best.

Kevin works at negotiating contracts and relationships which allow him to speak freely and honestly. Nevertheless, this honesty also requires courage. His clients value greatly his willingness to speak freely and perceptively and see it as a defining quality of a good consultant. Rick said: 'Consultants who do this earn the trust of the organisation.'

Finally, another aspect of Kevin's freedom seemed to me the absence of a need to be around senior people all the time. Nor is he burdened with the need to provide the answer or to be always at the centre of attention. Although he seems to enjoy being around people in formal positions of authority, he is able to work with people from all levels and all disciplines. Kevin has a genuine capacity to be a man comfortable in his relationships with people from all walks of life, a quality I admire.

Further reading

Bateson, G (2000) *Steps to an Ecology of Mind*. University of Chicago Press.

Block, P (1999) *Flawless Consulting*. Jossey-Bass, Wiley.

Jung, C (1964) *Man and his Symbols*. Aldus Books.

Nevis, E (1987) *Organisation Consulting – A Gestalt Approach*. Institute of Cleveland Press.

Schein, EH (1988) *Process Consultation: Its role in organisation development*. Addison Wesley.

Streatfield, P (2001) *The Paradox of Control in Organisations*. Routledge.

Watzlawick, P (1990) *Munchausen's Pigtail: Essays and Lectures*. Norton.

Watzlawick, P (ed.) (1984) *The Invented Reality: How do we know what we believe we know?* (Contributions to Constructivism). Norton.

Watzlawick, P, J Weakland, et al. (1974) *Change. Pinciples of Problem Formulation and Problem Resolution.* New York, London: Norton.

Weick, K (2000) *Making sense of the organisation.* Blackwell Publishers.

Bill's Postscript to Kevin's Story

LOOKING THROUGH SIX THEORETICAL FRAMES

This serves as a useful first story as, from a theoretical perspective, it touches all the bases of the AMOC programme.

It seems to me to exemplify the complexity perspective. This is most vividly demonstrated during the five-day workshop, when Kevin was working 'with the fear and vulnerability that people were experiencing at the edge of chaos'. Throughout this assignment he is concerned with the paradox of acting with decisiveness into emerging uncertainty. He eschews predictive models of planned change, but acknowledges the human need for some structure and certainty; hence he also uses scenario planning 'to prepare them for the uncertainty of the journey'. He reminds me of my colleague Patricia Shaw, an eminent complexity practitioner, when he says 'you need to forage, follow scents, rather than wait for issues to arrive on your desk'. He seems to be engaging in the art of 'changing the conversation in organisations'.

This is a rather different perspective from the one evoked by Hugh's earlier quotation from Kafka: 'You do not need to leave your room. Remain sitting at your table and listen... the world will freely offer itself to you to be unmasked'. Kevin goes forth and seeks interaction and provokes response; his is an active practice based on the tacit notion that there is nothing to be unmasked. Theoretically, we tend to conflate Bohm's notions of dialogue and an implicate order with the altogether messier notion of 'conversation' as propounded by Stacey, Shaw and Griffin in which order, or pattern, is created as we negotiate meaning in a process of continuous communicative interaction. This view makes more sense to me from my experience as an organisation consultant.

Kevin is also a consultant who lives in the present. Gestaltist Beisser's assertion that 'If you really want to change, concentrate on what is' seems to inform Kevin, whether he is aware of it or not. He says, 'I do not allow the baggage and history of the group I'm working with to invade the consciousness of my role as a facilitator'. What a bold statement! This is pure Gestalt and, as an 'old Gestaltist' I agree with the principle, while I don't entirely agree in practice, as a recent experience has brought home to me.

I was facilitating a group with a history of power relations of which I was unaware. This history informed how the group members were responding to each other while I became increasingly perplexed at what I constructed as apathy. Consequently my own interventions were increasingly ignored, until bar chats helped me understand what was going on. I was effectively disempowered by my ignorance. From Gestalt and complexity theory we know that both history and the future are enacted in, as Stacey puts it, 'the living present'. However Kevin is right in the sense that, as facilitators, we do not need to know the past as it was, only how it is being enacted in the here and now. In this focus on the present we are liberated from past constructions, but we do not become, as Kevin puts it, 'independent'. While we may be free to 'deconstruct' past meanings, we are never free of the constraints which are inherent in the process of social interaction. We are constrained by language, by the power relations inherent in any social interaction, by what has gone before, by the intentions of others and so forth. I think Kevin may be touched by a liberationist theology in which he values independence from social constraint, and theoretically, I think he makes a mistake. Maybe he constructs himself as a bit of a rebel and a hero?

Kevin combines complexity and Gestalt perspectives in his work, which are both central to the AMOC programme. He also draws extensively on the work of Watzlawick, and will therefore be aware of his caution against Utopian solutions. Watzlawick was interested in the phenomenon of stuckness which he attributed to the way the problem is being constructed, or the language and assumptions in which the problem is framed. He warns, like Einstein, that a problem cannot be solved from the mindset that created it, and identified four patterns in which a problematic situation can become intractable: trying harder, terrible simplifications, setting up paradoxes and Utopian solutions. He argued that in those situations the attempted solution becomes part of the problem.

I wondered whether the whole programme in which Kevin was engaged was an example of a Utopian solution: the programme 'looked to integrate changes in organisation and behaviour, business processes and the underlying technology platform of Sugarbrand *around the world*'. Where have we heard that before!

It seems to me that the whole change programme was too

grandiose, as so many 'managed change' programmes tend to be. I don't think that Kevin was necessarily seduced by its grandiosity, but if he was aware of it I would like to have heard more about the implications of this for his role. Was he actually seduced by its scope and the excitement of being so figural in such a major project? Did he go along with it expecting the opportunity to review it and revise its scope to occur naturally when the work was underway? Did he question or challenge its scope at the outset? These programmes tend to develop their own momentum, until the time is reached when we know, along with Macbeth, that:

> I am in blood
> Stepp'd in so far that, should I wade no more,
> Returning were as tedious as go o'er.

Most of us have been at these moments, not perhaps with the bloody hands of the Scottish King, but wondering whether we should have cried 'hold enough' a little sooner.

Jon – Man not Superman

Jon is an independent consultant, a subtle man, an ex-manager, someone filled with learning that he carries very lightly. There is a modesty and gentleness about him that, in my experience, makes him stand out in a world more accustomed to a 'baroque' consulting tradition. This subtlety carries with it a shadow: the risk that Jon remains unnoticed. In a world that shouts, many of us have lost the ability to notice the quiet voice of reason. Ironically this story starts with Jon being uncharacteristically significant, focusing on himself rather than on his clients.

A few days after Jon had agreed to take part in this research he had a stroke. I carried out the first interview with him about a month after he had returned home from hospital and Jon ended our conversation quoting the sculptor Brancusi: 'To see far is one thing. To go there, that is another.' Unlike some of his fellow artists, Brancusi personally sculpts his creations, rather than relying on the help of craftsmen and women. Jon likened Brancusi's approach to his rehabilitation process and his consulting work, and spoke of the challenge he faces in his work with management teams who seek to distance themselves from the implementation of their projects.

In a rehabilitation process there is no room for delegation. Every bit of recovery is the result of sustained effort. Since his stroke Jon has attempted a little extra movement every day: a bit more work, the first drive to the garage, the walk to the post box, all along reflecting on his experience of this additional effort.

In the two stories that follow there is a recurring theme of people stretching themselves, trying to do something different and reflecting on how their new experience has affected them. This process of action and reflection, with a personal and a collective dimension, is at the heart of Jon's model of adult learning: you try something a bit different, reflect on your experience and share that experience with others, hear how others have experienced your reflections (or their own take on the experience first hand), learn from this and prepare to start all over again. Whilst being similar to Kolb's classic 'learning cycle' (see Appendix 1), Jon's model is also subtly different in the emphasis he places on reflecting as a social activity, something best done in the company of others. Conscious of how very difficult I can find it to notice my taken-for-granted assumptions that continue to inform the way I construct my picture of the world, and thus become self-reinforcing, I think Jon has an important point here.

Working in Greystone – valuing difference and developing group awareness

At the time of our inquiry, and of his stroke, Jon had been working with Greystone, a not-for-profit organisation operating in the area of learning disability. Over a period of about 10 months Jon had consulted to the CEO and his immediate team, using the Myers-Briggs Type Indicator (or MBTI – see Appendix 1) to help team members develop a better understanding of themselves and each other.

Jon often uses the MBTI in his early work with teams. In his experience it helps to develop a shared language to reflect on and understand the dynamics in the team. I noticed how he also applies the MBTI in his sense making of his own reality. Thus he explained to me that he felt able to continue his work with Greystone shortly after his stroke, because the CEO, Stuart, had a similar profile to his own: one that shows a preference for an intuitive, open-ended approach, for decision making based on values and feelings rather than on rational analysis; and that values relationships as much as task completion (INFP – for a brief description of the different types please refer to Appendix 1). Jon's stroke occurred shortly before a two-day workshop at which the management team was to continue its conversation about roles, relationships and responsibilities in the organisation and the MBTI personal feedback process would be completed.

Jon was keen to facilitate the workshop, despite his fragile health. He knew that returning to work as well as having therapeutic value, would allow him to honour a long-standing commitment to Greystone, and not least provide some much-needed income. Since the workshop was designed to encourage thoughtful and reflective conversation, he didn't expect the work to be too demanding – an interesting assumption and one typical of Jon's consulting approach. Many other consultants would experience precisely this kind of work, with its lack of a tightly planned process and well-specified outcome, as exceedingly taxing.

Upon his return from hospital Jon contacted Stuart, Greystone's CEO, who joked about their last conversation hopefully not being the reason for Jon's stroke. Jon realised how, in the process of cautiously reassuring Stuart that he was up to the job, he was also reassuring himself. The work, he said, was straightforward, a simple process inviting equality of voice amongst the six people present.

Equality of voice is important to Jon. He firmly believes that in order to take sound decisions people must become skilled at speaking, inviting and hearing other contributions. Self-awareness and valuing voiced difference are recurring themes in his work.

Contracting with Greystone – getting permission to be different

Jon is keen to work with what emerges in a conversation and had designed the workshop with the management team accordingly. This approach is somewhat unusual, the more typical consulting intervention being designed to manage conversations tightly in order to keep them on course and safe. Of course the more conventional consulting approach is based on the underlying presupposition that there is one right direction for conversations to go in and that managers or consultants can know what that looks like in advance and can steer the conversation in the right direction. A presupposition that would be viewed as untenable within the philosophy of this research.

Jon had tested the organisation's tolerance for his unconventional approach from the very start. At the tender interview he had outlined his approach to adult learning in which participants are expected to take responsibility for the agenda. Arriving with some key pointers about his approach, summarised on not more than one side of A4, Jon resisted the temptation to offer an elaborate proposal, a more directive – and reassuring – approach which many clients have come to expect from consultants.

Although they were perhaps not entirely clear what working with Jon would entail, the selection panel decided to hire him – a decision Jon ascribes to the prevalence of MBTI 'NF' preferences amongst panel members. Quite quickly Jon realised that, despite his openness about his working style, the team still harboured an expectation that he would provide them with a challenging agenda. Instead he sought to enable the group's exploration of a shared agenda by offering some useful models, whilst also supporting Stuart's call for an initial focus on the roles of the different parts of the organisation and the relationships between them.

At this stage Jon also offered the MBTI as a means to develop a shared language with which participants could describe their personal style and preferences and explore the impact of their similarities and differences on the way they worked together.

Jon also used MBTI profiles to explain why Stuart was more comfortable than many of his colleagues with the unpredictable and ambiguous nature of their early meetings and with their seeming lack of progress. Whilst members of the team complained about the vagueness of the process and the difficulty of 'pinning it down' and asked for more structure and more predictable outcomes, Jon noticed how they had begun to talk about topics which were usually carefully avoided, and to speak more honestly with each other. Jon stuck with the process and the resulting discomfort because he believes in the importance of an engaging and adult approach to working through issues with a consultant. In my experience this contrasts with a more mainstream, parental approach to consulting in which the consultant is readily tempted to take up the role of the wise elder, someone who initiates the client in his enlightened view of the world. During the engagement interview he had emphasised that much of the work would involve 'learning to learn' and being responsible for oneself. Drawing on the work of Koestenbaum and Block (2001), Jon described himself as a consultant who demands of himself and his clients that they exercise freedom and take full responsibility for their choices.

I have come to think of Jon as an 'existential' consultant. Informed by the work of Smith and Berg (1987), he works from the rather sophisticated understanding that individual and collective identities coexist and inform each other. In other words, Jon does not see his identity as fixed and given, but as constantly emerging in the diversity of relationships with his clients. This perspective allows him to use the MBTI framework dynamically, as a means to help clients explore themselves as fluid in relationships, rather than to hold rigidly to a fixed notion of themselves.

Being a vulnerable consultant

By April the team had been joined by a new member and was ready to concentrate on creating an agenda informed by everyone on the team. At the workshop Jon's illness was explicitly taken into account. Whilst he found himself well looked after he also took responsibility to notice and share how he was feeling during pauses in the course of the day. Realising he would be unable to support the CEO in facilitating the planned dinner discussion at the end of the first day, which Stuart appeared quite relaxed about.

At the start of the second day, Jon sensed a feeling of care for him in the group and when one of the group members asked how he thought he would cope with the work, he took the opportunity to admit that facilitating this workshop was a big step in his recovery process.

The day worked out as Jon had hoped. People engaged in stretching conversations and he remained largely in the background. In our conversations

Jon explained how much pleasure he found in seeing others shine and how new this feeling is for him. Whereas in his early consulting days he would have considered it his responsibility to offer the sharpest insights and to be the source of major breakthroughs, he can now really enjoy others' insightful questions, well-framed observations and smart recommendations.

Jon repeatedly emphasised how he really wants to avoid 'talking at' people he is working with. It is, he explained, one of the reasons he avoids standing up and making use of audiovisuals: 'As soon as I stand by a flipchart or an overhead projector I fall into a more didactic relationship with my clients and become too much the centre of attention'. Jon takes those issues of power and power distance very seriously indeed. It means he challenges himself just as much as he expects his clients to challenge themselves. It is his main reason for investing heavily in professional support groups, where his views are robustly tested by peers. In his work with Greystone, just as the group members experienced and expressed discomfort with the ambiguity and the lack of predictable outcomes of their conversations, so Jon struggled with not knowing whether he would be able to make it through the two days or whether this was an appropriate step in his rehabilitation process.

Working with theory – making models available

As I mentioned earlier, Jon likes to use frameworks and models as a provocative invitation to reflective dialogue. On the April workshop with Greystone he chose the work of Smith and Berg (1987) on the paradoxical nature of group dynamics. Offering seven paradoxical statements (for example, 'trust only comes when you give trust'), he invited each team member to identify the paradox that most reflected their experience of working in Greystone and to share an experience that demonstrated their chosen paradox in action.

True to his style, whatever theory Jon works with is offered lightly and informally. No high-tech presentations, just a few bullet points on a flipchart; but his purpose is profound: 'We all hold and live by implicit assumptions about the nature of reality, about how the world works. By offering provocative frameworks I seek to help my clients articulate and challenge their implicit worldview. Reflecting on our experience from a different perspective can help us to notice patterns in our behaviour which may otherwise remain outside our awareness and therefore remain difficult to change. This can be quite an unnerving experience. For instance, in the Greystone workshop a couple of clients really had a hard time seeing the paradoxes as statements of contradictory truths rather than riddles to be solved.'

Jon used Smith and Berg's work to help the group develop a shared understanding of the complex and unpredictable nature of the world in which they are expected to lead. 'There's no need to mention "social constructionism". But I do think it is important that people come to terms with the messy and dynamic nature of organisational life where meaning is created over time in shared conversation and action, where the world does not work according to simple reductionist models of cause and effect.'

Jon uses models in the service of the group's learning and often decides in the moment what might be helpful. In order to heighten the team's awareness of the patterns in their conversation and decision making he briefly introduced Argyris'

'Ladder of Inference' (Isaacs, 1999), McLain Smith's 'Advocacy/Inquiry Model' (1994) and Nancy Kline's (1998) work on thinking environments in groups. Working with those frameworks helped team members to notice their tendency to include or exclude certain voices and how that resulted in a broadly or narrowly constructed agenda, or in a rich or impoverished set of recommendations. They realised that they needed to find a way to explore 'who is Greystone?' and 'what is our organisational identity?' amongst themselves, in the first instance, and subsequently with the rest of the organisation.

Working with others' frameworks, Jon has gradually weaned himself off the need to be *doing* things. Focusing less on the tasky side of consulting, he increasingly seeks to invite thoughtful reflection into habitual ways of thinking and, in the process, has come to value his own insightful contributions. 'Frameworks and models', says Jon, 'can really help people to uncover their personal and group patterns, provided the theory is grounded carefully in their experience. I need to remind myself to pay enough attention to the link between concepts and people's experience. Left unchecked I'm prone to stay quite happily at an abstract level.'

A parallel story – Rubco the industrial chemicals company

At the start of our inquiry, Jon and I decided it might be interesting to explore how different client engagements inform one another, since many consultants work with more than one client at any one time. Jon chose his work with Rubco as the parallel engagement to explore in our inquiry.

The invitation to work with Rubco came before Jon's stroke. He was well known in the organisation as he had worked there for a number of years before going freelance. The initial invitation was to explore with the outgoing MD, Graham, and the new MD, Andreas, the running of a two-day team building exercise. However, during the briefing it became clear that there was a larger task to be addressed. The German headquarters of Rubco expected the UK operation to produce a vision for the future of the UK plant, including a strategy for forging a new identity and overhauling current working practices.

During the meeting Jon noticed how his clients, despite talking about a 'vision based on our strengths', were mainly problem focussed and their language strewn with 'problem vocabulary'. In order to develop a process congruent with his clients' wish to build on their strengths, he suggested working with an appreciative inquiry (see Appendix 1) perspective, a framework that was new to both Graham and Andreas, but which they declared themselves willing to give a go. Jon subsequently proposed an extensive and participative process involving the whole site. The two-day workshop would now serve as an opportunity for the management team to develop their understanding of the proposed AI approach before giving the go-ahead for the wider process. The notion of taking an appreciative approach appealed greatly to the management team, as morale at the UK plant was low. A participative process also appealed. 'I wondered', Jon explained, 'whether people were confusing a genuine participative process with what we usually mean when we say "involving people". In a traditional patriarchal organisation that tends to entail making a decision and then "selling it". "Getting buy-in" is what we usually call it. I was very keen to explain that, for a vision to become reality, people need to be really involved in creating it, rather than have the vision sold to them. I also wanted to make it clear that, if we were serious about genuine participation, we would not be able to predict or manipulate the outcome.'

To Jon's delight his proposed approach, despite its challenges, seemed to be welcomed by Andreas, the new MD. 'A number of factors seemed at play here. First of all, Andreas was really open to new ideas, an openness which had stood him in good stead as MD of the Finland operation. In that role he had developed a deep understanding of the importance of cultural differences, and the discrepancy in views between HQ and regional operations. Secondly, Andreas saw organisations as considerably more complex entities than is suggested by the more common, engineering-based perspective. In my experience Andreas was the first MD in Rubco UK willing to consider an appreciative inquiry. Previous MDs, parachuted into the organisation to "sort it out", had arrived with preconceived ideas about what was required.'

When things fall apart

So far so good – but then the unexpected happened. The start-up workshop was planned for 8–9 March. On 3 March, Jon had his stroke.

It was a blow on both personal and professional levels. As well as the distressing concern about his health, Jon had been looking forward to earning some much-needed cash after a poor financial start to the year. He also realised that the workshop couldn't be postponed as Rubco's HQ was expecting Andreas to deliver the vision by the end of the first quarter. What should be done?

Jon's concern over such mundane matters as finances and work in the face of such a traumatic event may seem bizarre. However, it's what he was thinking about as he waited on his doorstep for the ambulance to arrive: 'Thinking about everyday matters, something normal, helped me not to drown in the potentially overwhelming health issues I was confronted with.'

After a day of frenetically wondering 'Why did this happen to me? Why now?' he quickly moved on to thinking about 'Who else?'

Mary, also an independent consultant, had taken her Masters in Organisation Consulting together with Jon. Although they hadn't been close at the time, they were now part of a mutual coaching group, where they supported each other in reflecting on their consulting business and practice. Until now, Jon had only ever toyed with the recurring question from his clients: 'What happens if you walk under the proverbial bus?' Well, now he had and the time had come to test the strength of his network.

Jon was confident that Mary was the right person to replace him: 'She had no prior relationship with the group and thus no historical baggage, which I thought was really important; she had a sound understanding of the process and philosophy of AI; and moreover, I was convinced that she would intuitively grasp my intention underpinning the design I had proposed. After all we had spent considerable time and energy learning about each other's approach, attachments and constructions in our shared learning group. This deep understanding is really important to me, I couldn't possibly have handed over the project to someone who'd only just read a book about AI.'

As soon as Mary had agreed to take on the work she called Andreas to inform him they could go ahead and meet the deadlines, provided he was happy to work with her instead of Jon. Andreas simply agreed, a testimony to his faith in Jon's judgement and to the importance of the quality of relationships between client and consultant.

On the afternoon of 10 March Jon had a call from Mary: all had gone well and there was nothing left to do until the next phase in late April.

Jon and Mary working together

Mary produced a written account of the workshop using the language of the participants, which simultaneously served as a strong piece of advocacy for the project. Whilst he was aware that Mary's approach was different to his, using the participant's language struck Jon as singularly effective. Another significant difference was Mary's single-minded refusal to manipulate the selection of volunteers which would have resulted in the usual suspects stepping forward. Instead she took great care in opening up the opportunity to anyone keen to be involved.

'I knew that Mary would do things in a different way, and I trusted her approach would be just as valuable' said Jon. 'My trust was based on the quality of our relationship, a key aspect of which is our deep respect for each other's differences and the shared philosophy that comes from our time together on AMOC. One of the differences between Mary and I is her courageous willingness not to fit in with others' expectations. She is really skilled at staying with the truth of her own experience and finds ways of sharing her truth with others that are carefully thought through. I know she refuses to collude with a general mood of "all is well" if that's not congruent with her experience. I'm aware that I find it difficult to break such a mood.'

Once Jon was out of hospital he and Mary needed to address how they were going to proceed with the project. Rubco had already mentioned that they hoped Mary was 'going to be around' as the process unfolded. Jon and Mary decided that they would let the client decide what they wanted in terms of working with Mary and/or Jon. They offered to work together on the project for the initially agreed fee, an arrangement which, not surprisingly, delighted the client. This arrangement also gave Jon and Mary the opportunity to work together and deepen their connection. Whilst their differences complemented each other, they shared an ability to work with what emerges, rather than being bound by a predefined script.

Taking the West Coast to the West Midlands

At the time of writing, the workshops at the different sites have not yet happened, although they are imminent. I asked Jon how he felt in anticipation of this experience. He admitted he felt quite anxious: 'I really do wonder how a bunch of "hairy-arsed" production people will respond to the language of AI. How will West Coast Americana land in the West Midlands? So far I have only worked with appreciative inquiry in coaching situations or in small groups, where asking people to describe themselves or their organisation at its best seems pretty straightforward. I'm not sure how this will work with 80 people from an industrial environment. What kind of language can I use to invite them to talk about themselves working at their best without the whole thing feeling like an import from an alien culture? What will it take to get people talking about themselves in a positive way? Secondly, I worry about the management team and their typical concerns. Will they really own and support this process? How can Mary and I respectfully challenge their likely attempts to position us at the forefront of the process? And finally, how can we ensure only a minimum number of decisions are made upstream (i.e. by the management team)? How can the process be transformed from a management initiative, or consulting thing to a genuine organisation-wide initiative?'

Jon has little anxiety about working with Mary and is looking forward to hearing her comments and questions as the process unfolds. 'I am convinced we will stretch each other. No doubt Mary will continue to stay with and pursue difficult issues that I have a tendency to avoid. I'm also looking forward to being able to step back and pay attention to the deeper patterns that are so easily missed when I'm swept up in the hurly-burly of the moment. By working with someone else I admit that I'm not superman, that I can't do everything. I know that working with a colleague I am so much more relaxed.'

Jon in his work

So what are the parallels in Jon's work with Greystone and Rubco? 'I think it is my fundamental desire not to be the centre of attention in my work and my belief that I add value through the difference I bring.' In my conversations with Jon I was struck by the humanity in both stories, the huge amount of trust. Much of the time Jon's consulting didn't seem to be as much about 'getting the job done' as about working with people who will provide the sort of value that he would hope to provide. At the heart of Jon's consulting are relationships, and when the work goes well it is because of the quality of those relationships.

Equally important seems to be a sound philosophy underpinning his work. Jon was at pains to explain that what he valued in Mary's contribution was not so much her ability to 'facilitate a workshop, do the work' as her deep knowing that enabled her to relate to Rubco. Jon is a big fan of theoretically informed action. He explained that one of the reasons he agreed to contribute to this inquiry was that it would provide him with an opportunity to share with his clients the depth he brings to his seemingly loosely designed interventions.

Jon admits to being a purist: 'I'm not really interested in working for a consulting organisation that "delivers programmes". Instead I want to work with the messiness of the actual here and now, I want to respond to situations as they emerge, weaving strands of theoretical insight and practical experience.'

At the start of this story I referred to Jon's appreciation of Brancusi's comment that 'To see far is one thing. To go there, that is another.' His experience of rehabilitation has brought home to him the difference between the two: 'The intellectual, emotional and relational state evoked by seeing a possibility is profoundly different from the one involved in actually "going there". As a consultant I want to "go there", and I want my clients to "go there" too. I don't want them to just sit back and catch a glimpse. There is a world of difference between thinking about doing something and doing something.' In our last conversation Jon recommended a Buddhist book to me *After the Ecstasy, the Laundry* (Kornfield, 2000). This text is deeply significant for Jon: 'We can all have the most transcendental experience possible but in the end we will come back to a messier and noisier world, where it is all right for us to get things wrong, so long as we notice and learn from what has happened.'

Sense from further reflective inquiry

The follow-up reflections with Jon were the most extensive and multi-vocal of the inquiries I conducted for this research. They included an interview with Jon and Stuart, two conversations between Jon and Andreas, Mary's own reflections on her experience as well as a final inquiring conversation between Jon and myself.

I was left with a strong sense of Jon's gentle thoroughness, both in his approach to our inquiry and in his work as a consultant, a quality easily overlooked by people who tend to equate thoroughness and rigour with analytical harshness.

Three themes stood out for me from this extended reflective inquiry:

- The consultant as an expert who can let go of his expertise
- The capacity to work with a plan and yet go with what is happening in the moment
- The consultant as a master of reflective practice.

The consultant as an expert who can let go of his expertise

Stuart expressed his view as follows: 'The client needs to know you're an expert before they can let go of the need for the consultant to be an expert.' In the course of Jon's work with Greystone he shifted from having to show demonstrable expertise, to making a difference through the quality of his engagement with Greystone's reality in the moment. Interestingly, and obviously in my view, Jon's perceived value increased as his explicit expert role decreased.

This brings a subtle nuance to the saying that in consulting engagements 'first steps are fateful', and reminds us that second and third steps are just as fateful. The challenge for consultant and client is not to get stuck in the pattern of their early engagement. In my experience many consultant–client relationships do get stuck in a pattern of the consultant as expert, so that the relationship does not allow the consultant's contribution to develop into that of participant and equally voiced expert. The focus of attention often remains on the presenting agenda and cannot evolve and deepen to an attention on the organisational patterns that caused this agenda to be the presenting agenda in the first place. I suspect that many consultant–client engagements get stuck into habits of working on a certain, narrowly defined set of situations in a certain way – typically, neatly rationalised issues that both parties hope can be addressed by a neatly rational, procedural approach.

Personally I find it hard to move away from this 'performing expert role' and I was really struck by Jon's ability to demonstrate real and practically useful humility – to work from a position where he sees his value as 'holding a space where others can step to the fore' – without denying the occasional need for advocacy. Jon does not allow his ego to get in the way. This humility seems to me to come from Jon's deep-seated belief that 'the people in the organisation can solve their problems better than anyone else'. Maybe the skilled consultant is the one who can voice his or her expertise in a way that means his or her voice is experienced as one voice alongside many others, rather than as a predominant or determining one.

The capacity to work with a plan and yet go with what is happening in the moment

Jon describes his facilitation process as full of holes, holes that get filled during the work itself by the people he is working with. He has a plan for how things could be, a good enough framing to get things going, but loose enough to allow disorder and frustration to emerge and to stay with it. Because Jon believes disorder engenders creativity, he offers his clients ambiguity rather than clarity.

In our conversations Jon talked of his love of imperfection, a notion that has taken him a while to get comfortable with – and one that I still only grudgingly accept in my life and work. As Jon put it, 'Imperfection is natural, it is the way people are. It is inevitable that we will make mistakes, do things in a way that doesn't suit others.' His reflections have led me to understand better the importance of the imperfect plan, a plan its creators know is always contingent, partial and in many ways wrong. I come now to see a plan as the creature of its imperfect creators.

Mary's reflections further clarified this for me. When she took over from Jon she was initially trapped into trying to emulate Jon's thought processes, whereas to be effective she needed to work in her own unique style. She needed to make Jon's plan her own, as much as Rubco's employees needed to make it theirs in the course of the workshop. Working flexibly with a plan, consciously letting go of what was pre-thought, is part of the discipline of working with the organisational reality as it presents itself in the moment. Stuart expressed his appreciation of this ability to stay with what is emerging in the moment and contrasted it with other consultants whom he experienced as pulling the conversation back to their own agenda. I associate this with a consultant's fear of losing control over a process, a fear I am well familiar with.

The imperfect plan provides a framework for frustration and creativity, for consultant and client to co-construct what needs to be addressed and how it needs to be worked on. The attention to the here and now gives co-construction vitality and makes change in the moment possible. Jon's belief is that change happens in the present: 'Shifts in patterns of relationship, in what is talked about, in how they are worked on can only happen in the now – talking about things needing to happen in the future will not result in change.'

The consultant as a master of reflective practice

Jon frequently referenced Reg Revans (1998) in our conversations and his belief that there is 'no learning without sober and active reflection'. Stuart expressed his appreciation of Jon's capacity to surface the patterns of interaction that informed how the Greystone management team was working. He also valued the theoretical interpretation Jon brought to the conversations. I had the impression that Stuart experienced it as a validation for much of what he was intuitively doing, whilst also providing a useful reflective discipline.

Jon is of a reflective disposition, as his Myers-Briggs profile illustrates. However, there is a world out there populated with people of very different dispositions for whom reflection can be quite a challenge. He needs to acknowledge those differences and illuminate the importance of reflection to people who are more motivated by action and experimentation. Jon is also aware of needing to quieten his ego: 'when my ego goes down I can stop being part of the established pattern of relationship, and the opportunity for reframing can occur'. This is especially so when it allows for questions and supportive inquiry that promote intelligence and insight in the one that is being questioned, rather than the cleverness of the questioner. But it is not simply a matter of subjugating one's ego, pretending to be an invisible consultant. 'If you're not able to see that you (as consultant) are both part of and observing a system or pattern of relationship, you will be stuck in it because your choices are limited. The artistry lies in being visibly present without being egocentric or self-referencing, being yourself in a way that encourages rather than stifles or overwhelms others.'

On the basis of Jon's story I'd like to offer the following contingent, personal and partial summary of what reflective discipline requires from a consultant: firstly, a capacity to invite self and clients into a slower rhythm of working than is normal in most organisational settings; secondly, a capacity to invite people into a more noticing and inquiring relationship with others and themselves; thirdly, an acknowledgement of personal presence and role, combined with an ability to quieten personal ego needs; and lastly, an ability to support intelligent inquiry in others through perceptive questions and observations that arise in the here and now.

Further reading

Argyris, C (1990) *Overcoming Organisational Defences. Facilitating Organisational Learning*. Englewood Cliffs NJ: Prentice Hall.

Argyris, C and DA Schon (1996) *Organisational Learning II. Theory, Method and Practice*. Reading MA: Addison-Wesley.

Isaacs, W (1999) *Dialogue and the Art of Thinking Together*. New York: Currency.

Kline, N (1998) *Time to Think*. Cassell.

Koestenbaum, P and P Block (2001) *Freedom and accountability at work*. San Francisco: Jossey-Bass.

Kolb, DA (1984) *Experiential learning: Experience as the source of learning and development*. New Jersey: Prentice Hall.

Kornfield, J (2000) *After the Ecstasy, the Laundry: how the heart grows wise on the spiritual path*. New York: Bantam Books.

McLain Smith, D (1994) 'Balancing Inquiry and Advocacy' in Senge, P, A Kleiner, C Roberts, R Ross and B Smith (1995) *The Fifth Discipline Fieldbook. Strategies and Tools for Building a Learning Organisation*. London: Nicolas Brealey, p.253–9.

Myers, IB and PB Myers (1995) *Gifts Differing*. Palo Alto CA: Davies-Black.

Revans, R (1998) *ABC of Action Learning*. Lemos and Crane.

Senge, P, A Kleiner, C Roberts, R Ross and B Smith (1995) *The Fifth Discipline Fieldbook. Strategies and Tools for Building a Learning Organisation*. London: Nicholas Brealey.

Schon, DA (1991) *The Reflective Practitioner – How Professionals Think in Action*. Aldershot: Ashgate Publishing.

Smith, K and D Berg (1987) *Paradoxical conception of group dynamics*. Human Relations, The Tavistock Institute, 40: 10.

Bill's Postscript to Jon's Story

LOOKING THROUGH SIX THEORETICAL FRAMES

This is the story of a 'Reflective Practitioner'. Oddly enough Jon does not mention it, but Schon's (1991) book with that title is on the AMOC core reading list. When we discuss, as we frequently do, what we see as our prime intention in the AMOC programme, we say that it is to develop organisation consultants as *reflective practitioners*. We explain this to our external examiners when they ask for more rigour in our research methodology, or to members of our academic board who cannot see enough 'content'. We are not seeking to turn out specialists in the practice of inquiry, or experts in complexity theory or Gestalt consultants or proponents of appreciative inquiry, but reflective practitioners. All contributors to this research demonstrate the reflexive stance, but Jon particularly seems to embody our aspiration by placing reflexivity at the heart of his practice.

The story starts with Jon's articulation of a simple, but profound, learning cycle that is the basis of reflective practice; and what is more, he includes this in his proposal to his client. I have a sense of Jon's implacable determination to be transparent with his client about his stance as a promoter of adult learning, in which people are challenged to pay attention to what they do, to experiment with something different, and to reflect on the consequences. Many consultants espouse this way of working, but few practise it as assiduously as Jon, who absolutely eschews the role of directive expert.

One of the subtleties in Jon's way of working which caught my attention early on in this story, is his insistence that the Greystone team create their own agenda for the workshop he is facilitating. Not simply because he does not want to do it for them, which would be reason enough given his way of working; but because he wants to draw their attention to their habitual pattern of agenda creation. I say this is subtle because many of us are well trained to notice the patterns of interaction in the life of an organisation, and yet do not draw special attention to the formation of agendas. Often, in creating a workshop, we take it for granted that it is our job to 'design the workshop' and even congratulate ourselves on our skills as designers of workshops. So, with this assumption about our role, we may miss something really important about the way the formal conversations taking place in the leadership team – which have a significant influence on the 'conversations' taking place in the organisation as a whole – are shaped.

Jon is here exemplifying a number of theoretical perspectives, not the least of which is complexity theory with its focus on the way themes shape and are shaped by patterns of conversation. As with Kevin, he is also informed by what Watzlawick refers to as first- and second-order change, intending to draw attention to their first-order pattern of habitual agenda creation. As a Gestaltist, he does this not through theoretical exposition, but by having them become aware of what they are doing as they do it. It is interesting that John Higgins refers to him as an existential consultant. Existentialism is, in its less academic sense, one aspect of the philosophy which informs the AMOC consulting stance – in the sense that we believe that what is happening in any organisational interaction is infinitely more important and interesting than constructions of what has happened or predictions about what might happen.

Jon also brings paradox into his work. Ralph Stacey argues that repetition and novelty are simultaneous characteristics of communicative interaction, so paradox is an inherent characteristic of organisation life. Leaders need some operational processes to produce consistency and repeatability, while simultaneously needing to create the conditions for innovation and initiative. They want their staff to collaborate at the same time as compete for promotion and rewards; to be good team players and to be held accountable for individual performance and so forth. Jon, in using Smith and Berg's work on the paradoxical nature of group dynamics, is challenging the managerial tendency to resolve paradox, or to eliminate the paradox into a comfortable 'both… and' way of thinking by locating the contradictory terms in different spaces or times. Instead, he challenges the team to hold the two terms of the paradox as inseparable and simultaneous, and hence potentially transformative.

Throughout these two stories I have a sense of Jon valuing relationship, but in a very low key sort of way. On the one hand there is something laudable about his own lack of ego and his propensity to keep in the background, but there are times when I believe a more assertive presence is needed. I sense that Jon takes an ideological stance on 'equality of voice', which may inhibit him from having an impact on the power dynamics that are an inherent part of group process.

So while I see him informed by the complexity perspective with its emphasis on paradox, power and unpredictability, he seems to want to create conditions in which the unfairness and inequality of organisation life are temporarily held in abeyance – which is not entirely consistent with his theoretical advocacy. This obviously suits his quiet, reflective style, and may be in many circumstances a healing balm to his clients.

Dominic and Liz – Not Just Doing the Do

Liz and Dominic work for Lane4, a consultancy of about 40 full-time employees and 30 associates, whose practice is informed by the insights of elite athletes and their coaches, as well as occupational psychologists and business consultants. Liz has a doctorate from Loughborough and Dominic is an Olympic-medal-winning pentathlete and an AMOC graduate. Their focus, and that of Lane4, is on improving organisation, team and personal performance. As will become evident during this story, their approach is less about the adrenaline of competing and more about the relationship between mind and body and how human beings create the world within which they experience, live and perform.

For the purpose of the research project Liz and Dominic chose to inquire into their experience of working with an organisation specialising in environmental engineering, which I have called The Institute. The Institute employs highly intelligent, highly qualified people, some of whom hold several PhD's. Many employees stay with The Institute at least for one or two decades, if not for life.

Lane4 was approached by the HR Director of The Institute, Patrick, to support him in a major change project, driven by changes in the regulatory environment that had started to erode the traditional monopoly of The Institute. Within a few years The Institute would have to operate within a genuinely competitive market, where purchasers of their services could exercise choice between suppliers.

By the time Liz and Dominic came on board, the project had been mapped out in classic engineering fashion, captured in a neat Gantt chart, outlining activities, deliverables, deadlines and responsibilities.

Culture change as a work stream on a Gantt chart

The Institute had identified that meeting the dramatic change in its competitive environment would require a culture change, although what was meant by culture change remained ambiguous. Nevertheless, in keeping with an engineering mindset, 'culture change' had been identified as a work stream within the overall change project. Rachel was put in charge of the 'culture stream' and asked to identify relevant activities to be incorporated in the Gantt chart.

However, both Patrick and Rachel were well aware that culture change requires something fundamentally different from, say, implementing an IT system. Rachel was interested in the messiness and a-rational nature of much of organisational life, and saw a key part of her role as helping the project's steering committee to develop a more sophisticated understanding of the process of changing cultures and mindsets.

'We felt really attracted to the work', Liz and Dominic told me. 'Not only could we relate to this client from a philosophical perspective, we were also invited to get involved early on, when the overall design and principles underpinning the change process were still being decided. However, we soon discovered we were not the only consultants on the job. Rachel and Patrick did not think of Lane4 as specialising in organisational change and had engaged two independent consultants, Peter and Chris for this purpose.' Peter had been a senior partner of a well-known HR consulting firm. He was very familiar with the considerable range of analytical frameworks used by his previous employer and had consulted in an independent capacity to The Institute for ten years. Rachel had worked with Chris before she joined The Institute.

'We were brought in', explained Liz, 'for downstream leadership development. The task was to offer support to between 100 and 150 executives, the scale of which was well beyond the capacity of Peter and Chris.'

Not a meeting of minds

Rachel and Patrick wanted the three consulting parties to meet before the work got off the ground. 'Although they didn't see us as design experts in the field of organisational change, they were keen we were at least party to the conversations at the start', said Dominic. 'I was quite keen that we could find a way to contribute over and above our assigned role of leadership developers, and thought that being involved right from the start would make that more likely. That's not to say that our first meeting wasn't really tricky. Our respective worldviews were not terribly compatible and I felt we were jostling for a spot in the limelight. I found myself becoming increasingly competitive, especially with Peter, who I experienced as rather patronising. I bristled at his recurring assertions "this is the way organisations work", "it is known that organisations change as follows" and "the qualities of leaders are well documented", which left little room for alternative views.'

'We suspected that Peter's view on leadership and change was probably quite congruent with that of The Institute', Liz added. 'Thankfully we found a kindred spirit in Chris. With an MSc in Change from Sheffield, he was very well read and, moreover, able to ground his well-informed theoretical perspective in the day-to-day reality. In his view, organisational change always has a paradoxical quality and involves a tension between different experiences that cannot be reduced to one another. He also emphasised the importance of the informal aspects of organisational life in understanding the dynamics of change. Although he was not a confrontational person, as the project evolved we discovered he was able to stand his ground and in the process we got to think of him as our "wise owl".'

Dominic found Chris's views sat comfortably with the perspective he was exploring in AMOC, particularly with the work of Stacey and other complexity-inspired authors. 'I was really pleased to have Chris at the first meeting', said Dominic. 'He helped me to keep my temper under control, and stopped me from getting quite childish in my frustration. At the end of the meeting I said "Of course we can work together", but in my heart I wasn't quite so sure. Because Rachel had brought us all together in this meeting I assume she didn't doubt our ability to collaborate, whatever our philosophical differences.'

Liz, while finding the meeting less emotionally charged than Dominic, struggled to connect with Peter and was frustrated by his apparent 'expert' (and I would add patriarchal) approach to consulting. Whatever their differences, Peter was well respected by Patrick and obviously had authority within The Institute; therefore Dominic and Liz needed to find a way to communicate with Peter, rather than continuing the battle of worldviews.

After the masterclass, the conversation

At the time of this work, the organisation was waiting for a new CEO to join, following the departure of the previous one. In that interim period the chairman had commissioned two masterclasses, one on change, lead by Peter, the other on organisational culture, lead by Chris, Dominic and Liz. The formal workshops for senior executives were intended to keep some momentum for change going in The Institute.

There was no attempt to integrate the perspectives underpinning both masterclasses. Peter ran the first one, with Chris, Dominic and Liz observing from the back of the room. Authoritatively, he took around 60 executives through their paces, engaging in team-building exercises and working with the Hey McBer Emotional Intelligence diagnostic tool.

At the second masterclass Peter was to observe his other three consulting colleagues in action. The evening before, Dominic, Patrick and Peter met up for dinner. Peter and Dominic fell into their usual pattern of light banter, entertaining enough but not truly connecting. After dinner, Dominic, keen to stretch his legs, offered to walk Peter to his hotel, a short distance from the conference venue.

'It was one of those chance moments', said Dominic. 'It was a beautiful still night. Walking along a Scottish firth, moved by the beauty of our surroundings, the nature of our conversation shifted. We talked about our childhood, about significant moments in our life, and Peter, a natural teller of heroic stories, started to show his vulnerable side. From that moment onwards I felt differently about Peter, and I had a sense that my feeling was reciprocated.'

The challenge of representing 'difference'

In one of their early conversations Liz and Patrick had discovered they had a different perspective on working explicitly with organisational values. Patrick didn't think it was feasible, whilst Liz held the view that, although challenging and difficult, it could be done and add real value. Peter had joined in the conversation, siding with Patrick, and to Liz's frustration her opinion was rather summarily dismissed.

'I was getting increasingly fed up with Peter. I seek to respect people, their values and their views, even if I don't agree with them, and I expect the same from others. Peter's definitive and judgemental statements jarred with me, leaving me feeling my view was neither heard nor respected, and in the process I didn't feel respected as a person either. I thought his facilitation style had that strong expert flavour too. It risked setting up a parent–child dynamic with the group, inviting participants to accept Peter's view without too much questioning.'

The situation became even more challenging for Liz. When she discovered she couldn't attend the first day of the masterclass she was co-facilitating, Rachel suggested she wasn't needed at all. 'I was quite taken aback', Liz explained. 'How had this been decided? By whom? Why? When I started to probe Rachel for a further explanation it emerged that Patrick wasn't quite sure I'd be right for the group, suggesting I was "too academic". It was a difficult situation. I suspected Peter's influence in Patrick's assessment of my style, but I didn't get an opportunity to speak directly to Patrick, only getting information second hand, via Rachel. I was frustrated with Rachel too for not challenging Patrick's statement. At least we managed to have an honest conversation about that. Thankfully Dominic showed himself a true partner. He refused to let me be sidelined and was adamant clients experience me as really grounded. So I stayed on the facilitation team for the masterclass, but I remember feeling less than charitable as I tore myself away from my son's birthday party to get to work!'

I was struck by Dominic's support for Liz. In my experience colleagues are often readily stepped down as a result of this kind of feedback from clients, without the underlying issue being addressed. Here I sense an unexplored generational/gender divide, as much as a philosophical one.

The second masterclass was very well received. Patrick was delighted and expressed his appreciation for Liz's contribution, admitting to Dominic later that he'd been wrong about her. Even Peter offered spontaneous and appreciative feedback noting that Liz 'was obviously an impact player', high praise indeed coming from Peter – although praise that could be interpreted as two-edged if seen through the lens of gender/generational conflict. Was Peter actually suggesting that Liz could behave more like an old man when required?

Protecting the interests of The Institute

After the masterclasses, consultants and clients turned their attention to the use of diagnostic tools, once again stumbling upon the fault line in the group. Peter, keen to take advantage of his considerable experience as director of diagnostics in his previous consulting firm, wanted to work with a proven, well-established approach, and therefore saw absolutely no reason not to use an existing instrument.

'At least we'd moved on', said Dominic. 'I think by that time we really did understand that Peter absolutely had the interest of The Institute in mind at all times. So while challenging his suggested tool, we tried to explain very carefully how we thought our proposed approach might be of more value to the client, rather than getting into an argy-bargy about "who's got the best toy". The real issue was that Liz and I had a fundamentally different perspective on the use of diagnostic tools than Peter. We believe they add value to the extent that they raise people's personal awareness and help to promote good, reflective conversations which might otherwise be difficult to initiate. Our perspective is at odds with the mainstream opinion that such tools reveal measurable and objective truths about people. Peter was not at all keen, not only on the Lane4 perspective on diagnostic tools, but also on the specific diagnostic framework we recommended; but at least we managed to persuade him to review the material.'

Reluctant and rather critical at first, over time Peter became impressed with the theoretical rigour that underpinned the Lane4 work and was eventually persuaded to visit the Lane4 research team. 'It's important to see Peter's questioning and probing in context', says Liz. 'We really felt that during those challenging conversations he did have the interest of The Institute at heart. As an organisation of leading experts in their field, consultants and managers too are expected to be rigorous in their choice of approach and materials. In line with those expectations Patrick too worked his way through the background reading on our recommended instrument, something not often done outside academic circles.'

I did wonder whether Lane4 were at risk of reinforcing the belief in The Institute that change could be approached with the same frame of intellectual understanding they employed successfully in their engineering environment. A more generous interpretation would be that they continued to pace their client well, so that their difference remained intelligible. I sense that they ought to have challenged an excessively intellectual perspective at this stage and that they became trapped in one of The Institute's and Peter's deep and unacknowledged assumptions – namely, that intellectual knowing would enable culture change to take place.

Changing the conversation between senior executives – unexpected support

Some time after the chairman's masterclasses a new CEO was appointed. 'We were asked to give an update on the leadership development work to the executive committee', said Liz. 'We couldn't but notice how anxious Patrick was about this. Understandably so, of course, since this was the first experience of the new CEO to a project that Patrick, in his role of HR director, was accountable for. Understandable, but therefore no less difficult for me to cope with, when I learnt that Patrick had once again voiced his concern about my suitability for this task. However Dominic remained adamant that he wanted to work with me.'

By this stage in the process, members of the executive team had met with their coaches and received the feedback from the completion of the various diagnostic questionnaires. 'We wanted the executive team of The Institute to make sense of the feedback they had received, both individually and in conversation with their peers. We believed that reflecting on how they were experienced in the organisation and making meaning of the messages they were getting, would help them to decide how they might want to engage differently with people when returning to their daily business. Our ambition was to contribute to changing the conversational patterns within the organisation.'

When Liz and Dominic briefly shared their plans with the new CEO before the start of the workshop he voiced his scepticism: 'Nice idea, but I'll be surprised if you get people to share their feedback. I recommend you keep some other ideas up your sleeve, in case the sharing doesn't happen.' 'We were pleased he felt able to share his doubts', said Liz. 'But he needn't have worried. The extent to which people felt able to share personal feedback with each other delighted us all, including Patrick who admitted to being really surprised that these were the same people who had historically been rather distant from each other and not willing to share much at all. We wondered whether the rather confrontational style of the previous CEO perhaps contributed to that "playing it safe" pattern.'

So what was different this time around?

When I asked Liz the above question she promptly replied: 'Well, it's not rocket science John, not much is when it comes to deepening connection between people. What is really difficult to understand is the extent to which we inhibit and disrupt the innate human capacity to connect in many organisations.' A modest-enough reply, but I was left with a sense that some of the aspects of the design were very intelligently thought out. Let me elaborate.

For a start they paid attention to the way they joined the 10 senior executives.

By 4pm the team members, in their role as senior executives, had been listening to formal presentations on various projects. It was important to change the dynamic and avoid Liz and Dominic being perceived as the next presenters, with the executives staying firmly in the role of audience and evaluators. Dominic also wanted to indicate that people would be invited to engage in a more personal way with one another. To set a more intimate tone he started off with sharing his own anxiety about joining this group and working with them in a different way from what had gone on before. After his own disclosure he invited the team members in turn to share how they felt in that moment.

Dominic also carefully modelled 'not being perfect' by opening the session in an informal, unpolished way, turning to the CEO with 'How shall we start?' 'I wanted to make it clear that there would be no need to keep up the veneer, that it was OK to show uncertainty, discomfort, whatever was going on for people in the moment.'

I also liked their clever use of metaphors. Dominic explained: 'We sought to create opportunities for people to find different ways of relating to one another, before going into the more sensitive feedback material. So our initial focus was on organisational issues. We tried to keep it light, without becoming patronising.

'We wanted to work with metaphors, because we find it often frees people up, and helps them to see their organisation in a different light. Chris had the fun idea of using "religion" as a metaphor. We asked some cheeky questions such as "What constitutes a sin in the religion of The Institute?" The question opened a way to talk about the shadow side of the organisation and within about fifteen minutes a rich conversation unfolded in which people felt free to talk about what it really felt like to be in The Institute at that moment.' I also like the way Dominic invited the participants to consider the power of language and of imagination in the way we construct our world by, tongue in cheek, asking this group of eminent physicists to explain the placebo effect.

Having done imagery work on the here and now, Liz invited the group to consider how this current reality might be held in tension with innovating for the future. Liz and Dominic managed to help the group stay with holding priorities in tension, rather than collapsing them, or resolving the tension through either/or scenarios. They offered short theoretical inputs as food for thought, from which small groups could develop insights about possible futures for The Institute to share with their colleagues. In the process a subgroup developed a simple metaphor in the shape of a kite, a reflection of how different people experienced the different strengths of the pull towards internal and external, present and future focus.

To bring the organisational focus to a close, different subgroups were asked to create an image of the future organisation, exploring what people would be doing differently. Dominic and Liz continually invited people to notice and explore each others' images in depth, paying attention to and amplifying the differences between the various subgroups, rather than allowing difference to go unnoticed or be quietly ignored.

In their conversations with the team, Liz and Dominic had advocated that the executive team members were key cultural role models and that how they conducted themselves in their day-to-day interactions with people in The Institute would be a precursor of how the culture of the organisation would evolve. No-one challenged this assertion and when the team's conversation moved on to what leaders would be doing differently in The Institute in two years' time, the personal challenge was obvious and clear.

Only after this careful groundwork did Liz and Dominic move on to the personal feedback material. On the second day, the executives were invited to share some of their feedback with colleagues in a small group setting, after a reminder that everyone could decide what and how much they shared. To their delight, the ensuing conversations were so engaged that the session overran! 'We were struck', they said, 'by the tremendous shift in the language we were hearing around us. Six months ago the conversations in the executive team were typically superficial and self-congratulatory: "Of course we're smart. Of course we're doing very well." Now people felt able to acknowledge their vulnerability in front of their new CEO! In fact, when they realised quite how honest they had been in the presence of their new boss, some team members felt quite nervous.'

A consulting philosophy: people need positive rather than negative stress

Liz is researching stress and coping behaviour among top sportspeople. 'When people experience stress, which they always do if something important is about to happen to them, it can either hinder or enable their performance. Stress is an enabler when the individual believes he or she has the necessary resources, internally or externally, to respond to the stress-inducing situation. In that case, the stressful situation is constructed as a positive challenge. However, if a person experiences stress and is not able to identify the necessary resources to deal with it, the situation is likely to be constructed as threatening and performance will be adversely affected. In my practice I seek to help people from all walks of life to explore new territory, without feeling threatened. Exploring what is important and new is bound to generate stress, but if people feel they have all the necessary resources available to them they can experience what's new as a positive challenge, rather than as a threat.'

Dominic's consulting work has changed significantly over the years. 'Drawing on my experience as an athlete, I think my work with organisations is really about creating possibilities to explore. When it feels appropriate I will share my views with the group I'm working with, but I no longer feel the need to be the expert who has the right answer to fix the problems of the organisation. I firmly believe that groups have the resources they need to work through their current or potential issues. That belief was borne out once again in our work with The Institute's executive team.'

Listening to Liz and Dominic articulating their consulting philosophy in relation to their work at The Institute, I found myself overwhelmed by their gentle optimism. I sensed that both of them deeply respect and care for the people they work with.

An evolving partnership with The Institute

No-one expected Lane4 to have the answer as to how the culture of The Institute was to change. The evolving team, despite its many challenges, managed to find a way to allow an 'answer' to emerge. The team had to work together in the face of considerable disagreement and uncertainty, by no means plain sailing. 'It was the strength of some key relationships that enabled us to continue our difficult collaboration. We needed to find ways to confront, and be confronted, when things were not working out, whilst remaining respectful of each other and ensuring our confrontations did not spiral into destructive arguments.' 'I am at my most resourceful', said Dominic, 'when I can express concern or differ in view. People in The Institute made that possible and I loved working with them.'

It was late on in my interview with Liz and Dominic that Rachel became really figural and the anticipation of her departure cast a cloud over our mood. On reflection they realised quite what an important role Rachel had played, Patrick always remaining somewhat distant. It was Rachel who enabled everyone to come to the table and play, without it turning into destructive sparring. Extremely skilled at diffusing issues formally and then working through them informally, she managed to lead the consulting team into the uncomfortable exploration of their philosophical differences. 'Rachel worked her magic across the organisation', said Liz, 'building commitment to the formal process and engaging in subtle negotiations about who was to be involved in what. In addition she had a very sophisticated understanding of the principles and practice of organisational change and was able to challenge Patrick when she thought it important. At the same time she was so very hard on herself when things took longer that she felt was necessary. I don't think she fully valued the importance of the relationships she had with people and how well she connected with them.'

With her impending departure, Liz and Dominic have a tangible sense of loss. They are concerned that the change work might deteriorate into a series of fragmented streams, that the sense of the whole will be eroded. 'Without Rachel's lived understanding that any culture change occurs through what happens between formal events rather than because of the events per se, we fear that the culture change work will deteriorate into a series of formal set pieces. But it is not her practical contribution that will be most missed. Rachel brought a commitment, an emotional energy and a willingness to challenge the organisation that was unique and can't just be magicked out of someone or somewhere else.' She embodied the more than simply intellectual understanding of change that Lane4 were trying to promote. The question is: did anyone else?

In the course of our conversation about Rachel the tone changed dramatically. The vitality and excitement of our inquiry into the masterclasses and the executive workshop were gone and there was a sense of apathy in the room. Liz and Dominic were aware that they would have to be really careful to avoid becoming passive in their work with The Institute. 'We must continue to actively draw attention to what needs attending to. If we don't watch out we're at risk of getting sucked into our work stream, the leadership development stuff, and losing sight of the bigger picture in the process. It was our relationship with Rachel that made this work sing for us, the sense of her door always being open and the sheer joy of her company.'

At the moment they cannot imagine establishing a similar relationship with Patrick. 'It seems unlikely we could have the same level of intimacy in our conversations with Patrick. And yet, who says things couldn't be different? It is a matter of recognising that it's going to take some work.'

As they began to reflect on what to do, it became plain to Liz and Dominic that the next design group meeting was an appropriate opportunity to reflect with Patrick, Peter and Chris on what it feels like now that Rachel has gone. And yet at the back of their minds the fear still niggles that, without Rachel, the focus will be on doing, on action, and change will become a task separate from the day-to-day work of the organisation – and so will fail.

Sense from further reflective inquiry

I received extensive, but one-sided, material for further reflection. Rachel and Chris confirmed Dominic and Liz's stories. However, I didn't get the voices of Patrick, Peter or people within the wider organisation. As a researcher I was quite gung ho about approaching Patrick and Peter, while Dominic and Liz thought that engaging others directly in the inquiry constituted an unnecessary risk to the relationships they had established, especially given Rachel's departure. Since their consulting work with The Institute is ongoing we decided not to pursue further interviews.

From the inquiry with Rachel, Chris, Dominic and Liz, the following reflections stood out for me:

- Introducing different voices doesn't guarantee a different conversation
- Being the alternative voice can be exhausting and hard to maintain
- Busyness is more comfortable than inquiry.

Introducing different voices doesn't guarantee a different conversation

Listening to Liz and Dominic's story I was aware of a growing sense of frustration and I caught myself rooting for Rachel's contingent to win against 'the forces of reaction'. When I shared this story with Bill he too was frustrated at what he perceived to be the inward-looking quality of this story, which seemed to concentrate on the dynamics of the project team rather than on how the consulting team did or did not make a difference to the wider organisation.

Bill's challenge provoked me into returning to this story with a fresh curiosity. What could I learn about change in The Institute if I started from the assumption that the dynamic in the culture change team mirrored in some way what was happening in the wider organisation? Was what happened in the consulting team a parallel of a more widely experienced organisational pattern?

From that assumption the difficulties and conflict in the project team would suggest that the organisation was struggling to find a way of approaching culture change it was comfortable with and the factions in the change team were representative of factions in the organisation. When Chris had argued that 'conversations' were a manager's primary tool, the chairman had replied that this insight had validated his whole managerial life. I interpret this statement as an indication that the chairman found affirmation of an approach to leadership he had adopted for many years.

For some people, including Rachel and the chairman, the notion of change being located in the informal, day to day, activities of managers and leaders rang true. At the same time many people in The Institute were deeply attached to a perspective on change as a formally managed, controllable, rational process, to be managed in a way most projects in The Institute were managed. Maybe most importantly, change was an intellectual experience to be understood much like a chemistry experiment.

In the end I sense that the latter approach got the upper hand with the formal workshops, mandated activities and external benchmarks taking precedence. From the start the habits of rationalisation, evaluation and justification, so useful in certain circumstances, choked off the space for experimentation, locally situated inquiry and personal experience. The project team's energy was focused on the debate about how to approach change, rather than on exploring how change was actually happening within The Institute. One anecdote from Chris seems to me a powerful illustration of this: 'During the chairman's workshops we emphasised the critical importance of informal conversations in bringing about change. A manager who had been glowing in his praise of the workshop was asked by one of his direct reports what had happened at the conference. Allegedly he replied: "I'm too busy to tell you and you should be too busy to ask!"'

Being a highly intellectual and analytic organisation, The Institute engaged in an intellectual way with an approach that was less analytic, more experiential and in the moment, and thus lost the potential and richness of this alternative approach. 'Formally inviting people to be informal' doesn't seem to have quite delivered a lasting effect. And yet, what would have been an alternative? After all, the change team had to work with where the organisation was at that time. Moreover, the work is still ongoing and, even if Rachel has left, Dominic, Liz and Chris continue to influence what happens next.

My rhetorical question to Liz and Dominic would ask whether they believe a real conversation took place between the two factions, each wedded to their different world views: I don't believe it did. I would have liked to see a genuine exploration of underlying assumptions and a profound challenging questioning of the potential collaboration in this kind of work between people who hold what, I think, are incompatible philosophies about change.

Being the alternative voice can be exhausting and hard to maintain

There was a lot of anxiety within The Institute and the culture-change project team. How could it be otherwise? In the view of those of a psychodynamic persuasion, such as Bion (1961), anxiety tends to bring out more conservative, familiar patterns of behaviour in people – a view that rings true with my own personal and professional experience. I wonder whether Dominic and Liz were aware to what extent their alternative approach to change raised the levels of anxiety in The Institute?

Peter's definitive statements about how organisations work were largely dismissed by them as incongruent with their understanding and experience. This rejection, supported by Rachel and Chris, may well have left Peter worried about the future of his relationship with this client, as well as making Patrick feel anxious about how he was to survive the coming upheaval. While Rachel did have conversations with Patrick about her desire to do this work well, 'for real', rather than merely going through the motions of formal workshops and events, I am struck by how little attention was paid to what it was like for Patrick and Peter, to have their deeply held views challenged.

I also noticed Rachel's, Dominic's and Liz's very low level of energy by the end of this inquiry. Rachel chose to leave, all passion spent I sense because of the lack of support from Patrick and her own self doubts – fuelled by the impression that Peter didn't rate her. By the time of my last meetings with Dominic and Liz they were full of enthusiasm for a new lead and another client who wholeheartedly, rather than simply 'wholeheadedly', engaged with them. When we returned to The Institute they gave me the impression of carrying a burden dutifully, rather than relishing the engagement.

Finally, as I have suggested on a couple of occasions, I have a niggling sense of a generational and gender dimension playing out. Rachel experienced herself as being undermined by Peter, while Liz never really fully recovered her sense of being valued by Patrick. The older men with the inside track kept the new ideas and practices held by the younger women at bay as much by undermining their personal confidence as by challenging them intellectually. In my conversations with some of my female colleagues, this was an experience all too recognisable to them, which actually made reading this story quite difficult for them.

Busyness is a more comfortable activity than inquiry

'At present,' said Chris 'The Institute appears to be caught in an activity trap, partly resulting from external expectations and partly of its own making. Almost thirty years ago Odiorne (1969) pointed out the narcotic effect that this can have on organisations. Although virtually everyone would accept that it is not productive to get locked into so many meetings and activities, it becomes almost something to glory in – a badge of honour. Unless this habit can be broken, the organisation at large will see little change in what is happening this time from what has gone before – as anecdotal evidence is beginning to show.'

What all this activity enables is an avoidance of inquiry. People are simply too busy to notice how they are behaving and what patterns they are stuck in. The pace of activity also makes individuals who would like to slow down, notice and reflect, stand out even more and not in a positive light: 'If I am so busy how come you have the time to stand and stare?' To be busy becomes a virtue in its own right and smothers the space for inquiry. Another feature of this busyness is that it is situated largely within the formal domain. It is about meetings and tasks and being seen in action groups. This further undermines the validity of any invisible work in the informal day-to-day aspects of organisational life, especially when it has been framed as an addition to the existing management workload rather than something that is a core part of that workload.

I would like to end this reflection on Dominic and Liz's story paraphrasing some lines from Macbeth:

> …formal change is a tale
> Told by an idiot, full of sound and fury,
> Signifying nothing.

Further reading

Bion, W (1961) *Experiences in Groups and Other Papers.* London: Tavistock Publications.

Odiorne, G (1969) *How managers make things happen.* London: Prentice Hall.

Stacey, RD, D Griffin, et al. (2000) *Complexity and Management: Fad or Radical Challenge to Systems Thinking?* London: Routledge.

Bill's Postscript to Dominic and Liz's Story

LOOKING THROUGH SIX THEORETICAL FRAMES

This seems to be primarily a story about relationships. It is interesting how the difficult dynamic in the relationship between the consultants seems to dominate the story, and it reminds me how hard it can be for consultants from different practices to work together. I have been asked if I would be willing to collaborate with a 'partner' on a number of occasions, and it is tempting to say 'yes, of course'. Who would not say 'yes' to collaboration; to do otherwise would mark one out as competitive, inflexible or superior. But I have learned from experience that collaboration with another firm is, in practice, extremely difficult, and from a theoretical point of view this is easy to explain.

Successful consultancies evolve a sense of *identity*, about who they are, what they offer, and how they are *different* from other firms. They develop this in their interactions with each other and with clients and their very success confirms their sense of identity and felt difference from their 'competitors'. Stacey sees this social process of negotiating similarity and difference in communicative interaction as fundamental to the way we make meaning of ourselves in relation to others, as the essence of identity creation. Therefore the invitation to two firms of consultants to collaborate potentially threatens their sense of identity. It means that much work will be required to create a good enough working relationship, which is usually underestimated by the consultants and rarely paid for by the client.

In addition to this inherent difficulty, at least one powerful male figure from each of the two pairs of consultants was informed by a different paradigm, so it seemed that the potential for conflict in this situation was evident from the start. I would have been interested to hear more from Dominic and Liz about how they thought about this at the beginning of the work. Did they underestimate it, or did they see the differences between the two firms as potentially fruitful? Of did they allow their interest in doing the work to override any concerns they may have had?

In AMOC we put a lot of emphasis on the process of relating, which we see as the core of consulting practice. Outcome research in other fields, such as coaching and psychotherapy, consistently identifies 'the relationship' as the main factor influencing successful outcome. Relationship tends to be understood instrumentally by most consultants as a skill to be applied in influencing the client about the work to be done or being done. From our perspective the process of relating is the work. We may use a number of artefacts, like models, frameworks, theories, or design workshops, meetings or events, but these are all in service of an emerging relationship.

What becomes interesting is how our involvement is making a difference. Putting it in the immortal words of Gregory Bateson, it is the 'difference which makes the difference' that is most interesting. In this case the potential for difference is high. The client organisation is famous for its environmental engineering and works through Gantt charts and meticulous project planning; while Dominic and Liz draw on holistic coaching ideas, occupational psychology and complexity theory. From a complexity perspective, change emerges through the amplification of difference, and this is indeed the same phenomenon to which Bateson is referring. Intuitively, we have all experienced this phenomenon: a chance encounter that leads to 'one thing after another', and changes a pattern in our lives forever. This is the stuff of organisational life – although this 'reality' still goes largely unaccepted because of the strenuous investments made in attempts to exert control.

We also have experiences where differences in the form of initiatives, plans of action, management programmes and so on did not in the end make a difference; and we were left wondering why. One of the reasons for this could be that the initial difference is too threatening for our sense of identity. We could hypothesise that Dominic and Liz appeared too different for this firm of engineers and that the threatening level of difference was largely contained within the consulting team where Dominic felt 'the clashing of world views'. We witness an ongoing dance around different world views and different methodologies.

Furthermore, we can view this dance through the lens of Kathleen's essay on relational psychology. She introduces the concept of two fundamental relational modalities in the existence of human beings: agency (the male modality) and communion (the female modality). This concept suggests two different development pathways. One is the familiar pathway constructed by Freud of an individual born into confluence or dependency, developing through becoming independent into autonomy, which is the ultimate goal of development. This she argues privileges the male experience of needing to *leave* the mother in order to identify with the father. The other pathway has received scant attention. The female gains her sense of identity from her mother with whom she is already connected. No leaving is involved, hence her orientation to connectedness and relationship rather than independence and autonomy. She argues that Western culture has privileged agency and that maturity could be re-conceptualised as an integration of the two polarities. I commend the essay to you.

It seems we have here an example of agentic relationship largely un-moderated by communion. Furthermore, the representative of the female modality, Liz, is dismissed as 'not fitting'. I greatly admire Dominic in his insistence in retaining her in the team and at the workshop, and I also noticed his discomfort at being constantly invited into an agentic mode by Peter.

I also appreciated Dominic's and Liz's persistence. Although frustrated in their desire to engage directly with the client on the change agenda, they nevertheless succeed in creating a different pattern of relating in one of the later sessions with executives under the new CEO.

The challenge as Dominic and Liz saw it for the working session with the executives was 'Could we help this group of leaders into a safe and energetic-enough place to want to share feedback and so change how they engage with people outside [of this workshop]?' The ambition was to do something to change the conversational patterns within the organisation.

In this encounter it seemed they did make a difference to the conversational pattern. Maybe they enabled the pattern to shift from pure agentic to embrace more communion, which is my sense of their intention. However, my overall sense is that, had they been able to confront more directly the differences within the consulting team, they might have had more impact on their client.

Francesca – Do Consultants Make a Difference?

Francesca chose to share a story whose outcome could easily be constructed as failure. It concerns her work with a part of the Information Management (IM) function in Omnia Healthcare Inc. (OHI). Norman, a manager in IM had approached her to 'do something about the perceived lack of engagement in the workforce'. Over a period of about nine months Francesca encouraged both management and workforce in the IM function to explore how they could improve their experience of working for OHI.

However, when OHI was acquired by an aggressive US corporation, Norman was increasingly preoccupied with the upheavals, multimillion-pound project cancellations and imminent redundancies associated with such acquisitions; and he became even more invisible and detached from his unit than he had been at the start of Francesca's engagement.

'They're compliant, passive and frustrating'

Norman's section of the IM function consisted of 45 people, mostly men, some working in shifts to provide 24-hour support and distributed across Norway, North America and the UK. Norman described his staff as compliant, passive and a source of frustration to him and to the wider IM management team and wanted Francesca to 'do something with them'. 'In some way', Francesca explained, 'the perceived compliance of this group was symptomatic of the culture of their tightly regulated industry, where strict compliance was expected at all times. The regulations covered all aspects of the business, from manufacturing, through distribution and especially R&D. In OHI there was also the added weight of a public-sector legacy.'

From the very start of her engagement with OHI, Francesca had views on the possible collusion, or even contribution of Norman and the management team to the passive and compliant nature of the workforce: 'I wanted to hold up a mirror to the management team, to show them how they were intricately bound up in the patterns that provoked and maintained passivity, but this was not the right moment. I firmly believe in starting where my clients are at in order to get a foothold. It would have been great if managers had seen their contribution to the prevailing passivity and compliance in the IM function, and a perfect place from where to start the process, but I would rather just get started than wait for such an elusive perfect moment to occur.'

Francesca proposed an appreciative inquiry (see Appendix 1), a process of inquiry predicated on the potential for generating change from the bottom up and seeking to help people articulate what they actually think and feel. This was a deliberate move away from the traditional hypothesis-driven approach, where it is assumed that someone (usually senior management or the consultant) already knows what sense the population of the organisation are making of their situation.

Getting permission to experiment

'I'm different. I brought something countercultural to OHI', Francesca asserted emphatically. 'I wanted to make the most of that difference, but needed to do that in a way that made sense to my clients. I needed to get alongside them so that they were prepared to embark on the journey with me, rather than alienate them by being too challenging to their established norms and conventions.'

When I met Francesca for the first time I did experience her as different. Her background in social work in South Africa seemed to have had a lasting effect on her. She had been exposed to the terror of AIDS and, in those early days, to the refusal of many white heterosexuals to accept it was a threat for them too. I sensed she had developed a deep respect for people, whatever their circumstances, and at the same time a willingness to challenge people where appropriate – including people in power. 'I grew up in a very different world,' she said. 'People in the UK seem so passive and accepting to me. Growing up in South Africa I had this tremendous sense of possibility. Our society was not very compliant. People wanted a better life and were prepared to fight for it in difficult circumstances. We believed we could make a difference. Social work was no picnic, and it taught me that in a masculine, macho even, culture subtle conversations with hairy-arsed managers about "how they make others feel", won't get you very far. You need to be direct.'

That was certainly how I experienced her: direct, grounded, speaking her truth. In the words of Norman, 'You call a spade a spade... I don't have to figure out what you are telling me.' In order to whet the organisation's appetite for an appreciative inquiry, Francesca painted polarised alternatives. One option was a survey-style process: develop hypotheses about what was going awry, test those assumptions in workshops and, from the outcomes, develop a plan of action, all the while keeping one's fingers crossed that employees would not respond in their usual apathetic way. Alternatively, people could be engaged in a participatory process that was congruent with the intention of the work. 'I did acknowledge explicitly that taking the AI approach would be more risky because it was countercultural, unpredictable and a million miles away from the habitual compliance-focussed way of working. In fact, I suspect that my clients didn't really fully understand what they were signing up to and went along with it because they trusted me or because everything else they had tried hadn't really worked. If what you're doing isn't working why not try something different?'

A messy start, but a start nevertheless

The lack of understanding about the principles and practice of AI in the Management Team didn't stop Francesca from getting started. As she observed, 'If I'd waited until everybody had a full grasp of AI, all my energy would have been spent before the project started. Also, given the fact that the IM management team from around the world met only once every four months, it was not just a matter of understanding but also of logistics.'

A working group was formed to be responsible for the project. 'In the process of planning for the 45 one-on-one appreciative inquiries, people became increasingly energised', recounts Francesca. 'We talked a lot about the philosophy underpinning the project and about our values. Unfortunately, Norman didn't seem really engaged with the project and I continued to challenge him. The union representative on the project team, on the other hand, was very much involved right from the start and had genuine concerns. He explicitly asked whether this was a management fix and whether the insights and quotations gathered in the interviews would be treated with due regard to confidentiality. His concerns were legitimate and, I discovered, the result of previous experiences with consultants. We talked about those experiences, what working for Norman was like, his doubts about the project and management's intention. I really could understand where he was coming from and encouraged him to talk directly to his managers. I tried to reassure him that if I was not truly convinced that the confidentiality clause in the contract would be honoured, I wouldn't do the work. In the end he was won over. I think he felt I understood and respected his concerns and really believed that the AI process would enable people to have a voice. Once he got to know me a bit better and after attending a number of meetings of the project group, he agreed that people could come and talk to me.'

I doubt whether many organisational inquiries address questions of the intention behind the work and the extent to which it is politically risky to speak with an authentic voice or whether people feel compelled to tell management what it wants to hear.

The inquiry in OHI was general and consisted of the following questions:

- What do you value about yourself, the function and your work?
- When do you think the function is at its best, what stories best illustrate this?
- Given your understanding of all that has been communicated with you, what is your understanding of what you are being called to become?
- What are the three wishes you have for this function?

Francesca's intent, assumptions and anxieties

Francesca started from the assumption that people would engage if they were offered an interesting, compelling experience. 'I wanted the management team to get out of the habit of making assumptions about what people thought and felt. Instead I wanted them to go out and find out. I knew this was a novel approach in OHI, but I was convinced it could work. In my work with disempowered communities I had discovered what becomes possible when people feel they have a genuine voice. I have a strong belief in people's capacity to be authentically authoritative if they are provided with a context within which personal responsibility and ownership can flourish. I am biased against traditional, bureaucratic organisations. I think their processes are inherently disengaging, a kind of "death by PowerPoint".'

Francesca knew that people had to be invited into the process in a truly engaging way, that 'engagement promotes engagement'. She also knew that she would have to start the process before all the stakeholders were fully au fait with the intricacies of AI and perhaps before they were all fully on board. So she just got started, well aware that the project would generate a considerable amount of anxiety.

I understand the anxiety to which Francesca referred to be the nervous uncertainty that arises in situations where meaning is shared sincerely, rather than ritually endorsed, and where the ground rules of how we relate to one another are changed. Managers feared to lose control – 'as if they can ever really be in control of meaning and understanding in the first place', as Francesca pointed out. 'Staff had a lingering suspicion that this was just another pretend-involvement, or even worse, that managers had dressed up a spying mission as an inquiry for the common good.'

Throughout the project Francesca felt concerned: 'Especially at the beginning I was nervous. I knew intuitively that I was taking a risk. I felt I was fighting for something even though this was not my fight. I was fighting for a space where people could talk together. I worried especially about how Norman and the management team would respond. I thought more then once, oh shit, what if this turns into a huge disaster? As my anxiety rose, I sometimes felt over-responsible for the work's success. But I did stay with the process and kept the sense-making firmly with the people who the inquiry was in service of, however difficult I found it. I was delighted to see how much energy people had in the one-to-one inquiries, and how much learning and insight the process seemed to elicit. I found myself personally very energised through the process too.'

'That's my style'

'I need to know that my participation makes a difference and that something gets better as a result.' For Francesca, 'better' means that a group of employees owns the change agenda and is responsible for deciding what needs to change, rather than management setting the agenda and steering staff through it. She firmly believed that if the AI process worked in OHI people would find a better, more engaging way of working. Her attachment to appreciative inquiry is rooted in its principle of involving people in the process. In short, Francesca wanted people to have a say; she wanted to help the employees reclaim their confidence in themselves, especially when dealing with a macho, 'command and control' style management team. As a result of her own upbringing she was able to model how to challenge the management team in a robust and constructive way.

The trouble with Norman

Francesca had a number of conversations with Norman about his repeated assertion that 'they [the workforce outside of the management team] don't engage with anything'. 'I used to say "Can we also talk about your engagement and your behaviour in this situation, Norman?"'

Norman spent much of his time in his glass-walled office with the blinds three-quarters drawn, busy on the phone or on his computer. Most of his interactions with his people took place within the formal setting of the team briefings during which he stayed firmly in telling mode, giving no opportunity for people to process the implications, for them, of his messages or for a dialogue.

'Not surprisingly, Norman became quite defensive during the first three of those conversations. He wanted to talk about the "trouble with them", rather than about "my problem". As my attempts to get Norman to see his contribution to the apathy and disengagement were not going anywhere, he started to complain about the lack of results after three months of working with me. I decided to write him an email. I had become increasingly aware of Norman's strong introverted nature and writing, rather than talking, to him would give him an opportunity to process the information and formulate his response in his own time, rather than feeling pressurised to respond in the moment.'

In the email Francesca reiterated that the inquiry process in itself was the major 'output' of the work. She emphasised the importance of paying attention to that process, and asked Norman whether he really valued this. She explained how hard she'd had to negotiate with everyone to have this process accepted, getting it to be seen as different from the usual consulting experience employees had known in the past. Most bravely, she told Norman she didn't feel he much appreciated her focus on genuine employee involvement since he only inquired about 'results', and never about how people were engaging with the inquiry.

Norman's response was robust and, significantly for Francesca, emotional. 'You plonker', he wrote, 'I really do value your work!' Their email exchange enabled Francesca and Norman to speak openly with one another. Francesca had succeeded in moving the conversation on from Norman's interactions with his workforce, to her experience of him and of their relationship. Instead of hypothesising about partially appreciated situations, they could now talk about their experience of each other and about their relationship. As a result, Norman was more able to hear that Francesca didn't feel valued by him, even if sending that signal had never been his intention.

They did talk about the project too, and Norman's relationship with it. 'You make me feel very important in this process, but I want other others to run with it', Norman explained. 'I told him how important his participation was', Francesca said. 'I needed his permission for what we were doing to be visible. You have to be engaged, I told him. I'm still not sure whether I ever really convinced him. I was always left with a sense that he felt misunderstood, without him seeing how he might have contributed to that misunderstanding.' Nevertheless, as a result of the project Norman did get out of his office more, he went to see people in their own locations and even joined in the odd soccer match. At the end of the inquiry people did say that they'd got to know Norman better. 'He's a good man, but he withdraws and makes it hard for us to connect with him.'

Making sense of the output

When all the one-to-one inquiries had been completed, Francesca produced an unedited outcome of all the stories and comments, a 29-page document of some 10,000 words. 'I collated the raw data because I wanted the responsibility to make sense of the material to stay with the organisation as a whole, rather than with me, the working group or – least of all – with the management team.'

Francesca's insistence that the organisation make sense of the data represents a significant digression from a more conventional approach to consulting in which consultants are expected (and seen to add value by their ability) to synthesise and make sense of raw data. People who do not understand the deep significance of personal participation by employees in the sense-making process might even consider it a dereliction of duty.

Given time constraints and the problems of getting people together who were expected to provide a twenty-four-seven support service, it was decided to hold two four-hour sense-making meetings, each of which was attended by about twenty people, including members of the management team. Having received the full transcript of the raw data, four groups were formed. Each group was invited to focus on one of the inquiry questions and asked to present back to the large group what they were learning about themselves and the organisation.

At every meeting, Francesca facilitated the overall process but did not participate in the small group work, which was facilitated by a member of the working group. 'I had worked with the facilitators to help them prepare for the task, looking at ways to involve people in an engaging, facilitative way. The workshops provided us with a wonderful opportunity to show managers how they could work with their staff in a different, more enabling way so it was important that the facilitators were well prepared. I wanted to give an opportunity for OHI staff to do that facilitation, to get the message across that it doesn't take a consultant to do this well, that the necessary expertise was already present in the organisation. I was comfortable that the focus on the questions that had already been agreed and worked with provided a robust frame for their facilitation work and that they felt confident about their role.'

Insights and initiatives

The two sessions drew out key themes in people's experience of OHI and the IM function and provided a picture of how they could imagine the place in the future. People drew images and gave examples of the function at its best and their dreams for the future. The function at its best, it emerged, was rooted in the practice and discipline of project management.

In terms of the future, three topics emerged. Firstly, the function needed to have stronger relationships with people both inside and outside the function and therefore people needed to socialise more in order to create a stronger social fabric. Secondly, people wanted communications to be better. They wanted more forums, greater transparency and meetings to be more engaging. Thirdly, they wanted the quality of documentation on the intranet to improve. At present they experienced it as so badly designed that people couldn't use it; the templates were wrong which made working with them very frustrating. Three initiatives were launched around the three themes, and volunteers were invited to step forward. No-one did. Not one person responded to emails or phone calls from the working group.

What's going on?

Surprised by the lack of volunteers, especially as people had been very engaged and even passionate about the issues at the working sessions, Francesca, together with members from the working group, set about finding out what caused this disengagement. 'It became clear that people were anxious about taking an active role in a change process they didn't really trust. I realised that taking a different, bottom-up, approach to change generates its own anxiety in people. I could understand that, but at the same time I found myself breaking out in a sweat and thinking "It's all gone horribly wrong!" We knew we (the working group) had to do something to make it easier for people to volunteer, and decided to be more specific, as well as more flexible, in terms of what was expected from volunteers. We sent out a message explaining that even an hour a week of people's time would be really appreciated.'

To her dismay, Francesca soon discovered that negative stories about volunteering started to circulate. Volunteering, so the stories went, meant being associated with failure. 'When I asked what lay behind those stories, I found people were blaming management once again. I listened carefully, challenged and acknowledged appropriate scepticism.' After a period, volunteers did come forward and managers too joined in the working groups. Norman joined the 'communications' group. The 'social fabric' group, which didn't have any senior management representation, simply wanted to focus on fun and overcoming a physical environment that did nothing to encourage socialisation.

Finding a new role as the working groups unfolded

Before embarking on any initiative, every one of the three theme groups conducted an inquiry into what people in the function wanted, demonstrating that they had taken on board the participatory approach that the initial inquiry had set out to model. The groups had varying degrees of success. Francesca contracted with each of the working group leaders, exploring what they wanted to get out of the experience and offered to coach them as they wanted. 'I saw the communications group as most successful. I think that was partly related to the way the group was led by Mike G, who was determined to use his role as an opportunity to position himself within the organisation and to make a difference to how things were done.'

The group began to experiment with novel approaches to information sharing. Francesca shared some examples with me. At a 'who's who' barbecue, attended by 27 people, over the course of the evening people populated a big chart with information about others they hadn't known before. On another occasion people were invited to an informal get together in a pub at which they could log anything they wanted to know more about. Table groups were then joined by managers who would respond to people's questions as best as they could. 'In a short briefing meeting I had reminded the managers that they really did not have to know the answer to every question, or didn't even have to feel obliged to answer everything. I thought it was a kind of "moment of truth" for managers, a time for them to face the consequences of their style. But it was also an opportunity for people to get to know each other "as people" in a more informal and relaxed setting, away from the formal fabric of the function and OHI. Although I know it's not very fashionable to admit it, I do think that a moderate amount of alcohol can be a good lubricant in a setting where people are not used to relaxing with each other.' In addition, the group also started to have an input into the design of other events, such as the Town Hall meetings, in an attempt to increase the level of participation.

Within the intranet management group the focus had traditionally been nearly exclusively on keeping people's technology skills up to date. The understanding of so-called soft skills was very slight, so it was a quite a shift for these people to develop a management practice informed by an understanding of interpersonal issues and an appreciation of what it takes to succeed as a change agent. Even the basic skills were hardly there. Quite early on this group was subsumed into a wider, pan-organisation quality initiative.

The social fabric group had all sorts of plans, but was thrown off course when its leader was hauled into a massive internal project that ruled out any further effective participation in the group's work.

Despite this mixed picture, Norman was pleasantly surprised at a review, held in the pub, of what had gone on in all three groups saying 'I can't believe the feedback, it's actually positive!' The passive and disengaged people of the IM function were getting engaged and taking an active part in creating a better workplace; and Norman had begun to do something different, building on this shift in what 'they out there' were doing. He started inviting people periodically to 'munch 'n' crunches' where, over a slice of pizza, he talked through what was going on.

And then the roof fell in

As the project seemed to be gaining momentum, OHI was taken over and Norman disappeared to the US to deal with all the fallout, becoming even more disengaged from the wider IM community than he had been before. Francesca said, with some regret 'I could see huge potential mileage to the project but when people are feeling threatened it is very hard to breathe life into the process and to do something positive.'

The acquisition left Francesca doubtful about the value of her work. 'It's hard to know the extent to which new behaviours have become embedded. I think I have contributed to creating a positive experience; but I can't see to what extent the participative approach I have modelled and promoted has been adopted as a way of being within the function.'

I sense that her uncertainty is not only a result of the acquisition, but also related to her approach, which sought to avoid creating dependency and attributing positive outcomes to her actions as a consultant. It seems to me to go back to the always equivocal and doubtful question: to what extent did her work contribute to generating change that is of lasting value to the client and to herself?

Francesca explained: 'I doubt the effect I've had on the IM function of OHI, nor am I clear about how I make a difference. I do know, however, that I can't separate myself from my clients' and my experience, that I am an integral part of it. I bring who I am into my work and use who I am purposefully and hopefully positively.' Sometimes this so called 'difference', as perceived by the client, is grounded in what they aspire to create/change in themselves. In the case of OHI the degree to which she did participate and engage with her clients may have been the significant difference from their habitual way of working. For Francesca, being enthusiastic and energetic provided a necessary pattern interruption, given that the people of the IM function of OHI had been described as passive and disengaged. She remains curious about how her clients would define the 'difference' she brought.

Francesca is left with a dilemma about her relationship with OHI. Should she let go as they deal with the new reality or should she help them think about how to maintain engagement at this time?

Sense from further reflective inquiry

As we engaged with the further reflective inquiry process Francesca was going through a difficult personal time. By that stage, her relationship with Norman had started to mirror that of most everyone in his department: she avoided him as much as she could, whilst feeling quite aggressive towards him. While Francesca and I continued to reflect on the story we had created together, she sought third-party feedback in conversations with Mike G.

The themes that stand out for me from this reflective round are:

- Getting caught in unacknowledged patterns

- Working with the light and shadow of personal presence
- Wanting to make a difference by humanising workplaces.

Getting caught in unacknowledged patterns

Bill's first response to Francesca's story was to interpret the non-engagement of the workforce as a passive-aggressive act. He suggested that the AI process had possibly helped Norman and his team to ignore an underlying anger. Initially I wanted to reject this interpretation, but the more I read Mike G's comments and remember Francesca's charged frustration with Norman, the more I am drawn to agree with Bill's assessment. At the same time I believe that Francesca's work did at least temporarily touch a number of people within the IM function, despite the fact that Norman is more invisible than ever, and the workforce talk together even less, with prizes having to be offered for any questions or participation in the open forums that do take place.

Often neither traditional consulting, with its focus on the rational, nor fashionable consulting, with its focus on the positive (as in this case), legitimise strong and/or negative emotions, or make it possible for them to be either acknowledged or expressed. Any consulting approach will contain an implicit or explicit invitation to engage in a certain type of conversation or task. The challenge for the consultant is to be aware, as far as possible, of the nature and limitations of their approach in the given culture of their client organisation. In other words, consultants need to be aware of the bias in the lens with which they are working, and of the variety of organisational lenses that will create their own biases in people's sense making.

This perspective directly challenges the notion, still much espoused, that a standard consulting process can be used to deliver a certain outcome. I believe that, even ignoring the limits of instrumental thinking, a standard consulting process will always play out uniquely in a given situation because of the local sense-making patterns. Unless biases of client and consultant are surfaced and attended to, unacknowledged patterns are almost certainly doomed to play out in the consulting engagement.

Working with the light and shadow of personal presence

'You make the difference because of who you are', Francesca told me, 'rather than because of your process or presentation. I have a real role to play in the quality of conversation that takes place when I'm there. I feel very responsible for my participation.' In Francesca's work the personal is an essential part of her belief in the redemptive power of participation which, based on seeing it work in South Africa, borders on the evangelical. She knows that lives can be transformed if people actively participate in making a difference. The shadow, in this instance, may be that her evangelism blinded her to the unexpressed anger within the workforce and to her own anger first of all towards the workforce (for being so bloody passive) and subsequently towards Norman (for not engaging with the process and then falling back into his old routines).

Francesca is a very energetic person. I suspect her dynamism and vitality shone out at OHI and enabled much of what happened to take place. She provided the missing ingredient and engaged vitality emerged as if by magic. The shadow of her vitality may well have been that she became a substitute for vitality in the organisation. She may have acted as the flame that fired people up rather than as the person who noticed, named and stayed curious about the lack of fire within the organisation.

Part of Francesca's power is her courage and willingness to say what others dare not say. The drawback of her power is the weight and figural importance it gives to her presence. She worked hard with Mike G to support him in speaking out more forcefully, in engaging more fully in the workplace, in taking responsibility for his reality. But his reflections speak to me of defeat, of an organisation that is ever more disengaged and uncommunicative, even if he personally feels that there is some spark still alive which may burst into flame at some time in the future.

The strongly principled and charismatic consultant always risks becoming the focus of the work, which can become dependent on their energy to get going. The challenge as I see it for such a personally present consultant is not to lose that personal vitality, but to hold it in a way that invites others to be equally present. Charismatic consultants must remain wary of not outshining their clients and consequently creating an unhealthy dependency. They need to hold their beliefs lightly so that they don't become blinded by them to other possible interpretations of what is going on.

Wanting to make a difference by humanising workplaces

Francesca works in organisations because she wants to bring about conversations and experiences 'in which people feel both heard and understood, in which they feel they have a stake in the outcome and able to be fully present in everything that is going on.'

This is a grand ambition, which I fear may be doomed to failure. I wonder how anyone can expect to achieve such an idealised and amazing transformation in entrenched organisations. Another part of me is in awe of her and her wonderful 'can do' attitude. If you're going to have a dream, it might as well be a fantastic one.

Francesca seems to be able to wear this ambition well. It is an integral part of her life's philosophy. However, I would wish for her to be well supported as she faces up to the inevitable tribulations that will beset her in dealing with all the sceptics who want her ambition to be a little smaller, a little more focused on the achievement of shareholder value.

I am drawn to conclude that one of the features that make a relational consultant is a humanising ambition. They are not passionate about efficiency or wealth creation per se, but about something that really matters to them personally. This personal passion fires their work, gives it an intensity and vitality that is unlikely to be present in consultants whose work doesn't matter to them on such a personal level – or is fuelled more by ego-need than personal values.

Further reading

Morgan, G (1997) *Images of Organisation*. London: Sage.
How to see, understand and manage organisations in new ways.

Wheatley, M (1999) *Leadership and the New Science*. San Francisco: Berrett-Koehler.

Bill's Postscript to Francesca's Story

LOOKING THROUGH SIX THEORETICAL FRAMES

This story is ostensibly about an appreciative inquiry, but in my view it is more a testament to the power of 'inquiry' per se. It is also the story of a consultant with commitment to values that she holds dear. One senses that she carries from her experience in South Africa a strong belief in people's innate potential, and a passionate commitment to emancipation. As John put it, she has a 'real belief in the redemptive power of participation', concluding that 'one of the features that makes a consultant relational is their humanising ambition'. So one of the lessons in this story concerns how aware we are of our beliefs and how we acknowledge and express them without imposing them.

There are also a number of interesting contradictions in the story. In the first sentence we are told that it is a story of failure, while the approach Francesca proposes is an appreciative inquiry. If her own process were congruent with her intervention, or as my colleague Adrian McLean puts it, if her consulting process were an analogue of her intervention, she would be looking for what worked well rather than what failed. It seemed to me that she was remarkably successful up to the point where the company was taken over. The main thing she demonstrates is the power of any genuinely participative inquiry process, appreciative or otherwise. I particularly admired her insistence on the sense making of the raw data staying with the organisation members. This takes courage because there is always considerable pressure on a consultant to earn their crust by interpreting the data.

The sessions were lively and productive. What an achievement! This was a group described as 'compliant, passive and a source of frustration to Norman and his management team', and I think this validates the practice of inquiry as the core of any consulting process. It validates the importance of clients and consultants sharing in the meaning making and insisting that everyone, including the consultant, acknowledges their own participation in the processes of the organisation.

John puts his finger on what appear to be some further

contradictions. Francesca sets great store on starting where her client is. According to their manager at least, the 45 people in the IM function were 'compliant, passive and frustrating'. From a psychological perspective this suggests suppressed or unexpressed anger, so to start with appreciation would seem at best paradoxical, and at worst misguided.

This may explain why, as Francesca puts it, the initiative started to fall apart when these people were faced with taking responsibility for acting on the emergent themes. From a psychological perspective, it is fairly well known that compliant, and passive people, often described unattractively as 'passive aggressive', do not readily move out of the shadows of avoidance into the light of responsible action without a great deal of long-term support and confrontation. And as John points out, Francesca may have fallen into the salvationist trap. Despite her attempts to avoid taking responsibility for the change, psychologically at least she provided the inspiration and source of hope, so when she talks of withdrawal, hope dies.

Finally, we have an echo of the previous story, in which the psychological dynamic within the organisation is played out in the interaction between the client and the consultant. We often refer to this phenomenon theoretically as 'parallel process'. Norman, and by extension the management team, were equally refusing to step up to their responsibility. Francesca is as frustrated with Norman as he is with his staff. There is an old adage in the psychotherapy profession that one cannot 'out passive a passive'. Metaphorically the therapist has to take them by the shoulders and shake them into some form of action while simultaneously holding their hand. It did seem to me that Francesca drew back from challenging Norman on his own avoidance and consequent failure as a leader, but maybe she was weary and sensed the futility of further challenge.

One of the lessons we might draw from this story is the importance for all of us of having good 'supervision'. It is difficult to see one's part in a parallel process, and see ways of breaking the pattern without a good supervisor to help. How often have we all been engaged in 'making a difference' – which I think Francesca was – when the context shifts through a takeover or major reorganisation? I think we all have to settle with making a difference to some people for some period of time. From a complexity perspective, working with the local situation in the living present is all we can do. What we can never know is the ripple effect of our work over the longer term on organisations and individuals.

Last words – Francesca's response to Bill's postscript

When Francesca read Bill's postscript she had a very strong (negative) reaction to what he had written. As she stayed with the feelings and wondered what it was about, she focused on Bill's comments about her stepping back from challenging Norman. Bill's provocation resulted in Francesca engaging in a sustained process of reflection, involving Bill and myself, that made her really question her reasons for not challenging Norman more.

In his first draft, Bill had made a comment about the habit consultants have of avoiding biting the hand that feeds them. Francesca was convinced however that her reluctance had not been a result of financial considerations, but of her weariness with the work and the challenge that engaging with Norman presented to her. She saw the strength of her reaction as evidence that Bill's comments had challenged her in her personal values. He had touched the very heart of her personally grounded professional practice.

Bill – The Old Gestaltist and the Global Media Company

'In the long run the only thing we can do with our life is to live it in as lively a way as possible; I am interested in increasing the liveliness in organisations and in social interactions. That's what I'm about', said Bill at the conclusion of my first interview with him.

We had been talking about Bill's potential contribution to changing the way people were leading in one of the world's great global media companies, from now on referred to as Glocom. He'd prefaced those closing remarks by lightly referring to himself as an 'old Gestaltist', having been a practising Gestalt therapist for many years, as well as an organisational consultant and academic.

A staff survey in Glocom had surfaced a number of issues not uncommon in large, long-established corporations. They related to customer focus, lack of creativity and the way leadership and management was exercised in the organisation – which included some evidence of bullying.

The organisation's response was to launch a co-ordinated suite of initiatives to address the various areas of concern. Improving leadership was considered essential to the success of the overall change effort and an invitation to tender for designing and delivering a leadership programme was duly sent to a number of reputable business schools in the UK. This is where Bill became involved.

First steps are fateful

Ashridge, keen to work with Glocom, appointed a team to prepare a response to the tender document. As various suggestions were considered, rejected, ignored, taken up and developed, Bill observed the proceedings with growing concern: 'I wonder', he said, 'how different we think our proposal will be from that of other business schools. Quite frankly, I don't think there's anything special or innovative here, and doesn't the tender document specify that's exactly what Glocom is looking for?'

Bill was living up to his reputation for making gritty interventions and for staying with challenging questions. On this occasion he also pointed out that the proposal of his colleague Caryn, unusual and out of the ordinary, had so far been completely ignored. One difficult conversation later, it was agreed that Caryn's draft proposal was to be revisited and developed.

Designing for innovation

In complexity thinking, as applied to organisations, increasing the level of diversity and the quantity and quality of connections is considered conducive to an innovative climate. Glocom's invitation to tender requested three separate streams of leadership development for senior, middle and junior managers. Complying with the request would mean inadvertently reducing the level of diversity, and hence the potential for innovation. Caryn and Bill, now actively involved in the design of the leadership programme, were keen to find a way of bringing leaders across the different levels together in order to maximise diversity.

From advocacy to inquiry

However, the ultimate design contained other elements inspired by complexity thinking, as Bill was keen to explain: 'When clients say they want to change the organisation, they have the formal system in mind: structures, processes, procedures. They don't consider the informal processes in the organisation. We have to work with this paradox, clients say they want to change, they think they want to, but they don't really.'

Here Bill alluded to the importance he places on working with the informal aspects of organisational processes. 'We need to engage with the informal processes, the patterns of everyday interaction by which people go about doing their job, the ingrained and recurring habits that can be described as the culture of the organisation; they are the ones that need to change.'

Struck by Bill's perspective on culture I invited him to expand. 'I think of culture as the consequence of a series of tangible and visible actions; it is the very fabric of organisational life, the persistent habits through which things get done', he explained. From this perspective, effecting change starts with paying attention to what is actually going on. It does not come about through close examination of formal procedures and practices that are meant to govern how people act, or by advocating a grand vision of what ought to be.

'From a leadership development perspective this means we need to inquire into what effective leadership in Glocom looks like right now, rather than advocating a guru's view. We therefore decided to start the leadership development process with some form of large group inquiry process. We sought to bring people together who would not normally meet and who represented different perspectives of the organisation. The focus of the event would be on inquiring into their current reality, rather than imparting an external view on how things ought to be, paying attention to the day-to-day practices of leadership, the informal processes, where I believe the potential for real change lies.'

This perspective was a radical departure from the original starting point, which had focussed on providing Glocom's leaders with models and frameworks of how to lead. For Bill it was about avoiding the compromise of embarking on a process that aspired to change, but would not really make a difference. As a consequence, Ashridge produced what Glocom acknowledged to be the most innovative proposal they saw.

Living congruently, living dangerously?

Caryn and Bill were keen that if Ashridge proposed an inquiry-based leadership development process, rather than a series of leadership workshops, their promotion strategy was congruent with the proposed process. They urged their colleagues to refrain from the standard PowerPoint presentation to Glocom's decision makers. They asked the Ashridge team involved in the meeting to model responsiveness and inquiry, rather than advocacy. Despite the nervousness of some of their colleagues, firmly wedded to the safety of a rehearsed presentation, the team engaged Glocom in a conversation at the selling meeting. The Glocom team, acknowledging afterwards the risky nature of the process, appreciated the occasion as well as the suggested design and Ashridge was awarded the contract.

The pull of performance over inquiry

Old habits die hard. 'While Ashridge had been chosen on the basis of its radical, inquiry-led process, Glocom's ingrained expectations of how a development programme ought to be delivered kicked in right from the start', Bill explained. 'While the rhetoric of innovation and collaborative co-creation was in place, the principles of participation and joint creation were not often adhered to. I couldn't help but notice and repeatedly challenged the client and the Ashridge team when I saw us slipping into putting on a performance (with fantastic production values) for the entertainment of Glocom. I felt we were continually fighting Glocom's habitual, and very successful, event management process. Given the nature of Glocom's business, this approach was of course deeply etched into the day-to-day behaviour of nearly everyone we encountered.'

The increasing fixation on the first pilot group and in particular the first large group event was particularly striking. The high-profile event generated a considerable amount of anxiety. The project team was told it had to be successful if the whole programme was to earn credibility. However understandable, the quick and visible judgements that would be made on what was intended as an opportunity to learn, were potentially hugely counterproductive.

Sand in the Vaseline

From the start Bill was aware of the unpopularity he courted by holding the process true to its informing principles. When the focus of the first event inevitably became on the quality of Ashridge's performance Bill continued to remind the design team that they were not offering a training event, and that concern for 'delivering a performance' should not be allowed to undermine the nature and purpose of the experience. While his role as 'the grit in the system' was formally acknowledged, he suspected that he was sometimes experienced as quite irritating.

'I was driven by a desire for our work to deliver something worthwhile, and for this to happen, I strongly believed that both Glocom and the Ashridge team had to preserve the innovative aspects of the programme.' Bill was referring here to the complexity perspective on enabling innovation, the focus on inquiry over exposition and the need to pay particular attention to the informal processes and practices within which each person's leadership practice took place. 'Unless people change the way things get done around here, the way they go about their everyday business, nothing will really change', said Bill. 'I feared that Ashridge would get sucked into a provider role, delivering interesting, even excellent, workshops, which made no difference. For me that amounts to selling my soul. And I wasn't prepared to do that. I know that many change programmes, and related initiatives, become part of the formal process. They exist in parallel to the day-to-day life in the organisations and therefore don't really affect the informal processes. I also know how hard it can be to interrupt habitual behaviour. It can become deeply uncomfortable for a consultant to help shift deeply ingrained patterns by working differently, by being different with clients.'

In other words, Bill considers the way a consultant engages with a client as more important than the delivery of any workshop or presentation. The consultant, as part of the difference that makes a difference, is at the heart of being a change agent and this may well be uncomfortable for both consultant and client.

The lure of the panacea

The first large group process began to turn into an end in its own right, 'the be all and end all', as Bill described it. At the same time the pressure to 'get it right' mounted as the leadership development programme became increasingly constructed as the cure to all the ills of the institution. For a brief, but intense, period it became the only initiative in town, the most expensive one, and therefore the most vulnerable to criticism. 'The impact of the messages that were fed back to the organisation from people's experience of the first gathering could hardly be overestimated, it was as if everything would live or die by how it went', said Bill. 'I tried to remind everyone that this was only a pilot, an opportunity to learn. I think it was near impossible for people to hear my message. Consultants and clients alike were swept up in the anxiety of the moment. The pressure to put on a brilliant show that would prove to be the salvation of the organisation was both intoxicating and terrifying.'

Bad news travels fast

Things could have gone better; in fact they went rather badly. It didn't help that Bill and Caryn, the lead consultants from Ashridge, couldn't be there for a variety of good reasons. However, the discrepancy between people's expectations and what the experience was designed to offer was probably inevitable.

By the end of the first day, some of the participants were on the phone to members of the Glocom board to say that they were wasting their time. Senior people fell into a habitual pattern of complaining to senior colleagues without making an effort to reflect on what might be going on. Although some more junior people informally expressed a genuine enthusiasm for the opportunity to meet senior colleagues and talk about the reality of life and leadership in Glocom, some senior people were not convinced and, not surprisingly, their voices made an impact.

Reflecting on this I am struck by the potential implications of this. If senior people do not value the opportunity to invest time in talking with and sharing experience with more junior colleagues, an important connection becomes disabled. This may lead to a lack of initiative at lower levels and overdependence on messages being passed down from on high – a level of the organisation with little understanding of what is going on at more junior levels.

The client–consultant team responsible for the design of the event met to process the formal feedback, which appeared to be overwhelmingly negative, and to lick its wounds. The main theme concerned the 'poor quality of presentation'. The Ashridge people acknowledged the need to improve the production quality, especially for a client organisation that prided itself on the quality of its productions. 'I stuck to my conviction', said Bill, 'and continued to emphasise that the negative feedback and discomfort with the process should not persuade us to turn the event into an all-singing, all-dancing production, rather than an inquiry. Indeed, doing so could involve colluding with keeping Glocom leaders well inside their comfort zone, instead of provoking change.'

The voice from on high

As the design team was reflecting on how to get the leadership development process back on track a disturbing edict arrived, apparently emanating from the most senior HR person in the institution, informing Ashridge that they must meet Glocom's quality standards, put some good content in place and get the large group process right.

Ben, the project leader for Glocom, who had been involved from the start, explained to Ashridge/Glocom joint team that they had no option but to fall into line. Not surprising, considering that he felt his job might be on the line, a feeling that he did not sense Bill was really aware of or sympathetic to.

'I had been working with Glocom for six months now', Bill explained, 'and I was beginning to notice a pattern concerning the way senior people intervened and exercised leadership in the organisation, the very leadership this work meant to change. When a senior person issued an edict, those on the receiving end felt there was no way for them to challenge it or to engage with the hierarchical chain of command. My suggestion that we seek a face-to-face conversation with the senior HR person fell on deaf ears and my attempts to inquire into the dynamics of this critical incident led nowhere. Increasingly frustrated, I decided to break the established pattern in order to give our leadership development work a chance of making a difference. This was, I thought, a de facto habit of hierarchical bullying, precisely one of the patterns that needed changing. So I took a risk. Without seeking Ben's permission I contacted the HR person directly. First I sent an email explaining the philosophy underpinning the leadership development work, the importance of starting with inquiry rather than exposition, the need to explore the leadership context. I concluded my message restating that this process was not designed to be entertaining. I then rang him up, and to my surprise got straight through. In a very good conversation we agreed the importance of staying true to the philosophy of the programme, the need to improve the production quality and to meet the expectations of participants by providing at least some more traditional content – in other words, meeting people on their wavelength whilst stretching their thinking.'

I think most people who have worked in large corporations will agree that Bill had taken a considerable risk. He could have seriously damaged his relationship with the Glocom people he had to work with on a day-to-day basis.

In the follow-up conversation Ben explained he had been trying to achieve a subtle, but significant change in who felt ownership for the programme within Glocom; and that he had not appreciated Bill's intervention, which had put a spanner in that particular works. Bill, in the meantime, had been unaware of Ben's intention. Although Bill's intervention did bring some respite for the Ashridge team, it did not achieve his intention of changing an ingrained pattern, whatever his fantasy at the time.

Engaging with the formal system

By now the board of Glocom was getting interested in what exactly was going on with the leadership development work. They wanted to experience it for themselves. 'I thought here's an opportunity for our work to connect into the formal organisation. Much as I believe lasting change is located in the informal systems, engaging with the formal system, the explicit power structure, is vitally important if what is emerging in the informal system is not to be quashed or undermined by lack of understanding in the formal system', explained Bill.

'By the end of our work with the board, I felt we were on a surer footing. I remember especially the robust response of the chief executive to the feedback of one of two people who participated in the infamous first large group inquiry: he demanded that people engage with the process and learn from it. I was also struck by how 'normal' the board was. As is often the case in hierarchical settings, the people at the top find themselves put on a pedestal and those who are engaging with them are exceedingly anxious, particularly in a system with high performance norms. I found the board to be composed of an open, intelligent bunch of people who were genuinely curious about what the leadership development work was trying to achieve and the way that it was going about its brief. By engaging with the board in a proper conversation rather than some form of presentational/propositional encounter, the formal system experienced what we were trying to encourage in the informal system.'

Sending a message of permission to experiment

One of the features of the large group process was a goldfish bowl conversation (See Appendix 1). One of the board members was invited to join in what turned out to be a particularly robust conversation, which went beyond the normal boundaries of what could be discussed, admitted and considered. 'I felt that this senior leader's engagement in this simple fishbowl process gave the message that it was acceptable to take risks. The formal and the informal aspects of the organisation had come together to create the opportunity for change to happen.'

Letting go of trying harder

Although things seemed to be settling down, Bill still wasn't quite satisfied with the large group events and sensed that Ben too was still uneasy. 'When we convened a small subgroup of the design team to explore our concerns, things came to a head. I was not a little surprised, and not best pleased, when a large contingent from Glocom turned up for what I had thought to be a small meeting. Design work is not easy in a small group, let alone in a large meeting with a whole lot of new faces. Ben is an inclusive person, and I sometimes got frustrated with the number of people he involved in our meetings. I started the meeting by asking whether we were here to continue to try harder to make the current design work (type 1 change), or whether we were going to radically change it (type 2 change). A rather awkward conversation ensued. We seemed to go round in circles. In the process I became aware that Caryn had a much stronger relationship with Ben than I had. Indeed, I suspected Ben experienced my involvement as rather erratic and was irritated by my self-assigned challenging role – not that he often showed it. When I thought we had reached a deadlock, I suggested that we wrote up the current design for the new people Ben had invited, so that they could offer their thoughts and suggestions. We got some interesting feedback about the lack of congruence between the design of the first morning of the event and the espoused principles. In the end we agreed on a design that was close to the original one, but more polished. We would start the day with an inquiry into what participants wanted to find out about leadership.'

In my conversations with Ben and Bill it emerged that they had felt rather cross with each other in the course of that meeting, although they had both valued the result. To their credit they had both been able to stay with what was happening in the moment, make space for the new voices to have a say, even though neither of them had planned or much wanted what was happening. My sense is that their shared philosophy, their mutual understanding of how new insight emerges, allowed them to stay with a process that was initially irritating to both of them.

At the time of writing the large group event works well and the process largely takes care of itself. Participants take responsibility for the way they lead, they begin to see themselves as able to have some influence within Glocom. No longer are they putting responsibility onto some idealised 'them', out there and separate from themselves, but they are seeing themselves as people who can make a difference.

The cathartic and unpopular consultant

Ever concerned about the value of the process, Bill asked for feedback at the end of the pilot programme. One participant responded that the second large group event was a bit of waste of time. 'When I asked "what don't you like about it and what do other people think?" the floodgates opened: a gruelling 45 minutes of negative feedback, with about 60 people in the room. It was a difficult experience, but I believe it had a significantly cathartic effect. I am convinced that even though participants hadn't necessarily enjoyed the process, for each person some significant change in their leadership style had happened.'

Engaging with people in the nitty-gritty of their daily work, seeing them do things differently, making a difference to themselves and to Glocom, is truly satisfying for Bill. 'I am moved when I see people taking risks, because if you're serious about changing you will need to take risks, breaking away from the life-sapping processes that people can so often find themselves part of.'

Bill's insights on large group inquiries in Glocom

'I have discovered that you can't simply invite 100 Glocom people into a room just to inquire. The invitation has to be more substantive. There has to be a clear reason for what we're doing, even if the process will actually be one of simple inquiry. For Glocom participants needed to be met halfway; they had to be offered something more than simply asking good questions, something that they would recognise as being of value. This meant we had to offer some content, some workshops on leadership and change. We also introduced an improvisational comedian who also happens to be literate in complexity theory and could make the bridge between the craft of improvisation and the practice of leading in dynamic, evolving, relationally constructed social settings. It also meant making sure that the production quality was acceptable to a media company.'

Prior to this work, Bill was somewhat dismissive of presentation and production. 'I was of the view that elaborate presentations got in the way of the purity of the inquiry. I've changed my mind. I realise that the look and feel of a gathering must be sufficiently Glocom-style for people to engage and sufficiently different to intrigue.' Glocom staff were deeply attached to the notion that on any development programme they would be trained and entertained. Preparing people to engage with a process of inquiry rather than 'knowledge and skills acquisition' required considerable work before people arrived on the programme. Practical issues such as lay-out, equipment and acoustics are important too.

'I think the role of facilitators is minimal if the process is well designed. However, they do need to be aware of their responsibilities. They need to give a sense of boundary, of what can and can't be done. People who are used to traditional workshops expect, to a greater or lesser extent, the facilitator to have an idea of what outcome is wanted. In the large group process, the outcome is more fluid, which can make people anxious. That is why the facilitator needs to provide a sense of reassurance that while the outcome is unknown, the process is robust. The final role of the facilitator is to judge when the moment is right to provoke, when people are shying away from engaging with the heart of the matter, and when is the time to get out of the way and allow for the natural energy and dynamism of the group to work its magic.' It is not unusual for the inexperienced large-group facilitator to want to demonstrate their value to the process by joining in too much, displaying their wisdom about a subject, a pattern I know all too well. This is usually fatal for both the process and the facilitator.

Two steps forward, one step back

Deep-seated patterns do not disappear overnight. The issue of negative feedback escalating through the hierarchy and provoking knee-jerk responses persisted, as did the need to hold the tension between performance values and learning. 'One particular example stands out for me', said Bill. 'The senior-leader workshops, part of the programme, had been really successful. When at the seventh or eighth occasion a couple of the participants felt unsatisfied they shared their view with board members.

'The by-now-familiar pattern was sparked off. We received explicit and specific instructions from on high: the team responsible for this workshop were informed "that it wasn't working"; were told new case studies had to be in place by 29 January (the date was that specific); and that the workshop had to be freshened up and rethought. Lastly, and most enervating to me, we were told there were to be no more "B-team" presenters. The message was clear: a new member of the Ashridge faculty who had contributed to the disgraced workshop was no longer wanted. I was told by Ashridge senior management that this was threatening our relationship with Glocom and instructed to "sort this out". There was even a suggestion that I might once again directly contact Glocom's senior executive who had sent the ignominious memo. I thought we were overreacting, unwilling to look at the issue in context, and landing the blame squarely landed on the so called "B-team" member of faculty, personalising an issue that was systemic in nature.

'I felt a repeat direct intervention was inappropriate and instead contacted Ben, who agreed vigorously. Ben also thought some of the issues raised substantive concerns. However, I didn't want us to just simply comply with the edict. In the end, after much "sound and fury", we agreed some design improvements.'

Bill also grew increasingly weary of the personal cost involved in preventing knee-jerk reactions, taking up the role of inviting people to be more reflective and see things in perspective. He was aware that, as the project moved into operational mode, his potency might wane and he would no longer be able to make the difference that mattered to him.

'I realised that key people at Ashridge and Glocom never sat down and talked about this particular pattern, because there was always too much going on, too much to do. I feared that Ashridge would fall into the comfortable Glocom pattern of becoming a production number, that the focus would shift to logistical planning and resource management, and that the whole programme would be neutered as it lost its novelty. It would cease to disturb the patterns it had set out to change. I wanted to explore how to engage more fully with Glocom, so that I could disturb the system without being ejected from it.'

Reflecting on his experience for the purpose of this research, sharing his story with Ben and getting Ben's feedback on his version of events, provided him with an opportunity to do this.

Sense from further reflective inquiry

After drafting the first versions of Bill's story to date, I met with Ben and Bill to find out to what extent Bill's experience resonated with that of Ben. Any differences in views I have included in the account you have read so far. I subsequently had another meeting with Bill to further explore his consulting practice as it emerged in this story.

Four themes stood out for me from these conversations:

- The consequences of the unexamined relationship between Ashridge and Glocom
- The tension between working with and against the grain of established organisational practice
- The flawed nature of consulting, the gap between what is known and what is done
- Bill's principles and the embracing of paradox.

The consequences of the unexamined relationship between Ashridge and Glocom

I am left with a sense of unexamined assumptions about the nature of the client–consultant relationship. I wonder what may have been possible if more explicit attention had been paid to the nature of this relationship and how best to develop it. There seemed to have been no agreed process, formal or informal, for doing so. The close collaboration and co-creation of the programme was a novel experience for both parties, and yet there never seemed to have been a thorough exploration of the assumptions each party held about this collaboration. Thus it remained unclear in which areas Ashridge was considered an equal partner and which areas Glocom saw as purely a matter for their own consideration. Similarly, Ashridge seemed unclear about the extent to which relationship issues between Glocom and the Ashridge faculty were up for discussion with Glocom.

I am also doubtful about the use of terms such as 'partnership' or 'client/supplier' to describe the relationship between clients and consultants. They seem to be insufficiently grounded, too general, and may mask rather than highlight some power dynamics. The incident that stands out for me in this respect is the absence of discussion about the risks and consequences of going hell for leather to meet the deadline for the first pilot, which meant that neither Bill nor Caryn, two core members of the team, could be present.

My sense is that the frank, robust and mutually respectful relationship between Bill and Ben could have been of more benefit to the programme. Trusting Bill's desire to ensure the work was generative for the client, Ben had sufficient regard for Bill to support him when he rocked the boat. He respected Bill's technical skills and shared his philosophy about how change happens in organisations. But in this kind of work people are nearly always too busy with the task to pay attention to the relationship, however much potential is left unexplored or unrealised.

The tension between working with and against the grain of established organisational practice

Ben pointed out that, as an internal consultant, he cannot afford the luxury of Bill's more purist stance: 'I always had to live the tension of not condoning behaviours that need to change, whilst having to work with the reality of where the organisation is at any moment in time. And I don't want to ruin my career in the process.'

While Ben felt frustrated by Bill's occasional lack of concern for his personal circumstances – something Bill expressed suitable regret and personal chastisement for when it was brought to his attention – he did hugely value Bill's interventions much of the time: 'Bill was always willing to ask the unspeakable questions, to do the right thing, even if did not make him popular.'

Bill often feels his willingness to be provocative is not valued by his clients. I sense he found Ben's feedback affirming – although it was not without caveat. Ben was quite clear that on occasions he valued the provocation in the moment, sometimes he didn't much like it at the time but valued it afterwards, and sometimes he found it plain irritating.

The flawed nature of consulting practice – the gap between what is known and what is done

Bill can be extremely, even excessively, self-critical. He described a number of occasions in his consulting practice where his personal preferences got in the way of doing certain types of work and pinpointed the occasional gap between what he knew and what he did. The one that stood out for me concerned the attention he pays to relationships. 'I may bang on about relationships,' he said, 'but do I pay enough attention to the relationships I am part of?' He knows the Gestalt principle that 'change happens in the crucible of a relationship. Therefore all I have to work with is high-quality relationships. It's an elusive concept but one you recognise when you see it.'

In terms of his preferences, Bill was aware that his orientation towards novelty makes it difficult for him to work from a set script – indeed he knows that he consults at his best when 'both of us [client and consultant] are off our scripts and responding to what is evoked in us'. He is also aware that he can be hard to digest, even socially: 'I have a disposition to being gritty that may not always be appropriate.'

Bill's principles and the embracing of paradox

Bill describes himself as a principled consultant, a description Ben could agree with. His principles concern his aspirations for his consulting work, rather than ethics or morality per se.

Firstly, he believes that 'change happens in relationships', that for something different to happen in an organisation the change must be located in the habits of relationship that exist between people in the organisation. Secondly, 'organisations are processes of communicative interaction' – a minimalist statement with very few normative overtones. It implies that if consultants want to make a difference in organisational settings they must engage with the processes of communicative interaction. Thirdly, novelty arises in conditions of messiness and difference. Therefore, to consult in the service of novelty requires a capacity to work with mess and contention.

Some people experience Bill as dogmatic. How can he hold such strong views (as described in the principles above), they ask, while at the same time asserting that people need to discover for themselves what their organisations are about through conversation? When I asked him how he lives with this paradox he replied: 'Easily. To live in our complex world we need to live with paradox. A paradox is not a dilemma. Truth and inquiry exist in the same breath.'

Further reading

Bateson, G (2000) *Steps to an Ecology of Mind*. Chicago: University of Chicago Press.

Perls, F (1989) *Legacy from Fritz*. Science and Behaviour Books.

Stacey, RD, D Griffin, et al. (2000) *Complexity and Management: Fad or Radical Challenge to Systems Thinking?* London: Routledge.

Bill's Postscript to Bill's Story

LOOKING THROUGH SIX THEORETICAL FRAMES

In reviewing my own story, it would be easy to indulge in some serious self-flagellation or coy self-congratulation. If I were to be self-flagellatory, I would say this is the story of a curmudgeonly consultant who relished to excess being the grit in the oyster, at the expense of the relationship with the client. If I were to be self-congratulatory, I would say that this is the story of a courageous consultant who held to his principles in the face of a powerfully self-referential client culture.

More dispassionately I think it is neither of the above. It has echoes of Francesca's story in that I was upholding a principle to which I became too attached. In Gestalt terms I made one aspect of the project figural, while not paying enough attention to other aspects, and not being sufficiently appreciative of our main client's position. However, as other team members were looking after these aspects, I would argue that I was legitimately taking up a useful provocative role.

In its broadest sense this is a story of a very large and ambitious leadership development programme, one intended to change the leadership culture in Glocom. It was based on a creative combination of large group processes, workshops, coaching and action learning, and has been in any number of ways extraordinarily effective. It has survived organisation-wide budget cuts and continues today. So it is a story of success through blood, toil, tears and sweat on behalf of both the Ashridge and the Glocom team.

It is also a story of a turbulent relationship between client and consultant, and here there is another parallel with Francesca's story. We knew that the dynamics of the relationship between Ashridge and Glocom were just as important as the programme itself. We frequently talked about how to raise our mutual awareness of our experience of each other, of the patterns and dynamics that we were co-creating. We knew that change occurs as much in client–consultant relationship as in the actual 'work'. We knew this and yet, like Francesca, we found it really hard. The pressure of simply meeting the project deadlines and the demanding performance expectations always took precedence.

For me it is a story of a consultant upholding some key principles about how innovation occurs. I don't consider this an ideology but a view about how things actually work – rather than how they should work. I think it's important for consultants to pay attention to the difference between how things are and how we would like them to be. We inevitably bring both into our work and I think a core part of being a 'reflective practitioner' is to be continuously reflective about how they are informing our practice.

In this case our clients had stressed at the outset that one of their goals was to become leaders in innovation, and that the programme should be innovative. Colleagues and I were upholding the view that innovation means the emergence of novelty, and that by definition novelty cannot be known in advance and therefore cannot be planned for: we can only create the conditions in which the novel might emerge. Critically, among these conditions is a certain amount of mess and disorder, diversity, and the reduction of power differentials. We were therefore keen on a programme which did not rely on all the usual ways of maintaining order, such as tightly planned schedules and smoothly delivered presentations, and that – in both its creation and delivery – challenged some of the habitual Glocom patterns, particularly some of the power dynamics.

Although I became overly attached to the principle of innovation, my reflections are that upholding it was largely appropriate and at times effective. However, as I write this I remember the sense of burden I felt, and realise that I took this upon myself rather than work with it in the team. What I now most notice in the story is my tendency to fly solo. Like Kevin, I am inclined to heroic consulting, and while I talk about the importance of relationship I do not think I paid enough attention to my relationship with the team, or with the client.

What an interesting way to conclude. Talking about being a reflective practitioner is one thing. Being one reminds me of what a challenge it really is.

Iain – Consulting with Conviction

Iain works in the area of brand strategy. He seeks to help his clients expound a clear sense of what their organisation is about and to develop ways of working congruent with that vision. A number of tensions arise in the course of that work: firstly, many firms see brand as little more than what appears in their advertising or websites and the logo on their letterheads. Secondly, there are possible discrepancies between what the firm does, what it says it does and what it wants to do in the future. Thirdly, there are the tensions that come from making choices.

Consciously or unconsciously, many of the more entrepreneurial firms operate on a Mintzberg-inspired model of emerging strategy (Mintzberg, 1994). They grow and evolve by taking advantage of opportunities as and when they arise, not necessarily in accordance with any grand plan. When consulting to those kinds of organisations, Iain seeks to raise his clients' awareness of the need to make choices about which opportunities to pursue, in order that the firm maintain and evolve a coherent identity so that its customers are clear about what the organisation stands for or is good at.

The consulting engagement Iain chose for this inquiry concerned Assist (a pseudonym, chosen for the purpose of this story), a very successful software firm with aspirations to position itself as a professional general consulting firm. Iain's work initially focussed on uncovering what the firm actually did, and how that compared with what stakeholders inside and outside the organisation thought it did. Having explored the organisation's capability, choices for the future could be identified so that the firm wouldn't find itself trapped in a successful but potentially vulnerable niche.

Similarity and difference

A recurring theme in Iain's story, as I see it, is the fine balancing act between fitting in, being similar enough to be acceptable on the one hand, and bringing a different voice, a fresh perspective on the other.

From Iain's description of Assist, I could picture the difference he brought more easily than the similarity: Iain is a stylish, elegant person who seemed perfectly suited to the light, airy and sophisticated environment he is currently working in. Assist, on the contrary, seemed to pride itself on its reputation for hard-nosed software engineers, who value pragmatism over sophistication and style. Most importantly, their perspective on the role and importance of 'brand' was certainly very different from Iain's.

So how did Iain fit in?

'I was struck by the highly entrepreneurial nature of the management team and their relative indifference to the technical skills and practices of the firm's work. This had advantages of course. People felt free to pursue different markets. On the other hand, it created all sorts of difficulties when it came to making strategic choices. There simply were no clear criteria', explained Iain. 'The strong cohesion I sensed in the organisation appeared to be a result of their recruitment process. Most people seemed to arrive with a personal recommendation, with a shared history with someone in the firm they knew, or through an industry connection, as many employees had worked in utilities and related industries. I caught my first glimpse of the importance of personal recommendations and connections in Assist when I was introduced to the board by Conor, my main contact, as "Iain Carruthers, recommended by Duncan for this work". Duncan was a member of the advisory board, a group of elders who supported Assist's management team. Every one of the board members had a track record in the utilities and transport sectors, core markets for Assist, was immensely well connected in the sector and exceedingly knowledgeable about the industry. I knew Duncan from my time as a board director at a major utility. Duncan admitted he had given a lot of thought to introducing me to Assist, but eventually decided I would be able to fit in.'

Iain also sensed a strong influence of the Celtic founders. The top team reminded him of a clan, and the whole organisation seemed cohesive more because of a deep relational loyalty rather than through shared technical or professional goals. 'Perhaps', he said pensively, 'it's not by accident that I too have a Celtic heritage. My mother's family left Ireland during the famine and settled in Glasgow.'

On a more prosaic note Iain also registered that his strong preference for learning through experimenting (as described by the Kolb learning cycle) was highly congruent with that of many employees of Assist. He described it as 'the engineer's way': the strong desire to pick something up and play with it to see how it works.

Building rapport

I was struck by the importance to Iain of congruence between his sense of self and his work and between his personal and professional values: 'I like to be with people, I like to be liked, and I want to engage with people emotionally as well as professionally. I believe that how you conduct yourself with others should be consistent with what you stand for in the world. Similarly, a company's best policy is to be as clear as it can be about what it's trying to do in the world and to make its actions coherent with its vision.'

I sense that for Iain the word 'company' could be replaced with 'human being'. The belief in, and need for, personal integrity and connection were at the heart of the way he conducted himself at an introductory meeting with senior Assist staff. Rather than doing the expected presentation to establish his basic credentials, Iain sought to engage Assist people in a conversation, inviting them to huddle around his PC, and to have a browse through a book he had published which described his work with other companies. 'I deliberately shied away from a more standard presentation. The formality of a projector almost inevitably creates a distance between client and consultants, something I sought to avoid.'

In the process of the conversation, Assist staff began to develop a different perspective on brand issues and to understand the importance of congruence between an organisation's identity and the behaviour of its people. Aware of the value Iain had added in their first encounter with them, they invited him to produce a short proposal, outlining what he thought he could deliver for the company. 'I realised', said Iain, 'that I was being treated in the way Assist had been treated by their clients in the past: as a provider of deliverables. It was exactly what they were trying to get away from. Nevertheless, on the basis of the age-old principle of starting from where the client is, rather than where the consultant thinks they ought to be, I obliged.'

The quest begins

Iain describes consulting practice as a kind of quest. 'My initial semblance of clarity is quickly overshadowed by confusion. I listen for signals that lead me along paths in a dark forest where I pick up clues that eventually bring me to "the grail", the insight that will benefit my clients.'

Iain's first foray into the forest consisted of meeting teams working on particular projects, clients and various non-executive stakeholders. 'I quickly developed a sense of empathy with Assist's employees. I admired their stubbornness, their sheer determination to keep working despite the turbulence in the infrastructure industry at the time. Although their work seemed rather boring to me, their pride and the sheer effort they invested in their work was awesome.'

A positive engagement with what is

Iain is an enthusiast. He patently believes in the value of what he does. Similarly, he seeks to work with the positive energy of his clients. Informed by an appreciative inquiry perspective, Iain explores the current reality of a client organisation from the question 'What's happening when we are at our best?' This approach informed his work with the wider Assist community as well as his conversations with the management team at the end of his assignment. 'The options for extending brand and markets I presented to the management team were based on acknowledging and valuing Assist's heritage as a solid foundation from which to move into new territory. I met strong resistance from some members of the team who were keen to dissociate themselves from the down-to-earth world, in the belief that it would tie them down to too narrow a niche. I remained firm though and insisted that they understood and valued what Assist stood for.'

A previous client once described Iain as 'using strong words, softly spoken'. I sense that describes Iain's approach with Assist well. Inviting Assist's staff to recognise and appreciate what Assist was about, he then helped them to see how this opened up rather than closed down the company's future options. Conor, upon reading this claim, tentatively agreed: 'In many ways Iain's work complemented the strategy work that was going on elsewhere'. I think Iain's position is similar to Stuart Kauffman's in *At Home in the Universe* (1995), that change can only take place by moving into the adjacent space. To attempt a leap too far away from a firm's current position simply requires too much of a stretch, and so results in the organisation reverting to its original position.

Iain's consulting work appears to me to differ from a more conventional approach in two ways: he looks to ask energising questions rather than to focus on problems and deficits; and he seeks to engage people emotionally. For example, in his work with Assist, he invited a team of exceedingly left-brain data analysts to create images, metaphors of Assist, from magazine pictures. 'They got really energised by the experience. Their favourite image was of an Assist consultant wearing a hardhat in the midst of some rail maintenance operatives in the back of beyond, in stark contrast with their daily reality of being stuck in an office analysing data. I think my enthusiasm was contagious and when I asked them to tell stories about their experience of working for Assist they really engaged with it.'

Iain ran a couple of appreciative inquiry workshops about the company and its brand in the UK, observed by Conor, who subsequently facilitated AI workshops in Dublin and Belfast with data analysts and software engineers. Conor was struck by the participants' level of engagement and creativity, which was much higher than he had anticipated. The workshops became a forum for people to share their pride in the value of their work.

Playing with the elders

Iain's engaging style served him well when he presented his findings on the uniqueness of Assist to Conor and the management team. 'You've nailed us' was Conor's laconic observation at the time.

The presentation was to be repeated at a meeting of the management team joined by the strategic advisory body, twelve people in all, mostly grey-haired men, a number of them hardened Scottish engineers, some smart infrastructure people and an ex-senior partner of one of the world's most successful consulting firms. This was an important event and Conor was somewhat nervous in anticipation of the meeting.

As well as wanting to make a good impression on the highest-profile group in the organisation, he wanted the meeting to achieve some real work with this group on the firm's current and potential future pictures of itself. 'It's part of the culture of Assist never to leave an asset under-utilised', Iain explained, 'and helping their clients to actively manage their physical assets is also at the heart of their business; so it's little wonder Conor was keen to make the most of this opportunity. Hence I thought very carefully about how I could stimulate the kind of conversation I believed we needed to have. I was aware that, for many of the people in the room, brand was an issue of the image presented in promotion materials rather than anything to do with day-to-day operations. I also knew that the board members had been cooped up in a room for most of that day engaged in left-brain, analytic work, either being on the receiving end of presentations or having "sensible" conversations. On top of that, this was a very male group, as was the firm as a whole.' Iain also expected the management board to treat the advisory board with the respect due to the 'elders of the clan'. Conor, on the other hand, thought it was less a matter of respect to elders as of the need to get best value from a group of highly paid people.

Taking a calculated risk, Iain decided to set the tone by working with metaphors. He suggested that each of the participants consider 'what this company, which you know so well, would be if it were a football team, rock band or car'. 'I was seeking to elicit people's hunches and intuitions, rather than their already well-articulated and familiar perspectives, by introducing a light and potentially humorous activity. Sometimes humour allows us to reach a deeper level than a serious, analytical approach as people can share insights without the risk of losing face.'

As the group engaged enthusiastically with the humorous opportunity provided by Iain's question, a rich discussion ensued around the implications of being akin to Charlton Athletic. Charlton were at that time a premiership football club, highly successful despite having relatively few resources and an unglamorous pedigree: a triumph of good management, team spirit and sheer bloody-mindedness. To Conor, though, it was more about being on the cusp of greatness.

This change of discourse allowed the men in the room to smile. It helped to create a receptive and creative atmosphere and it also met Iain's personal need for people to enjoy an experience that he had orchestrated. Moreover, this gave him an opportunity to share his findings in a style congruent with his belief in the power of narrative as a source of deep insight, telling stories that brought his PowerPoint presentation to life.

At the end of the session, Conor acknowledged it had gone very well and that they had been enthused – no small feat with this audience. 'It had helped them understand that brand is not about the logo or the brochure, but about the way you do business and what you stand for in the world', Iain reiterated. Conor confirmed that this presentation to the advisory board was pivotal and changed the conversation about branding. He ascribed this success partly to Iain's quality of presenting but mostly to the fact that they could recognise the company Iain was describing.

Harvesting the stories

'I believe that in the stories people tell I can find a clue to what is at the heart of the organisation and the treasure I can show to my clients. I know I'll hear dozens of stories and anecdotal nuggets. All of them help to provide an insight into the organisational dynamic, but from experience I expect some transcendent truth to emerge from about three to four of them. In the case of Assist one of those core stories concerned the way the Irish founder grew the firm, employing only people with social or family ties. Another highlight concerned the roots that fostered the firm's exceptional teamwork. It described a deep sense of kinship, going back to its Irish foundations, even though most of the people who now worked for Assist were Anglo-Saxons.'

The anchor against idealisation – being held within the Assist system

In our conversations about Iain's experience of Assist as a clan, he shared quite a bit of his own sense of his personal history, including details about his mother's ancestry and the connection to Irish history and I sensed a certain romanticism.

'I really appreciated the way Conor kept me attuned to the shadow of the clan, the problems and tensions that arise in a system of tight internal networks, where certain decisions can't be made unless particular members of the clan are present.' Conor was less convinced he played that role: 'I was keen to guide you. Once I'd decided to trust you with our family secrets, I wanted to be honest about the organisation with you. It was a very deliberate decision to "open the kimono", and having done that I didn't want you to trip up.'

Iain linked Conor's comments to his informing consulting metaphor of being a protagonist searching in the forest. In most of those stories the protagonist has one or more guides, some small or big mentors who help in the quest. Conor demonstrated the ability to have both a very strong affection for Assist, as well as a capacity to be ironic about it and laugh at its foibles.

I was struck repeatedly by the extent to which Assist seemed to take responsibility for getting value for money from Iain's work. In my experience, consultants are often left to plough their own furrow. Iain on the contrary seemed to be very actively guided in how to engage with the Assist system. I also sensed that Iain was excluded from certain discussions, and thus was rather hazy about the negative consequences of his work resulting in the loss of billable time on a particular occasion. Similarly Iain noticed that after each phase in the work the organisation would go quiet on him for a while, until they re-engaged with him to continue. I interpreted this as decisions occurring in an inner circle to which Iain was not invited. The clan is not a transparent decision-making body.

I also feel it is worth re-emphasising Duncan's role. I sensed that Duncan was responsible for the quality of Iain's work for Assist and at the same time acted as a badge of acceptance. Conor, on the other hand acted as Iain's guide through the rituals and unwritten ways of Assist, making sure that he didn't blunder and that the company got their money's worth from him. The presentation to the elders, for example, had originally been put to Iain as an opportunity for Assist to get a few more hours work out of him on a day when a workshop he was running finished relatively early.

What is striking about Iain's way of consulting

Iain works from the gut. He consults from personal conviction, which he trusts will in most cases address various counterarguments. There is more to this than rhetorical skill though. Iain's ability to be speak with conviction and confidence comes from his years of marketing and business expertise and a sense of what it takes for a company to succeed – together with an ability to bring to an organisation's attention the emotionally compelling logic of its stories. Working with this logic helps to short-circuit the potentially energy-draining tradition of more rationally grounded consulting.

For example, Iain could see the rationalisation of how Assist's recruiting policy was driving its extremely cohesive and effective team working. Iain shed a different light on this rationale when he quoted the operations director as having said 'It's not really teamwork, it's kin'. This privileging of narrative evidence, Iain believes, allows people within the organisation, as well as the consultant and client, to connect at a human level. People understand who they are in the context of Assist, through the stories that are told, rather than through reference to an organisational chart.

'Consulting in a way that seeks to establish human connection, rather than maintain professional distance', Iain admitted, 'means I risk being rejected. A more typical professional manages his boundaries with clients quite tightly and doesn't seek to be liked or to establish friendships. I need to be liked and I do seek out friendships.' His approach can leave Iain vulnerable and at risk of becoming too invested in a particular recommendation or in preserving a friendship at all costs. That is the shadow. The light, from the client's point of view, is a consultant who speaks his truth, doesn't sit on the fence and claim not to have an opinion, who speaks from a position of thoughtful and heartfelt attachment rather than from distant detachment.

I was also struck by Iain's perspective on consulting as a quest, in contrast with the more traditional 'hypothesis-driven' approach. Iain looks for clues for a treasure that he doesn't yet know. The traditional approach defines the treasure at the start and then looks for evidence that confirms this treasure as being the right one. This is unsurprising from a social constructionist perspective: the lens with which a world is viewed brings just that world into being. Iain's fear of engaging in his work as an open quest is that he won't find any clues, that by not knowing the desired outcome at the start, no outcome will be achieved. This 'not knowing' also provokes anxiety for his clients. To engage with a consultant who works from this principle requires an act of faith on behalf of the client.

At the end of our initial conversation Iain explained what he admires in the people he works well with in organisations: 'I admire people who are fully human and fully committed in an organisational setting, who are able to work at whatever task and still be themselves, who can express themselves fully'. I suspect his description is also a reflection of how he works with his clients and tallies with the perspective he advocates for firms: the need for consistency between how a firm operates at a day-to-day level with what it says it stands for.

He also touched on his motivation for being a consultant: 'I want to try and help people to access a human truth about themselves and their organisations, to find coherence between identity and values, and between identity, values and the market environments that my clients will continue to operate in and move into.'

Finally, I am struck by Iain's desire to help people recognise their qualities and resources. In the case of Assist, he wanted the firm to really appreciate what it had to build on, not at a level of bland generalities, but in specific qualities and skills, and how this was the best place from which to expand. Iain sees the world as a generative place and invites his clients to join him in a generative and creative exploration of what they are and what they could be. He invites his clients to engage with him in a spirit of robust friendship. It is from that position that Iain now wishes to re-engage with Conor, some months after he has provided his final deliverables.

Sense from further reflective inquiry

After Iain and Conor talked through the initial version of this story, I debriefed Iain. Conor had confirmed that the story was broadly congruent with his experience. Any exceptions are now incorporated in the story you have read.

The following themes stood out for me in our follow-up conversations, which concerned not only Iain's work at Assist but also another assignment which resulted in Iain being rejected:

- The importance of story and protagonist
- The preconditions for working with a consultant like Iain
- Whether a consultant can do good work if he or she doesn't like the client or the client organisation.

The importance of story and protagonist

Iain not only seeks to work with stories in his consulting work, he also talks of his consulting process in terms of a story. 'A story, a consulting assignment, requires the raw material of a protagonist who is willing to undergo stresses and challenges for what he/she believes in. When I meet clients, I'm looking for a protagonist... someone who has a set of beliefs, which may or may not be clear, that are upset or unfulfilled in some way. He or she feels called to do something. This quest is often part of someone's life journey.'

In our shared reflections we began to wonder, especially in the light of Iain's recent bitter expulsion, if hiring a consultant is sometimes a way for a client (a protagonist who does not want to face their calling) to avoid taking a particular test or challenge. Are consultants sometimes serving as unwitting emasculators of their clients? Shielding them from acknowledging their role in the patterns that they are part of? Certainly I would see the tradition of overly intellectual consulting and predetermined procedural consulting as approaches that can readily allow both clients and consultants to achieve this. In other words, the rationalistic consulting tradition provides an agenda and process that allows for significant aspects of organisational and personal reality to be ignored; and thus results in consulting engagements that are more about preserving the status quo, rather than challenging it.

The preconditions for working with a consultant like Iain

A consultant cannot magic into being what does not already exist within another person or an organisation. A willingness to change, a willingness to believe in what the firm stands for in the market are preconditions for a consultant's work. There needs to be at least some dissatisfaction with the status quo, some restlessness. Iain was quite categorical when he stated that he should really only work with clients who believe in their ambition. Assist were restless and they believed in their ambition. The firm that expelled him seemed to me to talk about their big ambition but appeared too fragile to really want to let go of how things were. For Iain, a key part now in recognising potential clients is an 'intuitive appraisal of their ambition, and a willingness on their part to explore robustly the beliefs that underpin that ambition and how those beliefs are expressed'.

Part of the restlessness Iain referred to is the never-ending search for a distinctively expressed identity – with emphasis on distinctive. Assist, as Iain politely put it, 'couldn't give a f**k what competitors thought of them'. They were comfortable with standing out from the crowd, giving their customers and potential customers a real choice by being authentically distinct. I would contend that this is also a healthy challenge to consulting work that looks to benchmark and compare one firm with another. Looking at others and learning from the external environment is of course vital for the health of any biological or social organism. But if this taking in from the outside is not carried out with a profound understanding of distinctive identity then the benchmarking will either result in a firm simply becoming a poor copy of everyone else or the external insights being rejected outright. This rejection, I believe, occurs because the organisation doesn't understand how its identity and belief systems are informing what can or can't be absorbed.

Iain really liked the people at Assist. Although at first they assumed that talking about 'liking the client' was part of his sales pitch, they eventually believed him. Conor also revealed that they chose to work with Iain because they liked him. I find myself wondering how many of those pseudo-objective consulting selection processes are simply extended exercises in justifying an intuited sense of liking and being liked.

This liking does not however mean abandoning all judgement. If Iain had failed at any stage he would have been out on his ear. But Assist did everything in their power to ensure he didn't blunder. Over the course of the engagement this mutual liking, Iain's delivering to deadlines and his behaviour at certain key meetings meant that Conor felt able to let him into more and more of the family secrets.

Intellectually, I can believe that it is possible for a consultant and client to work together well while having no positive empathy. Personally, I know that I have always done my best work when I have had a personal affection for my client and at least a passing regard for what the organisation does or stands for. Without the presence of affection or liking, I believe a consultant can be very skilled at the detached aspects of their work, but cannot hope to know the firm from a position of attachment.

Much consulting has traditionally emphasised the importance of detachment. This greatly restricts what can be known to a consultant as well as their capacity to intervene in the client system. By raising this theme in the context of Iain's story, I want to highlight how he marries attachment and detachment, personal liking and professionalism, and I propose that these dynamics are at play in all generative consultant–client relationships.

Further reading

Carruthers, I (2003) *How to move minds and influence people*. London: Prentice Hall.

Kauffman, S (1996) *At Home in the Universe*. New York: Oxford University Press.

Mead, G (1967) *Mind, Self and Society, from the Standpoint of a Social Behaviorist*. London: The University of Chicago Press.

Mintzberg, H (1994) *The rise and fall of strategic planning*. New York: Simon and Schuster.

Perls, F (1974) Ego, *Hunger and Aggression: The beginning of Gestalt Therapy*. Allen and Unwin.

Bill's Postscript to Iain's Story

LOOKING THROUGH SIX THEORETICAL FRAMES

This is broadly speaking a story about organisational identity. The opening sentence states clearly that Iain is in the business of helping organisations 'work in a way that is consistent with what they say they stand for'. Later Iain says his work is to 'help them realise that they have to choose which opportunities to pursue and which not, so that the firm maintains and evolves a coherent identity'.

This reminds me of Mead's (1967) essentially social constructionist view of how identity is formed through a process of negotiating similarity and difference. Individual identity is not a pre-given essence, but forms in relation to other, through 'identifying' with what is me and what is not me, what I am part of and not part of; and the process of organisation identity formation is clearly similar. So Iain helps organisations choose what to do and what not to do, how to differentiate themselves in relation to what they offer to which markets.

He does this by helping the organisation discover what it actually does, rather than what it espouses; and more than that, 'he demands that they acknowledge and admire their heritage. He demanded that the firm knew and admired itself for what it does.' This is bold stuff. He combines his understanding of identity with a strong appreciative stance, which is rooted in what is almost an anthropological perspective. He seems to assume that heritage is important and is the bedrock of identity.

The way Iain works is interesting. John describes him as working from the gut, from the position of personal conviction. What he seems convinced about is the power of an organisation's stories as a way of both confirming and acknowledging identity, and as a critical process in connecting people emotionally. He talks about the 'emotionally compelling logic of [an organisation's] stories'.

John also says that Iain seeks out friendship and needs to be liked – although this does not seem to inhibit him from speaking his truth. He admires people who are fully human and fully committed, who can work at whatever task and still be themselves, so I sense some strong humanistic values in play here. Later he says that 'he should only work with clients who believe in their ambition'.

While his work is congruent with some aspects of AMOC theory, there are also some striking contrasts. There seems to be a strong emotional and aspirational quality to Iain's way of working which contrasts sharply with Fritz Perls' notion of 'creative indifference' (Perls, 1974). What Perls, another old Gestaltist, was asserting with this somewhat laconic-sounding term, was that the role of a change agent is to work with what is, to heighten awareness of the patterns, constraints and possibilities in a situation, to enable something to emerge without investment in particular outcomes. I sense that Iain is quite invested in outcome. This can in some circumstances be a strength, but there are also risks: doing the work for the client, creating dependence, and subsequent rejection.

The second major contrast appears in his way of describing his work as 'a quest'. He 'starts off in daylight, encounters confusion and then listens for a call which leads him along paths in a dark forest, where he will pick up clues which will eventually bring him to the grail'. This powerful metaphor is also an archetypal structure for a story. This is not surprising given Iain's interest in stories, but it is intriguing that he chooses this archetypal myth of the hero's journey. In my own story and in Kevin's, I also notice the tendency to be heroic. Theoretically in AMOC we aim to 'decentre' the conventional, individualist model of consultant as diagnostician and expert, by using such descriptors as 'inquirer', 'co-creator' and 'participant–observer'. In our trade we are all prone to become heroes and rescuers, and most of us need robust help in the form of a good supervisor or shadow consultant to avoid the trap. I wonder how consciously Iain constructs himself as hero, and if so, what he sees as the implications of taking up this role.

A final contrast lies in the implicit assumption that there is a grail to be found. From a social constructionist and complexity perspective there is no 'truth' or identity to be discovered. Each story is a construction of recalled events, and in the re-telling a new story is created, which will be similar and different to the previous time it was told. Each person will construct their own story of events in a way that will be similar and different from those of other people. There is no one true version of events – a problem that throws many a jury into confusion and turmoil. So from this perspective, organisational identity is permanently under construction.

I like the work Iain does. Although he does not actually say this, he invites us to think about the strategy process very differently from most traditional strategic models, as being intimately connected to the evolution of organisational identity. I find this a much more satisfying and humane view of strategy than the rather militaristic or Darwinian models which have populated the literature. It seems to me that the risk Iain runs is in the influence he may bring to bear, through his own energy and attachments, on the construction of that identity.

Last words – Iain's response to Bill's postscript

I felt prickled on reading the phrases '[the] risk Iain runs is in the influence he may bring to bear... on the construction of that identity' and 'I wonder how consciously Iain constructs himself as hero'. It's that prickle you get when unwelcome feedback rings true. I have to monitor myself constantly in my interpretations of a client market or environment. I am often poised between inquiry and advocacy and have to be conscious of which way I turn. Three reflections occurred to me.

Firstly, I and my co-consultants are involved in the organisation's construction of its identity. We have been invited in and if our interpretations are accepted, that is a legitimate part of the construction. One of the tenets of the new science is that everything is an act of participation, changing the nature of the outcome. You cannot not have influence: although I acknowledge you have to be mindful about the level of influence you are bringing.

Secondly, Bill's observations remind me that I'm not an organisational consultant. I'm a marketing and sales consultant who is organisationally informed. My interest is not primarily in an organisation's identity or self-meaning, but in how it uses that identity to engage others. This implies that the organisation must come to a clear view about itself – albeit a 'holding' view – otherwise it ceases to be coherent to the people it seeks to serve. Of course, it may choose to continue to be incoherent. Many organisations make this choice.

Thirdly, of course, there is no 'grail', no one version of events. I am convinced, though, that there is a charge of meaning in every resilient organisation, created by events and available to those listening for it. An organisation needs some form of vocation or calling, otherwise it unravels under pressure. My starting point is that there is some form of calling and that my job is to help create the circumstances that allow an organisation to hear, acknowledge and articulate it – and to hold back from trying to do it for them!

SECTION **4**

Concluding Chapter

A PUNCTUATION IN AN ONGOING INQUIRY

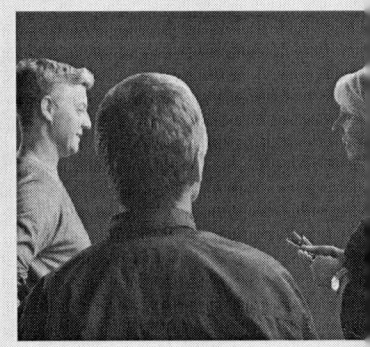

Not surprisingly perhaps, finding a suitable way to close this book has proved to be something of a challenge. John and Bill were keen to draw some conclusions, to find a provisional answer at least to the question: 'So what does consulting from a relational perspective look like then?' or put differently 'What seem to be some of the common characteristics in the consulting practice of AMOC graduates and faculty?' As ever, John was keen to differentiate 'AMOC consulting' from more mainstream work, of which he retains such unholy memories.

At the same time it seemed important to bring John's voice more directly into the foreground. Thus far John has taken a role of narrator, making the occasional observation or sharing some of his impressions of his co-inquiring consultants or their work. Reading this book you may have had little sense of John or of the significant impact his presence has had on the shape this research has taken.

Finally, from the start of this research, Bill and John had thought of the research report as a mere punctuation in an ongoing process of inquiry. Following the publication of the report, all AMOC alumni who had expressed an interest in the research (and purchased the report) were invited to a follow-up day in Ashridge. Some thirty people turned up to an exciting and lively occasion, one of the outcomes of which was the development of further collaborative inquiry groups.

A particular incident, described below, brought into sharp focus the important role John had played in the research and the importance of his voice being heard. At the same time people did express reservations about closing any publication about the inquiry in too decisive, too definitive a fashion. A consensus emerged: 'John ought to write the final chapter and it needs to incorporate this conference, which is a significant moment in this ongoing inquiry'. John set about writing the first drafts, in his inimitable personal and somewhat charged style. As he engaged in a number of cycles of inquiry, Kathleen doing her usual demanding editing, John became increasingly aware of the extent to which the principles he had recognised in the practice of his co-inquirers also showed up in some form in his experience of the conference. Eventually he settled on an account of his experience of the conference which highlights those core principles as John has come to articulate them in the course of the inquiry and which seemed to resonate so strongly with the wider AMOC community.

This chapter then is John's account: his masters' voice.

An Ongoing Inquiry – John's Story about a Conference

This is a story about finishing and not finishing, about the marriage of the formal and the informal, the tension that exists between relationships, conversations and text. It raises issues dear to any consultant's heart: what does it take to let go of a piece of work? What can co-creation cost and give to everyone involved? Is it possible to retain an enlivening sense of exploration and uncertainty while also providing some form of distillation and framing?

At its heart, though, this story is about endings. It is an example in its own right of what is involved in a consultant stepping out from a process that continues to have a life after the consultant's departure. It is the story of a significant piece of Batesonian punctuation in my relationship to this project.

Setting the scene

In September 2006 a conference was arranged to continue the inquiry into the practice of relational consulting. Bill, Kathleen and I invited all those who had participated in the research and anyone who had bought the research paper. Prior to the conference we had also started work with Peter Critten at MU Press and, much as he was an enthusiastic supporter of the research, he felt that the way we'd finished the research paper was out of keeping with the espoused and practised philosophy we had otherwise worked with. A philosophy that privileges the multi-facetted, non-definitive experience of sense making rather than its boiled down, expositional cousin-by-marriage.

The research paper had finished with a slightly tongue-in-cheek piece called 'The Seven Habits of Relational Consultants', a weak joke and a summary list that inevitably invited (as I discovered when seeking feedback from a more traditional consulting friend) readers to a fast snack on a few summarised sound bites rather than a sustained and rigorous inquiry into the text as a whole.

I am very struck now by how difficult it is not to collude with certain consulting habits that I used to value above all else. The ability to summarise on behalf of clients. The ability to make complex ideas easily digestible. A set of skills that frequently resulted in important work not being done by my clients, namely the hard and necessary work of really thinking things through for yourself – albeit in the company of others.

The conference was not only, therefore, an opportunity to engage in a further round of inquiry and seek out possibilities for establishing the work to date within a visible and ongoing process of inquiry; it was also an opportunity to mark an end to the writing of this book, while positioning that end in an ongoing process. But this is too neat an exposition: there were other dynamics afoot for me and the work at that time.

Shifting contexts

Throughout this book, the informal aspects of organisational life have been privileged and the research process was carried out along similar lines. The formal framing came in the invitation to participate but from thereon in I conducted the research in a very intimate and personal way. Each relationship was different and my way of being with each person was either subtly or quite distinctly different. To some I was a tutor, but others talked of me being a coach, a friend or a shadow consultant. I don't remember anyone labelling me as a 'researcher' – a term that may be associated with the formal frame of the work and, historically, with a distancing and separation that was not how I went about things.

The conference, however, marked a high point for me in the re-establishment of the formal aspects of the research. It was hosted at Ashridge and was in service of the Ashridge-sponsored ongoing inquiry and an Ashridge-owned book. It was a very visceral reminder that the days of intimate conversational inquiry were, for me, at an end. It was also a reminder that I needed to come to terms with my changing role, the changing visibility of the work and the need to close things down enough so that a book could be finished – while continuing to amplify those conversations that would encourage further inquiry.

As I reflect on the transition I was going through then, certain parallels with consulting experience stand out. Throughout the stories, consultants are having constantly to move between formal and informal contexts, between the requirements of providing enough of a script to demonstrate sufficient boundaries and order, while leaving sufficient opportunity for the unscripted and spontaneous to emerge. There is also that delicate process of readjusting words and phrases, which were safe for their original use in confidential conversations, so that they can live well in a more public and less contained arena.

The morning of the conference – turning-up and tuning-in

I travelled to Berkhamsted station on the morning of the conference and was picked up by Kathleen and Bill who took me up to the college. I was struck by their apparent insouciance and my actual nervousness. I anticipated an unappreciative audience, an exercise in destructive inquiry; they anticipated a constructive and appreciative gathering and they proved right. They also seemed to have a confidence in their group facilitation skills that had eroded in me.

When I shared my nervousness with them, Bill seemed surprised – these types of events are after all the meat and drink of his professional consulting practice. Reflecting now, I believe that part of my nervousness came as a consequence of my attachment to the report: I had invested significantly in it and to a certain extent felt it as an extension of myself. I was not in a state of sufficient creative detachment to allow myself to move on from my strong feelings about the day. Bill and Kathleen seemed to have a found a good mix of concern, for good process and constructive outcome, and professional distance from their ambitions for the day.

Up at the college we went to the Lady Marian Alford room, one of Ashridge's grand spaces, to review the layout and refresh our mutual understanding of the process for the day. Our design planned the day to start with people having brief, private conversations about what had drawn them to come to this conference. After this they would be invited to physically congregate around the one story that had most grabbed their attention. To make this possible, we positioned a dozen metaplan boards around the room with the twelve story titles displayed.

I was very struck by how much I missed having the opportunity to lead some form of expositional inquiry – or in other words, a lecture in which I could indulge my fantasy of controlling the sense-making process of others. This resonates with Caryn's piece, where she also talks of wanting to manage people's sense making, even though she knows this can't be done in any substantive, meaningful or ethical way. This attachment to demonstrating value to a process through exposition and content is something that had enabled me to thrive in the early, positivist, years of my consulting career and is a historic construction that can often reappear in my present. Fortunately my colleagues Bill and Kathleen were there to hold me in check and bring me back to this specific present.

As we were talking through the design for the day, going through which roles each of us was to take at each point, I became aware of people arriving and became distracted by whether they were being well received. This has always been a concern of mine, but one I used to dismiss as unimportant. Emboldened by my experience of Kathleen and the textual friends she introduced to me in her essay on relational consulting, I now found myself acting on these requirements for good hosting, paying attention to the social fabric of any professional situation.

My anxiety and negative historic projections subsided immediately when I left the room where the conference was to be held and bumped into a number of the people whose stories I had co-created or helped come into being. I felt myself shift from feeling I was going to engage with a flock of strangers, into an anticipation of meeting with people for whom I felt considerable affection. I was able to let go of my unhelpful legacy of defensiveness and engage fully in an appreciative present. These were people I knew, whose judgements I trusted, who I knew as skilful and generous inquirers.

The conference attracted a good-spirited group of about thirty. These were people who started from an informed understanding of social constructionism and had chosen to come to this conference. As a group we had enough in common to be able to connect; in retrospect the only question I would ask is whether there was sufficient difference to make a difference.

Reflecting on these observations and the story I've told so far I believe that some important points can be made about what makes for a generative relational consulting praxis. My first point concerns the importance of choice, of people voluntarily choosing to invest part of their professional lives (in this instance) in coming to the conference. They had made the effort to buy and read the research report and were now committing another day to make further sense of what they had read or been involved in constructing. These were not people who had been unwillingly corralled into some institutionally mandated activity, quite possibly wanting to be somewhere else. I have a sense that this personally owned experience of exercising choice is at the heart of much generative human interaction; and it may be that demanded participation is what makes so much programmatic, managerially enforced consulting so potentially unenlivening.

My second point concerns giving time for people to connect personally. Even though many of us at the conference knew each other, there were still some strangers and, as a collective, many of us had not met in months, even years. Rather than brusquely demand that we start exactly on time at ten o'clock, we let the socialising take its course for a while. Much of the value of a conference such as this comes not only from paying attention to the figural task, but also from allowing for people to have the opportunity to explore each other's current realities and so allow for the possibility of chance assistance or common cause to emerge. A generative relational consulting praxis allows time for people to explore and disclose unknown hinterlands and so make possible ways of going on together that no-one can have known ahead of time.

'What drew you here' and 'moving to the story that engaged you most'

We had deliberately designed the start of the conference to be personal and unintrusive. Right from the formal beginning of proceedings (the informal had of course begun already) we were holding in tension the opportunity for experience to be shared and explored in the whole group, with the more intimate but less commonly available small group conversation. I sense that a relationally informed practice will give more time for the intimate and private conversations at the start of a meeting as this allows for people to find their feet and establish some sense of relational context. This may provide a greater sense of security and confidence for people when it comes to expressing themselves within a larger group context; most optimistically it may improve the voice-giving potential of the group as a whole.

Now that the conference was underway I found it a terrific relief not to be holding the boundaries of the process, as Bill was doing at this point. I knew I was too attached to the work to facilitate well. I was also wonderfully relieved that I was not having to give an exposition and was with a group of people who threw themselves into the work of connected, but individually chosen, inquiry. I had become free of my old need to own responsibility for other people's sense making.

When Kathleen invited people to choose the chapter that most spoke to or engaged them, the act of physical movement reminded me of the importance of bodily action when it comes to living a choice. To walk across a room and be with others who share your passion or fascination makes for me a whole-bodied sense of joining with others. I wonder if relational consulting invites an embodied consulting, a consulting with the whole self rather than simply with the intellectual or verbal self. Certainly our process at this stage invited us to reflect on our chosen chapter with more than our verbal conversation. Kathleen had shared with the group that one of our hopes for the day was that we would collectively produce some creative expressions of what each of the chapters meant to us; creative expressions that could be photographed and used in the book.

I chose to go to Jon's chapter, 'Man not Superman', a story that I hugely admire of a modest man working in a way that resonates with how I would wish to practice. The five of us who came together were soon busy idealising the story and had Jon on a pedestal that would have shamed a god. To abuse Jon's Brancusi quote, 'appreciation is one thing, but idealisation quite another'. As we were beginning to take a more rigorously reflective position, wondering about what we were projecting onto Jon's story and what the shadow of his approach might be, I overheard Bill and a couple of others talking at the next door chapter. They were talking about the meaning they were making from Dominic and Liz's story, 'Not Just Doing the Do'. I was particularly engaged with their conversation because Bill and I have had such different reactions to this story throughout its construction.

An overheard conversation about 'Not Just Doing the Do'

A new face at the conference was Chris, who'd had such a significant role in Dominic and Liz's story. The initial temptation for Bill and the others gathered around the chapter was to seek Chris out, to find out more about a story that Bill had on occasion found infuriatingly self-referential, obsessed with the project team dynamics rather than the job of work to be done in the organisation. I learnt that, both during and after the conference, Bill and his co-inquirers had fallen into the consulting habit of wanting to seek out ever more about the story, as if there was some form of definitive truth to be found – much as in writing this final chapter I have found myself often wanting to write as if there was some quasi-definitive set of conclusions to be put down.

In the case of Dominic and Liz the narrative had already included five voices (including Chris and myself) and the two major voices that were absent were so

175

for the very pragmatic reason of wanting to keep an established stream of work on some sort of track. In the end, having flirted with the desire to seek out more, Bill and co. went with the Gestalt-informed principle of paying attention to what is. Rather than seeking out more fruit, they chose to examine the light and shade that was being cast by the fruit of an already-rich text and their reaction to it.

The temptation can often be not to stay with things as they are, not to pay attention to our relationship with what already is, but to move away from it with the excuse of finding something more – in other words, different. This habit of wanting to find out more, as if the extra information would complete some definitive jigsaw, can result in a paucity of understanding of the patterns that exist in what is already present and a lack of attention to our relationship to what is already known.

I am reminded of Kevin and Robin at this point. Kevin talks of 'holding and holding' things, as he gets people to stay with an uncomfortable but critical point in a group's framing of a situation. In Robin's case, I recall how he valued his colleague Sarah and her ability to stop him rushing on from quick conclusions. She was the anchor that got him to join her in the full richness of the present, including those disquieting and/or unexpressed feelings that feed the desire to move on.

In the practice of relational consulting, the collation of a mass of quickly processed data is not privileged. Relational consulting stays with an inevitably partial story that is mused on slowly and in which one's own relationship to the data is an important part of the analysis. Part of the practice I am trying to model as I write this.

A fishbowl conversation

In our design we had wanted to provide an opportunity for the subjects of the stories to share their experience of being present while others talked about their work and also share their reflections on being part of the wider research process. In an on-the-hoof decision it was agreed that I would hold the process, while Kathleen and Bill joined the other story participants/authors/co-creators in the middle. I sense I went along with this for fear of becoming the sole focus of interrogation – a dynamic that I had managed to establish in earlier expositional inquiries with the research. I also went along with it because of my attachment to the work and my fear of feedback in such a public setting. I was also finding myself ambivalent towards the work as it continued its transition into the formal, public and collectively owned arena.

The people in the centre of the fishbowl shared very different stories. Kevin spoke of his frustration with the story as it had finally been written up, how it still didn't do justice to the experience he and his client had been through. He framed his sense of disappointment with the story by contrasting the liveliness of our conversations with the comparative lack of liveliness in the written text – a tension that has run through this book and which exists in any consulting situation where text and conversation co-exist. I find myself wondering now about the extent to which the movement between text and conversation is both a metaphor for, and an actual expression of, the movement between the informal and formal domains of organisational life.

At the time I was also struck by the way Kevin distanced himself from the story, which he described as mine. What I think of as his story, he constructs as being my story. Interestingly, neither of us constructs it as our story, which is what it is. Maybe this is one of the potential shadows of relational consulting: it can become possible to lose a sense of self if the relationship is all and, as the self gets lost, so the sense of personal responsibility or commitment fades.

Other people shared different experiences of the research, finding the process of inquiry a hugely valuable aid as a framework for either making sense of their experience or as a catalyst/stimulus for enabling them to write what they needed to write as well as they could.

The most common resentment concerned not the inquiry- or story-drafting process, but Bill's presence as a reflective voice. Their contract and experience of the research was with me and, while they intellectually knew that the research was being sponsored by Ashridge and in particular Bill, his arrival into the process was often uncomfortable. One comment in particular stays with me. It concerned Bill being experienced as 'doing an audit on their practice', which Bill never intended and was very surprised to hear.

There are a number of points that this highlights for me about a relationally informed consulting practice. Firstly, the enlivening part of an inquiry is the intimate and personal part, the activity that is most closely bound up in an actual experienced relationship that is taking place in a creative present. Done well this does not evoke a feeling of being judged, but does evoke a feeling of being invited to inquire rigorously and well. Secondly, once the results of the inquiry are taken outside of the context of the relationship in which they were constructed, then people can feel much less well held – unsafe even. Thirdly, Bill's commentary on the stories lacked a present-tense relational context and instead evoked the historic relational context that existed for all the graduate practitioners, that of the AMOC Programme Director who had at some time marked and assessed their work – either directly or indirectly.

The fishbowl process again revealed the problem that comes with a lack of creative indifference. I was absolutely entranced by the conversation, hungry to hear what it had been like. So it was Bill who stepped out of his role as participator in the conversation and asked how it was going from the perspective of those sitting outside the inner circle – an example of Bill applying his Gestalt principles of paying attention to the present and owning his authority to act (rather than waiting for me). It was the second remark from the outer circle that shifted the process: why wasn't I, as the most widely present author, present in the centre? Put like that, it seemed absurd that we had constructed a process in which the person who was most relationally connected to everyone in the research process was not in the conversation.

The reflection I want to draw from this is not to do with why we had constructed the fishbowl the way we had, but around the importance of working with and responding to the now. At that moment, it was obvious that I needed to step into the centre of the fishbowl and join the conversation. Any defensive fantasies I may have had were simply not present. At many times in the stories the notion of holding onto plans or scripts lightly has been referred to. I believe that this ability to hold a plan or script lightly is a significant aspect of relationally informed consulting. Yes, sometimes (nearly always) I go into conversations with some sense of intention, even outcome. But then sometimes (nearly always) comes a point where that intention or outcome is superseded by something wonderfully obvious that emerges in the here and now.

Lunch

We had originally planned to repeat the conversational inquiry in the afternoon, with people choosing a second chapter to meet and reflect around. The lunch break gave Bill, Kathleen and I an opportunity to reconsider our plans for the afternoon. I found myself quite attached to the issue of what to do with the last chapter and wanted to seek confirmation that Peter was right – that the last chapter with its list of attributes didn't fit with the spirit of all that had gone before.

Meanwhile, Kathleen was committed to inquiring into where next to go with the research, an enthusiasm sharpened by the expressions of regret some had made during the morning that they had not had the opportunity to participate thus far.

We decided to offer people a threefold, parallel inquiry after lunch. They could work with me on the last chapter, with Kathleen on what an ongoing inquiry could look like or choose a second story to reflect around. With our design work done the three of us went our separate ways.

I found myself talking with Kevin, wanting to test the state of our relationship after his public expression of disappointment with the story. Back in conversation with him, I found my resentment towards him for not appreciating our story washed away as we shared the context for where we were that day. As so often happens for me, once I am in intimate conversation with someone, their public behaviours and my responses to them become more intelligible.

This habit of moving in and out of public and private settings seems an important part of relational consulting. If all remains public then the situation can often remain mysterious and strange; there is a lack of private context. If all remains private, then the opportunity for collective endeavour is lost and the world can turn in on itself – collapsing into a series of hot narrow intimacies. If I look at the tensions between Bill, Kathleen and myself, I can sense that at our best we complement each other well. Bill has a comfort and confidence with the public domain and I enjoy the private, while Kathleen acts as a bridge between the two.

I notice now how we have happened upon working with our individual strengths to achieve something that none of us individually could have achieved; and for me, this highlights the importance of working in collaboration with others. Through our collaboration I have been able to work from a position of attachment and a privileging of the private and personal; Bill and Kathleen have brought the creative indifference I couldn't achieve given how I'd bound myself up in the inquiry process. I find myself wondering if one of the arts of relational consulting is the division of roles in the consulting team, with some working from the position of attachment and others from a more detached perspective. Some writers have suggested that a single consultant needs to shuttle between these perspectives, or always remain at some level disinterested – but for me this doesn't work. Both positions provide a particular inquiring perspective, but to do one means not doing the other.

Inquiring into the last chapter

The points of view of the ten or so people who joined this inquiry were not in agreement. Some found the synopsis of the stories into seven habits useful – it gave them a helpful framing when it came to engaging with the stories. Others agreed with Peter and the suggestion that I should write a more personally present ending – a suggestion that resulted in two drafts being rejected as being excessively self-referential and insufficiently attentive to the requirements of the community of practice this work was in the service of.

This to me is one of the great tensions of being a consultant who seeks to be both personally and relationally aware, while also retaining a clear focus on what is figural in a particular piece of work. Without self-awareness I can become a slave to my own unacknowledged scripts or the scripts that others are inviting me to join in with. With an excessive attention to self-awareness, or to what by then is simply self-regard, I can become obsessed with the wonder and magnificence of my own story and my own psychological and professional development takes centre stage.

The inquiry at the conference identified that something different needed to be done at the end of the book, something that was personally situated but also in the service of a wider readership. It did not, however, write my words – the responsibility for doing that rested with me, Kathleen, Bill and Peter, each bringing our particular perspective to bear. I could write from a position of personal attachment; Kathleen could edit from a position of empathy with my position and consideration for the wider reader; Bill could review from the perspective of good AMOC practice, looking for evidence of a reflective practitioner in action; while Peter would have his eye on the wider population outside of AMOC. This is authoring in a relational context, rather than seeing myself as a solitary and independent agent. It does not, however, give absolution from personal responsibility.

Affirmation and endings

We came together for a large group conversation at the end of the day. I remember vividly a sense of people owning their responsibility for their experience and learning through the day, a reminder that as a consultant I can only have so much responsibility towards others. It was also personally affirming, with people appreciating the work that had been done. Having been brought up in a culture of depreciative inquiry, the appreciative always appears as a strange and exotic beast. It is this appreciative frame that has kept me going at the difficult end of this work, and has kept me connected with this book – something quite firmly situated in the public and formal domains.

The conference broke up with Bill and Kathleen immediately being drawn into absorbing conversations. I drifted away with Iain, frustrated at not having a chance to reflect on things with the two of them. But now I see another construction: I wanted to create something exclusive and possibly valedictory with the two of them; they, however, were behaving in an inclusive way and engaging with the messy dynamics of the now. I was focused on an ending; they were paying attention to the ongoing and emerging energies of people in the group.

Last words

It is now nearly two months on from the conference and I am still conscious of the use some people found in a synopsis of the principles of a relationally informed consulting perspective. I am also aware of how glib and obvious many statements of good practice can seem when they are presented apart from the situational complexities of their application. But I would still like to offer a perspective on what has stood out for me after over four years of immersion in the principles and practice of relational consulting. So, here's my synopsis of that perspective:

- There is no single, definitive story for describing reality.
- Every person and organisation has a number of story-making processes, some of which are given more weight than others. A consultant joins in, notices and (maybe) makes a difference to these processes.
- A consultant cannot do somebody's thinking and feeling (sense making) on their behalf.
- Knowing from a position of attachment and a position of indifference both provide important perspectives. Maybe a single consultant can't know from both.
- Be self-aware, but be aware of the trap of self-regard and self-obsession. Oh, and by the way, self-awareness can be a much richer experience and process if done in relationship with others.
- Work with what is, not what you or somebody else thinks should be. The opportunity and energy for doing what needs to be done is in the here and now, not in the future, the past or in somebody else's office.

I'll stop here. Of course this list is partial and will be different when I sit down to write it next week. But that's the nature of inquiry: it never ends, but it does need the occasional piece of punctuation.

SECTION 5

Appendices

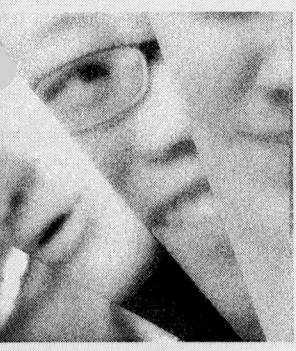

185 Appendix 1: Glossary

190 Appendix 2: Overview of the Research Philosophy

195 Appendix 3: Original Research Plan and Letter of Invitation to Contributors

201 Appendix 4: Overview of the Syllabus of the Ashridge Masters in Organisation Consulting

205 Contributor Photographs

Appendix 1
Glossary

Action learning set

Action learning is a process involving four to six people who meet to work on each other's individual challenges in the workplace. The focus is on providing the space and support for people to explore the nature of their situation and to commit to trying out particular courses of action that they will then report back on to the group. For further insight on this refer to Reg Revans' book, *ABC of Action Learning*, in the Mike Pedler Library, published by Lemos and Crane, 1998.

Appreciative inquiry

Appreciative inquiry can be defined as the art of discovering and valuing those factors that 'give life' to an organisation, group or individual. By this we mean those things which make them unique, powerful and the best that they can be. It aims to stimulate innovation, connectivity, relationship and improved performance by helping people collectively realise their full potential and become great at what they do and how they are at work.

It is more than a method: it is a philosophy, or a way of thinking, which leads to a new way of working together.

In appreciative inquiry, primarily through structured conversations and storytelling, the best *real* examples of the past and present are recalled and rigorously understood. This sets the stage for a well-grounded imagination of what could be possible in the future. These future possibilities are decided upon by the whole group working together, rather than being imposed by a few people, and are felt emotionally, as well as understood intellectually. From this process spring new possibilities for action in the present.

This ideal of the future (or collective 'dream') is seen as a stimulant, challenging people to consider how they are behaving and deciding *now* in the living present. It differentiates this approach from the more traditional, deterministic view of a 'vision' as something that you work towards with a sense of certainty (and a step-by-step action plan) that will make it happen. It is a pragmatic, powerful way to develop individuals, and organisations that leads to a welcome combination of novelty and innovation, alongside preservation of key elements of organisational or individual character. Whilst it draws energy and learning from the past, and stretches forward compelling ideas for the future – the change is always seen within the day-to-day present experience of complex patterns of interactions and conversations between people. In this sense, at Ashridge Consulting, we believe it is a way of engaging pragmatically with the idea of 'radical' or 'provocative incrementalism' as a change strategy. Paradoxically, it is our experience that taking this approach allows for deeper and more sustainable change than pursuing approaches which aim for 'blue sky' leaps and fast transformation.

Sources:

Barrett, F and A McLean *Appreciative Inquiry. A Constructive Approach to Organisation*

Development and Social Change. A workshop for Consultants and Leaders of Change. Aptos, California.

Cooperrider, D and S Srivasta (1987) 'Appreciative Inquiry in Organisational Life' in *Research in organisational change and development*, Vol. 1, ed. R Woodman and W Pasmore, pp.129–69. Greenwich, CT: JAI Press Inc.

Cooperrider, D et al. (1999) *Appreciative Inquiry: Rethinking Human Organisation. Toward a Positive Theory of Change*. Stipes Publishing.

Ludema, J, D Cooperrider, et al. (2001) 'Appreciative Inquiry: the Power of the Unconditional Positive Question' in *Handbook of Action Research*, ed. P Reason and H Bradbury. London: Sage.

Fishbowl conversation

A fishbowl conversation, sometimes also referred to as a 'goldfish bowl', attempts to provide an opportunity for a dynamic and intimate conversation in the context of a gathering of many people. It consists of a small inner circle of chairs surrounded by a larger outer circle. The conversation takes place in the inner circle only. People are free to occupy one of the empty chairs in the inner circle if they want to contribute to the conversation. There are different ways of enabling free movement between the inner and outer circle. Frequently there is an agreement that one person in the inner circle will vacate his/her chair when someone from the outer circle joins the conversation.

Kolb's learning cycle

Kolb designed a simple model that helps us to understand how people approach learning. It is based on a four-stage cycle:

- **Practical experience** – this stage of the learning cycle emphasises personal involvement with people in everyday situations.
- **Reflection (learning from watching and listening)** – in this stage of the learning cycle, people observe and reflect on events.
- **Conceptualising (learning by thinking)** – in this stage, learning involves using logic and ideas, rather than feelings, to *understand* problems or situations.
- **Experimenting (learning by doing)** – learning in this stage takes an active form – experimenting with influencing or changing situations.

It is unlikely that a person's learning style will be described accurately by just one of the descriptions above. This is because each person's learning style is a combination of the four basic learning modes.

Kolb identified four learning style types as follows:

- **Accomodator.** People with this learning style have the ability to learn primarily from 'hands on' experience. The accomodator has the opposite strengths to the assimilator. Their greatest strength is in doing things – in carrying out plans. They may tend to act on gut feelings rather than on logical analysis.
- **Diverger.** People with this learning style are best at viewing concrete situations from many different points of view. They have the opposite learning strengths

to the converger. Their greatest strength lies in imaginative ability. Their approach to situations is to observe rather than take action.

- **Converger.** People with this learning style are best at finding practical uses for ideas and theories. They tend to be less emotional, preferring to deal with things rather than people, and are often more at ease dealing with technical tasks and problems rather than with social and interpersonal issues.
- **Assimilator.** People with this learning style are best at understanding a wide range of information and putting it into concise, logical form. Their greatest strength lies in the ability to create theoretical models. They tend to be less focused on people and more interested in abstract ideas and concepts.

Source:

Kolb, DA (1984) *Experiential learning: Experience as the source of learning and development*. New Jersey: Prentice Hall.

Large group event

A large group event is a process which can involve anything from 50 to many hundreds of people from many parts of an organisation. It seeks to avoid a split between idea generation and action by having a representation in the room of all those who will need to own, understand and bring to life new ways of acting.

Myers-Briggs Type Indicator (MBTI)

The Myers-Briggs Type Indicator is a psychometric instrument based on Jung's theory of psychological types. The information provided by the instrument aims to enhance a person's understanding of herself, her motivations, natural strengths and potential areas for growth.

The MBTI was developed by Katharine Briggs and Isabel Myers who studied the ideas of Jung and applied them to understand people around them. After more than 50 years of research and development, the MBTI is the most widely used instrument for understanding normal personality differences.

The MBTI reports preferences on four dichotomies, each consisting of two opposite poles:

1
Extraversion (E) – Introversion (I)
Concerns the questions: where do you focus your attention?
Where do you get your energy?
Do you like to focus on the outer world of people and activity (E) or do you like to focus on your own inner world of ideas and experiences (I)?

2
Sensing (S) – Intuition (N)
Concerns the question: how do you prefer to take in information?
Do you prefer to take in information that is real and tangible, to focus on what is actually happening (S) or do you like to take in information by seeing the big picture, focusing on relationships and connections between facts (N)?

3
Thinking (T) – Feeling (F)
Concerns the question: how do you make decisions?
Do you prefer to base your decisions on the logical consequences of a choice or action (T) or do you like to consider what is important to you and others involved (F)?

4
Judging (J) – Perceiving (P)
Concerns the question: how do you deal with the outer world?
Do you like to live in an orderly, planned way (J) or do you like to live in a flexible, spontaneous way (P)?

Every one of these preferences, according to the MBTI, identifies normal and valuable human behaviour and there are no right or wrong preferences. The combination of these different preferences leads to 16 different types, each with identifiable and predictable characteristics.

Source:

Myers, K and L Kirby (1994) *Introduction to type dynamics and development*. Palo Alto, CA: CPP.

Type 1 and type 2 change

In the course of their family therapy work, Watzlawick and colleagues developed a typology of different approaches to change. With 'Type 1' they refer to change that is pursued by trying harder, doing more of whatever it is that is currently being done. 'Type 2 change' refers adopting a new course of action, taking an approach that does not fit within the common sense view of what is an appropriate course of action, and which may feel to be counterintuitive.

Source:

Watzlawick, P, J Weakland, et al. (1974) *Change. Principles of Problem Formulation and Problem Resolution*. New York, London: WW Norton.

Open space technology

Open space technology was created in the mid-1980s by organisational consultant Harrison Owen when he discovered that people attending his conferences loved the coffee breaks better than the formal presentations and plenary sessions. Combining that insight with his experience of life in an African village, Owen created a totally new form of conferencing.

Open space conferences have no keynote speakers, no pre-announced schedules of workshops, no panel discussions, no organisational booths. Instead, sitting in a large circle, participants learn in the first hour how they are going to create their own conference. Almost before they realise it, they become each other's teachers and leaders.

Anyone who wants to initiate a discussion or activity writes it down on a large sheet of paper in big letters and then stands up and announces it to the group.

After selecting one of the many pre-established times and places, they post their proposed workshop on a wall. When everyone who wants to has announced and posted their initial offerings, it is time for what Owen calls 'the village marketplace': participants mill around the wall, putting together their personal schedules for the remainder of the conference. The first meetings begin immediately.

Open space is, as Owen likes to say, more highly organised than the best planning committee could possibly manage. It is also chaotic, productive and fun. No-one is in control. A whirlwind of activity is guided from within by a handful of simple open space principles.

The most basic principle is that everyone who comes to an open space conference must be passionate about the topic and willing to take some responsibility for creating things out of that passion.

Four other key principles are:

1. Whoever comes is the right people
2. Whatever happens is the only thing that could have
3. Whenever it starts is the right time
4. When it is over it is over.

Open space conferences can be done in one day, but the most powerful go on for two or three days, or longer. Participants gather together briefly in the morning and the evening to share experiences and announce any new workshops they have concocted. The rest of the day is spent in intense conversation. Even meals are come-when-you-can affairs that go on for hours, filled with bustling dialogue. After a few days of this, an intense spirit of community usually develops that is all the more remarkable considering that participants are all doing exactly what they want.

Source:

http://www.co-intelligence.org/P-Openspace.html

Appendix 2
Overview of the Research Philosophy

The research was approached in a way consistent with the AMOC programme philosophy and can be described as being grounded in social constructionism, with particular attention being paid to the relational dynamic within which the stories were told and written up. It also paid attention to the reflective discipline of both researcher and graduate practitioner, as well as the reflective relationship that existed between the two editorial voices (Bill and John).

- This social constructionist stance meant the research eschewed the notion of an objective or essential truth that was to be found about the experience of either the graduate or faculty practitioners. It also eschewed the notion that the researcher was an independent and impartial observer who was able to see and capture some essence that existed outside of himself or the processes of inquiry and advocacy.
- Reported stories of people's experiences are not truths, but stories that are co-created by researcher and graduate/faculty practitioner, both of whom are actively participating in influencing what does and doesn't get said and written down.
- The authors of stories are not writing objective truths, they are writing stories that are heard through their own relationally and personally situated sense-making processes.
- Stories and reflections on stories acquire some form of validity through the discipline of reflective practice, where authors and reflective partners pay attention to the assumptions that are informing their sense-making habits.
- Inquiry and advocacy, the habit of knowing and not knowing, are present at all times in the researching, authoring and editing processes. What is 'known' to the graduate/faculty practitioner, researcher and editor is subjective and partial and is mediated by a disposition towards inquiry.

With explicit reference to the theoretical frames discussed by the faculty practitioners in their essays, the creation of this research paper can be understood in the following ways.

A) As an example of researching from a complexity perspective

- The graduate practitioner and researcher stepped into the process not knowing what the outcome would be. The researcher was not attached to any particular hypothesis that he wished to have proven or not proven.
- The research focus on consulting practice sought to amplify the consultant's voice rather than that of the clients.
- The research did not look to discover/construct cause-and-effect relationships, but to notice the web of conversations and relationships within which the consulting experience took place.
- Attention was only lightly paid to the formal domain of the work, as typified by

workplans and formal deliverables. The main attention was on the unpredictable cut and thrust of how things were actually taking place and being talked about within the informal domain.
- The researcher inevitably interfered in the sense making that the graduate practitioners were making of their work. He was intervening by being part of the conversation about that work.

B) As an example of researching from a Batesonian social constructionist perspective

- The focus was not so much on where John stepped into the web (i.e. whether it was an historic piece of work, work in progress or work anticipated) but on *how* he stepped into it. It was a matter of working with as much as possible of what he noticed of the experience of immersion in the research, rather than 'researching on a consulting project'.
- The research looked to pay attention to the ecology of relationships that the work took place within, which meant talking not just to consultants but also to clients and other parties involved in the work and then noticing together how these relationships were interacting.
- The ambition for the research was to support graduate and faculty practitioners 'to step up' rather than 'drill down' their thinking. The intention was not to reduce or distil what was said to some bare bones, but to support researcher and practitioner in stepping up into being able to see their work differently – to provide potentially insightful reframings for all.
- During the research, John attempted not just to immerse himself in the intellectual understanding of the work being examined; he also sought to pay attention to the feelings and intuitive insights that were evoked in him. This is consistent with Bateson's multi-facetted methodology of knowing, where all aspects of one's noticing of a situation are of note.
- In keeping with the Batesonian notion of 'arcs of meaning', the stories are not intended or believed capable of being definitive. Their depth comes from the connections that are made between arcs, between consultants and clients, between practitioners, other parties and both researcher and editor. And possibly most importantly from an AMOC perspective, between theory and practice.

C) As an example of researching with a dialogic orientation

- The research sought to acknowledge the totality of things (cf. Bohm); it worked with the evolving personal and professional situations of the practitioners and the personal values and dispositions of the editors/researchers. It also stayed with multiple projects and multiple perspectives in the belief that all of these things were somehow connected, even if these connections could not be causally expressed.
- The research also worked with a view of reality as unending, never static or complete (cf. Bohm). The stories rarely had a sense of closure, but more of a sense of situations shifting and evolving. This may not satisfy a Western desire

for stories to have a dramatic architecture, to go somewhere, but it is part of the dialogic orientation. Part of this lack of narrative clarity is also a response to always speaking within a wider context than we, as researchers, editors or practitioners, can understand.

- In Hugh's essay he talks of people always being involved in situations that are more complicated than they can control. The experience of this research bears it out. Who is available to speak; whose stories become available; how the storytellers and the researcher find themselves speaking of these stories do not fit within the controlling influence of the researcher or the commissioner of the research.

- The last point for John that this research highlights from the discipline of a dialogic and also Gestalt orientation is the virtue of creative indifference, or not trying too hard to force conclusions. At times John sweated blood to identify themes and draw conclusions, carefully examining the texts to see what was there (as if something existed independently of his process of inquiry). The vast majority of the conclusions and summaries came when he let go of the sweated thinking, when he let go of the need to grasp his thoughts and instead engaged in a dialogue with the material.

D) As an example of researching in a way informed by relational psychology

- One of the notions that stood out for John from Kathleen's essay was the notion of mutual growth-in-connection. The research experience was something that John found to be a growing experience, both personally and professionally. Both graduate and faculty practitioners also commented on how they had benefited from simply telling their stories and being in a reflective inquiring relationship. Research when practised from the standpoint of relational psychology is an experience of connected mutual growth.

- Part of this connectedness comes from paying attention to, and working with, relational logic (cf. Fletcher). John is struck by the importance he found himself placing on the need to be empathetic towards the situations people described, both in terms of the stories they told and the challenges they found in talking about them. His retrospective belief is that he sought a non-exploitative engagement with all involved in this, taking care that what was written down could be lived with (losing some of the 'juicier' pieces, as he saw them, along the way).

- The research process uneasily held the tension between agency and communion. At times John wanted to disappear himself as author, hide his presence behind the words of the others, and attribute the work to the intelligence of the others and to his co-editor. The challenge has been to acknowledge the agency of both Bill and John, while also realising that this work could not have happened without the presence of the faculty, practitioners and other third parties who had formal and informal involvement along the way.

E) As an example of researching in a way informed by Gestalt psychology

- John's ambition when engaging with practitioners was to have full-blooded contact, so that both he and they were able to experience each other vividly. In the service of this good contact he looked to himself to think strongly and feel intelligently; to pay attention to his thoughts and feelings so that they could be present in the research without becoming its focus.
- Bill talks of one of the Gestalt qualities being toughness, a willingness to name things that are unnamed, to offer a provocation. In his reflective pieces at the end of each of the graduate practitioner stories John sees Bill exercising this quality of toughness, through the naming of patterns that had otherwise gone unmentioned. At times during the interview process John felt himself able to do this, but always sensed that this quality of toughness had to be held in tension with the quality of respect for the other, which sometimes meant that John may have been overly appreciative and insufficiently tough.
- A focus on 'what is' is one of Gestalt's 'right-minded' principles. The implications for the research being that John worked with the professional stories and personal situations as they presented themselves, not necessarily as he had anticipated in his framing questions or in the formal invitation. This meant that inquiring questions arose in response to what was being expressed, during the research encounters. While being mindful of what was figural, research into AMOC practitioner consulting practice, John sought to work with the reality as expressed by the practitioners and the responses this evoked in him in the moment. The most practical consequence being that he researched without a script.

F) As an example of researching in a way informed by inquiry and reflective practice

- The research process provided a frame for the inquiry; John did not arrive empty handed or headed when he met with the practitioners. He offered an invitation for them to look at the work they were doing anew – or at least in the company of a fresh pair of eyes. What was particular about the inquiring stance adopted was not so much its focus as its non-attachment to outcome. Neither John nor Bill had a view as to what to expect in terms of narratives or findings.
- John and Bill approached the inquiry with interest and curiosity. They both felt strongly about the figure of the research and were also curious as to how people actually practised consulting within a social constructionist frame. This was an inquiry that mattered to researcher, editor and practitioner.
- An unplanned but important part of the inquiry was the time taken to create the stories and also to comment on and draw insights from them. An important part of the discipline of reflective inquiry is to stay with data for longer than normal, to give an opportunity for insights other than the normal to emerge. Because of the three-month-or-so delay between each of the three rounds of graduate practitioner inquiry, we stayed with data longer. The review process by the editors took many months and many iterations, and also involved staying

with the sensation of being at a bit of a loss at times.
- Reflective inquiry is a relational and interactive activity. One person cannot know all that can be known. Throughout the inquiry, John, Bill, practitioners and others have been talking about what has been emerging for each of them and the nature of their relationship to the research. It has not been a simple matter of collecting stories and then either Bill or John drafting insights. It has been a frustrating, evolving and accidental process of finding out what can be usefully written up – and how it can be written up.

Appendix 3
Original Research Plan and Letter of Invitation to Contributors

Inquiring into what can be usefully written down about the AMOC experience (Draft for discussion with Bill Critchley)

Summary

This paper describes a raison d'être and possible process for recording in book/manuscript form aspects of the AMOC experience. The ambition at the start is to produce something akin to *The Fifth Discipline Field Book*, i.e. a text that weaves in personal experiences and tips set within a rigorous academic context. A working title could be *The Ashridge Field Book of Progressive Consulting*.

The raison d'être

Two reasons strike me for embarking on this inquiry into what can be usefully written down about the AMOC experience. Firstly, there is a gap in the market for a consulting book written with the consultant practitioner, rather than consultant theoretician, in mind that works from a complexity/social constructionist/psychologically literate perspective. Secondly, the AMOC experience could be enhanced by making available to future AMOC students the narratives, experiences and theoretical musings of the rich bag that makes up the AMOC community. In the long run this could become a living document, in which future generations rewrite and build on what has been written already.

Thoughts about the consulting book market

Much of the consulting book market would appear to be (based on a recent subjective tour of the relevant section of the Waterstone's bookshelves in Gower Street) dominated by a naïve, objective observer, model – in which an intellectual process of organisational intervention is over-privileged. Other books tend towards the anecdotal and lack an explicit philosophy within which the anecdotes and prescriptions sit.

Thoughts about 'documenting' AMOC

Reflecting on my AMOC experience and the rich use made of textual sources, the calls made by some participants for an AMOC text, and enthused by the recent research by ACL into leadership – which demonstrated to me that useful texts can be written while being consistent with a more complex and socially situated sense of truth – I believe that an AMOC text can be produced which does not undermine the experiential and personal dimensions of the AMOC journey.

Pitfalls and contradictions

If any text is produced, it has to be made available in a way that avoids falling into prescription but then also avoids falling into a sense that 'anything goes'. It has to hold up exemplars of good practice in a way which informs how people set about conducting their own consulting work/AMOC journey but does not invite people to try and copy what has already been done. It is the difference between encouraging enlightened comparison and blind copying.

The implications of this are, I sense, that the text must have the feel of a work in practice – also all stories and narratives must include some sense of the messiness, the dark side, that accompanies any success.

I also sense that it will be the personal narratives that will bring it to life, something which shows how the personal worms and frames inform why particular consultants work in particular ways. This gives room for the idiosyncratic as well as the rigorous.

Possible outcomes

There are two outcomes: firstly a text that can be used within the AMOC programme; and secondly a book for the wider consulting market.

My early thoughts about the content of the first text (which will then provide the foundation for the second) are:

- Six to eight narratives in which people reflect on how their consulting practice has evolved as a result of their engagement with AMOC and how changes in their consulting practice have been affected by, and also had an impact on, the wider context of their lives. This is not as pure as the leadership research, but I hope can provide a sense of the complexities of the changes and the personal context for the changes.
- Six to eight essays around the key informing theories and principles that shape the AMOC perspective on good consulting. These would be written with an eye to both the theory but also as to how faculty members live up to and tailor their work in the light of practice. My understanding is that the AMOC faculty has recently identified the six or so theoretical roots of its philosophy.
- Anecdotes and top tips. A wide collection of short stories that show how people worked with and learned about particular techniques. Here again, something on the personal context that drew a particular person to a particular technique or client situation would add depth to this.

The hope would be to weave these all together, with particular narratives having a natural affinity to a particular informing perspective.

A way for getting started

The first step is to engage with the AMOC leadership team to agree that this is a useful exercise, working with a version of this document. The second step is to identify what the first step is in engaging with the wider AMOC community. I would not want to just send out a simple request to the whole community and see who comes back; I sense that some deliberation and care needs to be exercised in identifying whose narratives provide the stories around which other more theoretical and anecdotal perspectives are weaved – while at the same time allowing opportunity for chance to have its inevitable rich mix with whatever is planned.

The role of an outsider and their relationship with ACL and the AMOC community

For this to happen requires it to be figural in someone's life. My memories of ACL are that it is very hard to turn down the demands of clients, and the other day-to-day requirements and distractions of belonging to the Ashridge community, when one is trying to give long-term attention to an internal project.

I am also aware that many consultants and members of the AMOC faculty find the act of writing down their stories and their theories a painful process. I would hope to be able to act as an intelligent ghost writer for people, being able to produce something which people are able to identify as being a good expression of what they are about even if they didn't have to sweat the words.

Given that many of the AMOC community are working consultants, I would hope that the offer of 'ghost' support would make possible a task which otherwise would be too onerous given their consulting workload.

John Higgins

30 October 2003

Researching *The Ashridge Fieldbook of Progressive Consulting* – description of inquiry process and supporting protocols

A) Overview of the entire research process

- Identify 8 consultant subjects and make requests for them to participate
- Bill to identify the 7 subjects other than himself (plus 4 back-ups) from the AMOC participant list
- Bill to make request/invitation to each to participate
- Subjects to identify clients and obtain their agreement to participate
- Task 5 AMOC faculty to write the theoretical framing pieces (see section C of this document for protocols and responsibilities)
- Carry out first consultant subject inquiry with Bill as subject to test inquiry process (see section B of this document for a description of this process)
- Carry out remainder of the consultant subject inquiries (8 in all, including test)
- Hold a group review process for all consultants and clients involved in the process
- If all participants want to be involved hold as a 2 group process of 4 consultant–client dyads
- Each dyad talks about their story and other dyads share what strikes them
- Research paper is drafted and proposal for book developed (see section D of this document for initial proposition for outline of the research report).

B) Description of the consultant–client inquiry process

- Conversation between consultant and researcher (John) around these framing questions (2 to 4 hours):
    - What is the work being done?

- ♦ What have been the critical incidents?
- ♦ What were your intentions in doing this work?
- ♦ What is it about yourself that is invested in this work?
- Researcher drafts story which is agreed with the consultant
- Story is sent to the client and the client is asked to reflect on what strikes them about the consultant's story and its relationship to the client's experience of the work (Should the story be sent by the consultant or the researcher? I sense it should be the consultant)
- Conversation between client, consultant and researcher leading off with the client's response to the consultant's story (4 hours)
- Researcher redrafts story that is agreed with consultant and client (Is this so Bill?)
- Final conversation between consultant and researcher around these framing questions (4 hours):
  - ♦ What does this piece of work (with the client) tell you about your consulting practice?
  - ♦ Why did the things that worked, work in this case?
  - ♦ Why did the things that didn't work, not work in this case?
  - ♦ What sense are you making of this from a theoretical perspective?
- Researcher finalises story that is agreed with consultant.

C) Responsibilities and protocols for AMOC faculty

The following members of the AMOC faculty will be invited by Bill to write a piece around major theoretical frames:

- Caryn on complexity
- Robin on inquiry
- Kathleen on relational psychology
- Hugh on dialogue
- Adrian on social constructionism.

A possible set of questions they may want to work with are:

- How does this theoretical frame inform your consulting work?
- What are the aspects of this theoretical frame you believe are of particular importance to consultants?
- Why are you attracted to this theoretical frame?
- What have you learned about working with this frame?

It is assumed that the faculty will write their own pieces unsupported – although the researcher could work with them if requested to help them draft their piece.

D) Initial outline of research paper (to be held lightly)

- Overview – this will provide a summary of those informing axioms about good

consulting practice which emerge from the work
- First consultant–client story, based around the questions worked on and issues identified during the inquiry process
- Second consultant–client story
- First theoretical frame (e.g. complexity) – it is hoped that certain stories should lend themselves to the exposition of particular theoretical perspectives; if not, the theoretical frame chapter will refer backwards to those stories that have been covered and forwards to those yet to be touched
- Third consultant–client story
- Second theoretical frame
- Fourth consultant–client story
- Fifth consultant–client story
- Third theoretical frame
- Sixth consultant–client story
- Fourth theoretical frame
- Seventh consultant–client story
- Eighth consultant–client story
- Fifth theoretical frame
- The challenges of consulting in the way described in this book:
  - How it fits and doesn't fit with established norms of client/consultant behaviour and client expectations of consultants
  - How to bridge between this type of consulting and other consulting and managerial discourses.
- Appendix – research methodology.

E) Next steps

- I can begin the first inquiry round, which will be with Bill and then Bill and Ben of Glocom, early in the New Year. I can meet any day in January after Tuesday 6th except for the 27th and the 29th.
- I would request that there is a two-week gap between the first meeting with Bill and the subsequent meeting with Bill and Ben, to give time for the draft narrative to be worked on, agreed and sent out to Ben.
- Before then I would ask Bill to engage with the AMOC faculty and also to identify and approach consultant subjects. I can begin to book other rounds of inquiry before we complete the pilot first one.
- Issues of location we will sort out with each consultant–client pairing.

John Higgins

10 December 2003

Letter of invitation to contributors

Dear

I am writing to ask if you'd be willing to take part in what I think will be some ground-breaking research into consulting practice informed by AMOC philosophy and principles.

The ambition is to produce something akin to *The Fifth Discipline Field Book* i.e. a text that weaves together personal experiences and a rigorous academic context. The working title is *The AMOC Field Book of Radical Consulting*.

At the heart of this will be eight narratives, constructed from eight consulting relationships. Our request is that you and a current or recent client be one of those consulting relationships.

The inquiry process would consist of your being interviewed for about two hours by John Higgins, an AMOC graduate and for five years a member of Ashridge Consulting, who would then draft a story that you would mutually agree. This story would be based around four framing questions:

- What is the work being done?
- What have been the critical incidents?
- What were your intentions in doing this work?
- What is it about yourself that is invested in this work?

The agreed story would then be sent to your client prior to a meeting between the three of you, in which the client starts by reflecting on what strikes them about your story and its relationship to their experience of the work. A narrative would then be constructed, drafted by John, which incorporates the client's responses. During this final drafting we will also be interested in exploring what this piece of consulting is telling you about your work from both a theoretical and practical perspective.

Our ambition is then to bring together groups of you, consultants and clients, to identify the important themes that all your stories speak to.

I do hope that you feel drawn to take part in this research and would appreciate it if you could let Debbie Karydis know of your willingness to participate.

With best wishes

Bill Critchley

Appendix 4
Overview of the Syllabus of the Ashridge Masters in Organisation Consulting

AMOC Overview Document

Rationale including details of how AMOC's aims and learning outcomes are ensured by the learning and teaching strategy, supported by the curriculum, and measured by the assessment.

1.1 Rationale

The Rationale comes in three parts:

Part One

Ashridge Consulting, which has been in existence for some fifteen years, has been developing a philosophy and style of consulting, broadly informed by a phenomenological and participative philosophy, and practised through forms of inquiry and dialogue. This philosophical stance underpins a purpose which combines commercial success with a number of ethical considerations. Such considerations would include our intention to work with organisations, rather than imposing solutions upon them; to develop organisation members in the course of our work; to foster learning and a spirit of inquiry; to encourage diversity, and promote quality relationships.

Our consulting stance is based on the theoretical view that organisations are complex social processes which are largely socially constructed, and based on this premise, we have developed a number of theories, perspectives, processes and methodologies in the service of our purpose.

The MSc in organisation consulting emerged out of the energy and commitment of a small group of people within Ashridge Consulting to promulgate this philosophy of consulting as an alternative to the prevailing positivist paradigm which we believe creates unsustainable expectations, and tends to ignore important ethical questions.

Part Two

Ashridge launched the MSc in order to position itself, and become better known as an organisation consulting firm within the context of the wider Ashridge, which is mainly known as a management education establishment. We also wished to differentiate ourselves in the market as a radically challenging and ethical firm of organisation consultants, with a practice grounded in the broad principles of 'action research'. We see action research as congruent with our phenomenological and participative philosophy, while meeting the need for an underpinning qualitative research methodology.

So we see the programme as a means of promulgating Ashridge's consulting philosophy and experience, as well as supporting Ashridge's overall purpose as a Centre for Management and Organisation Development.

Part Three

When we were planning the launch of AMOC, we believed that the consulting profession was not well served by a dedicated and systematic educational process; and that the distinction between management and consulting education was by and large blurred. Since the launch of AMOC, more interest has been shown in education for consulting, as evidenced by the British Academy of Management's Special Interest Group on the topic. However, when in 2001 the Director of AMOC was invited by the BAM SIG to offer an overview of the AMOC programme, we were recognised as offering a radical consulting proposition to a niche market. So within the field of consulting education we seek to offer a broadly social constructionist, or post-positivist alternative to the largely positivist perspective on consulting which prevails, for those who seek to develop an ethical and thoughtful consulting praxis based in this emerging paradigm. The challenge this presents us is that many of the professional assumptions and practices, and much of the language which configures the positivist tradition of consulting, is paradigmatically incommensurable with those of social constructionism. Similarly, post-positivist epistemology, and hence our stance on research and evaluation, is radically different from that of the mainstream academic community. We are continually looking for ways of bridging the two paradigms, which do not breach the integrity of the ideas and praxis we are seeking to promote, while recognising the practical need to connect creatively with clients and members of the academic community who represent other traditions.

1.2 Programme Aims

The overall aims of AMOC are:

- To promulgate organisation consulting as a distinctive and ethical practice, informed by the perspective that organisations are complex social processes and that consulting is a participative act with consequences which may be anticipated but not predicted.
- To provide experienced practitioners with a forum in which to develop their practice within a learning framework intended to stimulate:
    - their understanding of themselves and the complex array of attitudes and beliefs they express through their practice, and
    - their critical appreciation of organisations and the perspectives they bring to bear.

The framework adopted by the AMOC faculty is fundamentally participative, drawing on a number of strands:

- An appreciation for the significance of relationship and its co-constructed nature, as expressed through practice. This strand reflects the philosophical and psychological underpinnings of Gestalt and related phenomenological ideas, and the perspective on sociology represented by thinkers such as George Mead and Norbert Elias.
- A view of organisations as socially constructed phenomena subject to development through conversation.

- Approaches towards change, based on complexity thinking, and methods compatible with social constructionism such as appreciative inquiry.
- An interest in experimental forms of organisational intervention utilising, for instance, large group processes and other dialogical forms.
- An insistence on the development of rigorous awareness of participants' own epistemology through the application of action learning and action inquiry.

1.3 Programme Objectives

The broad intention of the programme is to equip practitioners with:

- A coherent set of interrelated theoretical strands which participants will learn to use to reflect on their own perceptions of organisations, their own relation to organisations, and their evolving praxis as organisation consultants.
- A rigorous process of self-development based on the principles of action learning and action inquiry. Participants will be expected particularly to exploit these processes during the final dissertation phase of the programme, and leave it well prepared to maintain an action inquiry orientation to their continued development.
- A network of colleagues with whom they have shared significant moments of their development, with the potential for future collaboration, and a growing alumni network, with a shared interest in radical organisation and consulting perspectives.

1.4 Learning Outcomes

We envisage a number of specific learning outcomes which participants will gain:

- Broader perspectives on the phenomenon of organisation; a particular understanding of organisations as complex social processes; and the implications of this perspective for leadership, change, and organisation consulting.
- A heightened awareness of themselves as individuals and how they engage with, and impact on, other individuals.
- An increased awareness of group dynamics and how they typically engage in such processes.
- Increased ability to work effectively with group and power dynamics in organisations.
- An enhanced sense of personal presence and confidence, enabling participants to respond appropriately in uncertain and emerging situations.
- An increased competence in designing consulting processes, and facilitating small- and large-scale events and activities.
- A broader awareness of ethical considerations and how they currently and potentially take account of these in their practice.
- Understanding of, and ability to work with, various forms of 'action research/action inquiry', and thus develop a rigorous basis to their development of self and praxis.

1.5 Learning and Teaching Strategy

1.5.1

The Ashridge Learning and Teaching Strategy was written subsequently to the launch of AMOC, and substantially reflects aspects of the approach to learning and teaching developed during the course of the AMOC.

We wish to reproduce here Principle 1:

'Our programmes are postgraduate programmes designed for experienced client populations. Our approach to teaching is based on developing an adult partnership with participants, rather than a dependent relationship as found in the traditional teacher–pupil, classroom-based situation.'

One of the participants on the first programme described faculty as 'guides', rather than teachers; people who knew the territory to be covered, but did not know the exact nature of the journey which would be jointly undertaken. Faculty provide a learning structure, relevant reading material, and carefully designed learning experiences, and participants take responsibility for their own learning, subject to the broad assessment criteria. This co-created stance is a hallmark of our teaching philosophy.

1.5.2

AMOC is designed and delivered by practitioner–academics. Each member of the faculty is currently engaged in consulting work, and this is one of the unique selling points of the programme. We see the programme as a temporary organisation formed for the purpose of learning, and hence the programme provides an analogue of what is being taught. We believe the learning experience should be congruent with the themes being covered, so that if the theme be 'self organisation and emergence as a phenomenon of organising processes', so the learning will be exactly that, emergent and self organised. Hence learning outcomes can only be intended, not predicted in detail. Each workshop is thus designed somewhat in the way a consulting intervention would be designed, and faculty act both as consultants to an ongoing organising process as well as tutors.

1.5.3 – The overall teaching and learning structure

The AMOC programme is designed in such a way as to introduce theoretical and methodological strands through a mixture of:

- Guided pre-workshop reading relating to the background of the themes to be covered.
- Presentation and discussion in workshops, supported by:
- Experiential sessions designed to elicit the practical implications for participants and embed their learning.
- Consulting Application Groups in which participants apply action learning as way of translating the themes and insights of the programme into their practice.
- Tutorial support for a programme of written assignments which provide a basis for consolidating learning in a rigorous process of reflection.
- This aspect culminates in a dissertation in the fourth module.

Contributors

Liz Campbell

Iain Carruthers

Bill Critchley

John Higgins

Kathleen King

Robin Ladkin

Dominic Mahony

Adrian McLean

Hugh Pidgeon

Kevin Power

Francesca Talevi

Jon Townsin

Caryn Vanstone